THE NAKED COMPUTER

E. ZACHERY

THE NAKED COMPUTER

A Layperson's Almanac of Computer Lore,
Wizardry, Personalities, Memorabilia,
World Records, Mind Blowers and Tomfoolery

Jack B. Rochester
and
John Gantz

William Morrow and Company, Inc.   New York   1983

For Mary

You are the sweetest song I sing

and Joshua

Warrior-son and muse extraordinaire

J.B.R.

For Shelley

Whose empathy, culinary art, and untethered soul

make life worth living

And infant Jesse

Who can slobber on a computer with the best of them

J.G.

ACKNOWLEDGMENTS

Many people helped make *The Naked Computer* happen. First and deepest thanks to H. Michael Snell, our agent, who suggested the idea for the book. Mike and his wife/partner Susan saw us through our writing with wit, wisdom, and sometimes a whip. We would like to thank our intrepid researchers, David Needle, Managing Editor of *InfoWorld* magazine, Mary Greene Lamb, and Edward Allen Milkow for their thoughtful work. Special thanks to Errol Zachary for his title page and chapter-opening illustrations and for designing the "naked computer," and to Rich Tennant and Tim Eagan for their cartoons.

Our appreciation to the following people, who spent a great deal of their time sharing the history of the computer industry with us:

Richard A. Bennett, Synapse Computer Corp.
David Henry Goodstein, Inter/Consult
Joseph C. Jablonowski, *American Machinist* magazine
Charles P. Lecht, Lecht Sciences, Inc.
Walter Pitts, International Data Corp.
Charlotte F. Scott, IBM
Robert Strayton, The Strayton Corp.
B. L. Trippett, NCR Corp.
Russ Walter, *The Secret Guide to Computers*
Edward N. Yourdon, Yourdon, Inc.

And our appreciation, in memoriam, to James Peacock, who would have loved this book and enhanced it with advice and information had he lived.

"Isn't it interesting that the industry is so dynamic, much more dynamic than I had predicted," Thomas J. Watson, Jr., former president and chief operating officer of IBM, told us in an exclusive interview. "The innovative changes seem more rapid than in any other industry, possibly anywhere."

So rapid, in fact, that many great events went undocumented and, today, live only by virtue of the oral story-telling tradition. We have striven to uphold the highest standards of journalistic integrity in researching and writing *The Naked Computer*. Our material is as accurate and authoritative as possible, but inevitably, differences of opinion will arise; our "first" is someone else's second, something or someone wasn't included in a list. We hope you'll take comfort in the knowledge that we've made every effort to be responsible in the arduous task of preparing this book.

We are grateful to Pat McGovern, Chairman of the Board of International Data Group, for sharing his experiences, reviewing our manuscript and for creating *Computerworld* and International Data Corporation, without which this book would not have been possible. We gratefully acknowledge the editors and writers at *Computerworld*, both present and past, who provided us with a treasure trove of stories, and to the staffers of IDC research and publications departments.

Many thanks to NEC Information Systems, Inc., Lexington, Massachusetts, for loyally supporting our computers, and to Robert G. Tepper and the gang at Standard Software, Avon, Massachusetts, who nursed us through software glitches and provided technical and moral support above and beyond the call of duty.

And most special thanks to the people of the computer industry, the poets and programmers, heroes sung and unsung, visionaries and videots, without whom this book would have been boring, difficult, unnecessary, or worse. You are part of mankind's cybernetic renaissance; we hope we have unfrocked your creation with humor, grace, and awe.

CONTENTS

9

INTRODUCTION

The Mating Call

You're in love. You just don't know it yet. The tail fins you were so enamored of in the 1950s have long since gone to ferrous oxide heaven, the psychedelic posters of the 1960s are decomposing with the bead curtains deep in the bowels of the condo storage area, the self-help books of the 1970s are lost in the bookshelf amid a clutter of video game cassettes.

There's a new musk in the wind. Silicon dust, mylar motes, and electron charges. It's the computer's spoor.

You can resist the lure, like Raymond Schoolfield, who stood naked in front of the IBM building in Atlanta on September 23, 1968, carrying a sign that said, "Computers Are Obscene." Or Harvey Matusow, who formed The International Society for the Abolition of Data Processing Machines in the same year.

But you might as well join the orgy, succumb to the pleasures of the information age.

After all, a computer has already changed your life—for example, that metal bank teller that ate your cash card last Saturday night, the overbooked airline flight that left you spending the night in Newark, the new no-goof-off digital time clock down at the factory, your last electrocardiogram reading, that IRS audit that discovered the medical deduction you took on your dog's distemper shot, the Pac-Man cassette you threw out the window when your kid flunked English.

In 1960, there were about five thousand computerlike "things" in the world. By 1985 there will be fifty million. One out of two white-collar workers will have an electronic "computer Friday," one out of fifty blue-collar workers will be a robot. The average home will have more computers than motors (currently forty) in it.

Big computers, small computers, egghead computers, working-class computers—they're coming out of the closet. Like little green space men, they're landing at the rate of a thousand a day before our very eyes. Now that they're in Times Square, we can't ignore them.

If five years ago we thought of the computer as a mysterious box filled

11

with multicolored wires, festooned with lights, and somehow out to get us, today we may *still* think of it as a mysterious box filled with multicolored wires and festooned with lights—but Jones down the street just bought one. And our kid is bugging us for one.

Forget the boring stuff—accounting, payroll, inventory—that computers were bred to do. Today doctors, artists, mechanics, mad scientists, firemen, hookers, bird watchers, and Mafia dons all use computers. Even computers use computers.

There's an advantage to all this. Now that computers are being booted out of their dust-free, glass-walled enclaves into the street, more of us get to see them in their birthday clothes—warts, birthmarks, flat feet, zits, and all.

If we want, we can even buy one—only $49.95, sold in drugstores—and fold, spindle, and mutilate it just for revenge.

So relax. Computers can do all the dumb things we can do; they just do them a lot faster. They can be both boggle-minded and mind-boggling. Poke around the next twenty chapters and you'll see.

THE NAKED COMPUTER

CHAPTER 1

THE INVASION:

Computers by the Zillion

Picture ENIAC, the first computer. In 1946 it was the scientific marvel of the day, a thirty-ton triumph, standing two stories high and covering fifteen thousand square feet. A boxcar could fit inside it. Yet today, a $1,500 Radio Shack TRS-80 computer, smaller than a stereo, can add and subtract twenty times faster. Just the cost of the electricity to run ENIAC for a week could buy a couple of Radio Shack computers; an hour's worth could buy its computational equal in hand-held calculators.

The human equivalent of today's average computer is one million mathematicians working twenty-four hours a day doing sums, consuming a ton of scratch paper a second. The level of miniaturization in today's computer memory matches that of inscribing the Bible on the head of a pin.

Had automobile technology advanced at the rate of computer technology over the past thirty years, a Rolls-Royce would cost $2.50 and *would get two million miles to a gallon of gasoline.*

Mind-boggling? No more than watches that play Space Invaders, electronic bartenders, cars that talk back, calculators that sing, smart bombs, computer-drawn cartoons, digital records, or intelligent carburetors.

Consider the following. Computers perform one hundred thousand calculations per citizen every second. The average citizen's name pops up in a computer thirty-five times a day, gets passed between computers at least five times a day. The U.S. census alone collects five billion facts about us—all of which are good computer fodder.

But that's nothing. The collective brainpower of computers shipped in the next two years will equal that of all computers shipped from the beginning of time to now. By two years after that, the installed computer capacity will have doubled again.

Apple Computer was incorporated in 1977. Tandy didn't ship its first Radio Shack TRS-80 computer until 1978. Together they have shipped over two million computers by now—more than IBM has ever shipped.

And this isn't counting computers disguised in other products: microwave ovens that talk, bionic limbs that twitch to brain-wave signals, missiles that have eyes, or games that gobble quarters.

No nook, no cranny of society will be spared the invasion. For better or worse, they're with us—whether you consider them milestones of progress or just so much electronic kudzu. But weep not. The little devils seem benign. Almost friendly, even.

When IBM did its first market forecast for computers in 1948 it decided not to invest in the business. The market was too small. By the end of 1983 there were thirteen million computers in use in the world. A total of $200 billion will have been spent buying them, and many more billions making them run. Between 1981 and 1982 the number of computers in the world doubled; between 1982 and 1983 they doubled again. In twelve months IBM shipped more of its personal computers than all the computers it had shipped up to 1983.

You think computers aren't "in"? Well, how much trendier can you get than to be the subject of a Jerry Rubin "Networking Salon"? That's right, Jerry Rubin, number one Yippie war protester of the 1960s. In 1968, he said, "My goal is at the age of thirty-five to act like I'm fifteen." Now pushing forty, Jerry's turned businessman: He keeps busy running The Business Networking Salon at Studio 54 every Wednesday and Sunday. Here business professionals from various areas of interest—finance, advertising, real estate, and such—can exchange business cards and home phone numbers in an atmosphere that gyrates between carnival, singles bar, and convention. Some of New York's most delightful and debonair show up—and computer professionals now have their own night. At the first computer salon, held on December 8, 1982, your intrepid authors were in attendance. Part variety show, part college mixer, the salon said this about computers: Even the BPs (Beautiful People) are getting into them.

Maybe attending a computer-people networking salon wouldn't be so bad after all, especially if you've got your "Jerkfinder" with you. Radio station WIND of Chicago has a program called the "electronic producer" that runs on an Apple computer and helps talk-show hosts screen incoming callers. Instead of handing the host a piece of paper, the show's producer, who receives incoming calls, can send a description of the next five callers on the screen. The host can determine which callers get on the air in which order.

The first French restaurant to use computers for waiters was located at Valenciennes, France. In 1981 proprietor Georges Guillaume, a graduate of the famed École Polytechnique, installed computer keyboards at the tables. Customers now order by pushing buttons that call up different menus—bar, entrée, hors d'oeuvres, etc.—and then pushing the buttons for their choices. Customers seem to like the system.

Technology may save rock 'n' roll. The largest on-line data base of popular 45rpm recordings—over one hundred thousand going as far back as 1947—now takes up seventy million characters of computer-disk storage. Paul Mawhinney, owner of Record-Rama in Allison Park, Pennsylvania, started collecting the information in 1968 when he bought a hundred forty thousand singles, which he sold for $0.99 a pound. He computerized in 1978; now the data base is so big that commercial information services won't carry it. When laser disks replace 45s, Mawhinney's data base may be the last available oracle for determining who put the bop in the bop-she-bop-she-bop. Or the ram in rama-lama-ding-dong.

The first home computer? Not the Apple II or TRS-80! No, it was the Honeywell H316 "Kitchen Computer," offered in the Neiman-Marcus 1969 catalog. The $10,600 system—mandatory teletype terminal not included—could be programmed for menu planning and other household duties, including keeping track of golf scores, charity ball membership lists, and stock investments.

Drawing by Rich Tennant

Rev. Apple is ordained. Nuptial nonsense? Now you can get married by computer. Rev. Ron Jaenisch, ordained in the Universal Life Church as an "archbishop," performed the first computerized wedding on Valentine's Day 1981. An Apple computer displayed the text of the ceremony on its screen; the all-critical "I do's" were executed by punching the "Y" key for "yes." The computer, to perform the ceremony, was ordained.

Rev. Apple retires. Besieged by the media because of his use of a computer to perform weddings and finding couples eager to wed electronically,

Rev. Ron Jaenisch announced in September 1981 that he would no longer marry by computer.

Rev. Apple returns. Six months later, by spring of 1982, Rev. Ron Jaenisch is back in computer weddings—this time using two Apple computers, one to run the music system, the other to perform the ceremony. The ministerial Apple can also output digitized speech—four seconds of Jaenisch's prerecorded voice at a time—to add a humanizing touch to the wedding. The system is now so automated that Rev. Jaenisch no longer has to be present. "This is what we call 'second generation,'" says he. "If we ever get around to 'third generation,' we'll just put the whole thing inside a robot so it can throw rice and slap on water at a baptism."

In 1957, two thousand people attended the Western Joint Computer Conference, the biggest of the day. In 1967, fifteen thousand people attended. In 1969, forty-one thousand attended the Eastern (Spring) Joint Computer Conference, causing the largest traffic jam in Boston's history. In 1983, one hundred thousand people attended the National Computer Conference. (Another three hundred thousand people attended various other exhibits, conventions, and shows about computers.)

The Naked Computer's *favorite show.* It's the 1976 National Computer Conference in New York at which Data General displayed one of its computer chips in the navel of a belly dancer.

In 1968, according to the annual *Computerworld* salary survey, a computer programmer made about $6,900 a year, a data processing manager, $12,800. By 1982's survey, a junior programmer made $28,000. Managers made $52,000. The both beat inflation (Consumer Price Index) by 40 percent.

In 1962, computer industry revenues were $1 billion for the first time. In 1983, IBM has more than five times that amount in cash; industry revenues were $55 billion.

For the techie who has everything, including money. Posh advanced-technology condominium, The Terrace, in Fort Lee, New Jersey, comes with built-in wall system with stereo controls for speakers in every room, room-to-room intercoms, smoke and burglar alarms, all computer-controlled. No big deal, right? But try the bedroom, which comes with a nine-by-four-foot enclosure, called The Environment, in which the occupant may simulate exotic environments. A few computer commands and the sunlamps and suitable sound effects come on; a push of a button and a tropical rain falls. Fans stand ready to provide wind or dry off occupants. Also unique to The

Terrace is the building's talking elevator, which can greet condo owners by name, store personal messages, deliver stock quotes, etc. If you don't have $400,000 to $750,000, though, don't bother hopping the bus to Fort Lee.

For computer junkies on the road. Check into Ottawa's Teron International Hotel. Each room has a computer terminal, connections to a larger office system, large screen for text, movies, and video games, and electronic mail. If you can't get in there or you're not going to Canada, try to find a hotel that offers Roulabette (Vegas, Reno, Atlantic City), a computer connection to downstairs gaming tables that allows betting from your hotel room. To play, you get a special credit card from the casino cashier that fits in your Roulabette room terminal. It keeps track of your winnings. (You wouldn't have losses, would you?)

Medical trouble, right here in River City. The cavalcade of illnesses brought on by contact with computers is growing. . . . Dr. Gary Edward Myerson of Atlanta has catalogued video-game-related hazards such as calluses, blisters, arthralgia, tendinitis, ganglion cysts, numbness, and "video elbow." . . . Dr. D. N. Rushton of London traced an epileptic seizure in a patient to the space war game of Astro Fighter; lights flashing at fifteen cycles per second apparently set off the seizure. . . . T. K. Daneshmend and M. J. Campbell, neurologists from Bristol, U.K., reported a patient having epileptic seizures from playing Dark Warrior. Say the doctors: "Electronic Space War Video Game Epilepsy is a special category of photoconvulsive epilepsy. Video games other than space war games—for example, Super Bug or Munch Man—appear to be less epileptogenic." Whew.

High-tech Torah. Rabbi Irving Rosenbaum of the Institute for Computers in Jewish Life has compiled an extensive data base of texts and commentaries on Jewish life, dating back to the eighth century and up through the present on an IBM 370/168 mainframe computer. Called the Reponsa Project, the "rabbinical data base" can help people find answers—often more than one—to their questions and concerns, ranging from women's rights to shipbuilding, euthanasia, vegetarianism, and war.

Like any good filing system, everything is indexed, but since it's all in Hebrew, the task is more complex. "In Hebrew, the word 'steal' can appear two hundred ninety-seven different ways," says Rabbi Rosenbaum. "It's a monumental task to search for every variation."

For the less Talmudic, the institute also sells software for home computers that helps Jewish kids learn the text and chanting for the Bar Mitzvah, and teaches Jewish history. The number one best-selling program is "Jewish IQ Baseball," a quiz on Jewish history that is scored in baseball parlance. Faster answers mean more bases stolen, more runs, etc. The program also includes a special code, for Apple computers equipped with sound, to bleat the ram's horn, called a *shofar*, which is sounded on Rosh Hashanah.

The King James version of the Bible is now on floppy disk—all 4½ million characters of it. The diskettes, available from Bible Research Systems, cost $199.95 and can run on Apple, IBM, and Radio Shack computers. The six-to-eight floppy-disk set also comes with an indexing program that allows you to search for particular passages.

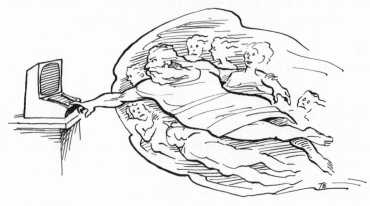

Drawing by Tim Eagan

The most ubiquitous computer? The Commodore VIC/20, one million strong at year-end 1982. The least ubiquitous: CDC's G/20, of which there is one left.

The first electronic digital computer. The University of Pennsylvania's Electronic Numerical Integrated Calculator, ENIAC, which weighed thirty tons and took fifteen thousand square feet to house. It contained eighteen thousand vacuum tubes, seventy thousand resistors, ten thousand capacitors, and six thousand switches. It is said that when ENIAC was turned on, the lights in Philadelphia dimmed. ENIAC could add five hundred numbers in one second.

The smallest computer. The Intel iAPX 432, the equivalent of a medium-size IBM computer packed onto three coat-button-size silicon chips. It can address sixty-four million memory cells—thirty-two thousand times as many as ENIAC—and can add five hundred numbers in one one-thousandth of a second. (In 1967, the smallest computer, the CDC-449, weighed thirteen pounds. It couldn't do much besides the limited tasks it was required to do as an onboard computer for Grumman planes.)

The wettest computer. The 4½-pound Husky computer (based on a Zilog Z-80 chip), which can operate underwater. Sold by Sarasota Automation for $3,000.

The next wettest computer. The hydraulic computer, designed to work on fluid dynamics rather than electricity. See Chapter 16.

The first naked computer. The "Naked Mini" sold by Computer Automation. So named because it was sold with no frills to technologically sophisticated buyers. Over six thousand installed worldwide.

The spookiest computers. The two Cray-1 computers, code-named Lodestone and Carillon, that anchor the National Security Agency's nine-story espionage complex.

The most expensive computer. The $40 million one-of-a-kind Illiac IV, financed by the army, designed at the University of Illinois, built by Burroughs, installed at NASA's Ames Research Center at 1972, finally working right by 1975, and dismantled in 1981.

The heaviest computer. The IBM FSQ-7, three hundred tons.

The lightest computer. The twenty-six-ounce Hewlett-Packard HP-75C.

The cheapest computer ever built. The $2 million computer built from $20,000 of scrap parts by William L. Eaton and Gary L. Forbes and assembled in a barn in a cornfield in Liberty, Indiana, during the years 1968 to 1973. The result was mostly a GE computer, although it had plenty of hybrid parts. The toughest part to obtain was a maintenance panel, which had been bought by an art-lover as an *objet d'art* (once he knew how badly they wanted it, he became reluctant to sell it). The easiest was a full set of programs on printout and punched cards, being sold at scrap value. It's not clear that Eaton and Forbes ever did anything with their computer.

The world's most powerful computer. The Hitachi-Hydra, capable of performing two hundred million instructions per second. The world's most miniaturized computer: the human brain, with ten *trillion* circuits jammed into an area the size of a cauliflower.

Famous users of computers. Douglas Hofstadter, author of *Gödel, Escher, Bach: An Eternal Golden Braid*; Todd Rundgren, rock star, composer, and digital light organ inventor; Jimmy Carter, President-turned-memoirs-writer; Bill Rogers, marathoner; William Safire, who uses it to research meanings of words; Edward Adler, made famous by the Apple Computer ad

Photo courtesy of Cray Research, Inc.

The Cray-1, the first designer computer. You can order it in colors to match your decor, and even get genuine leather upholstery for the surrounding bench, which houses the power supplies.

that describes how he programmed his computer to rock his baby's cradle when she cried.

Neat technologies. If the ocean were as clear as the glass used in fiber optic cables, you'd be able to see the bottom at its deepest, 35,800 feet; Josephson Junction circuits, the world's fastest, operate at a few degrees above absolute zero, at which temperature electrons form mysterious tunnels through materials; IBM's mass memory system uses a mechanical picker, jukeboxlike, to retrieve data stored magnetically on cartridges, holding 472 billion characters, enough for a short résumé for every person in the world.

Most disgusting product. Sonic Productions' Sexus Chronograph, a digital watch made in Hong Kong by Cheong Koon Company that displays explicit sex acts and four-letter words on its face and plays "cancan" music when its alarm goes off.

Next most disgusting product. Custer's Revenge, a porno video game that depicts the esteemed general dodging arrows to rape a trussed Indian maiden.

Woodstock meets Silicon Valley. On September 2, 1982, the US Festival turned Southern California on with the music of the Police, Tom Petty and the Heartbreakers, Fleetwood Mac, Pat Benatar, Talking Heads, the B-52s, Santana, the Kinks, and the Cars, their music belting out over three hundred speakers at three hundred thousand watts of power. Flanking the stage were the two largest closed-circuit video screens ever built. And along with all the music, Apple cofounder and US Festival sponsor Steve Wozniak and friends sparked, "booted up," as computerniks say, the first-known outdoor computer show—with the Apple hot-air balloon floating overhead—as well as a communications and ecology fair. In true California fashion, a new freeway offramp was built for access to the Glen Helen Regional Park near San Bernardino especially for the event, which hosted over two hundred thousand attendees. Billed as "the end of the 'me' and the beginning of the 'us' decade," it lived up to its promise—"Woz," as Wozniak is affectionately known, lost $3 million on the gig. The US Festival allegedly cost $12 million—quite a weekend—although Woz will get some of the dough back on record and tape rights. Besides, thanks to a stock market rally, from Friday to Tuesday Apple Computer's stock rose enough to increase Woz's net worth more than the $12 mil he spent on the show.

Naked computers for naked computing, or computer buffs in the buff. Club Med, that famous (or infamous) French resort network where anything goes, has added computer classes to its lessons in tennis, scuba diving, and sailing. Club Medders seem to be taking to the idea; instructors admit that, since students are already in varying states of casual dress, the experience seems less intimidating. Classes run for a few hours each afternoon during which people learn graphics, music, and simple business and household programs. If you find that it's cutting into your beach time, you can duck in for a quick game of Star Raiders during the cocktail hour or in the early morning to balance your checkbook.

The dinosaur egg-eating award. Back in 1972, engineers were still using the slide rule for their calculations. Bill Hewlett, one of the founders of Hewlett-Packard, thought it would be easier and more accurate to give them a scientific calculator to do the work. H-P's management was skeptical; subsequently, market research proved there was no market for a $400 calculator when slide rules cost only $20. Bill reportedly said, "I don't know if anyone else wants one, but I do. Build it." The HP-35—with performance comparable to old ENIAC—was introduced. The HP-35 was the hottest product ever advertised in the computer trade press, and by 1980, scientific calculators had driven the slide rule makers out of business.

First known use of the word "computer." A scribe named Trevisa wrote in 1398 of "compotystes . . . departed by twelue mones, in sixe euen and sixe odde," a reference to maintaining the calendar. Turns out the word was used to refer to those involved in day-reckoning for some time; Sir Thomas

Brown spoke of "the Calendars of these computers" in 1646. Seven years later, Blaise Pascal sparked riots by inventing the first working model of the automatic calculator, dubbed the Pascaline.

The first known computer? Johann Martin Zacharias Dase, 1824–61, employed by various European governments to perform computations. He could multiply two hundred-digit numbers in his head *and* get the right answer!

In 1799, Edward Ludd, who may or may not have had a full wit, destroyed some stocking frames and became the spiritual talisman for a cabal of disgruntled workers who traipsed about England destroying machines. Ned Ludd's followers, who adhered to the motto, "No General but Ludd Means the Poor Any Good," rampaged from 1800 to about 1815 smashing the looms, workshops, and mills they thought would put them out of work. Although this wasn't the first time the citizenry turned against technology— in 1529 a German inventor of the ribbon mill was drowned—it was the only movement out of which a word was coined. "Luddite" has today come to characterize a worker who resists new technology. Most recent reoccurrence: anticomputer protesters calling themselves Processed World picketing the U.S. Office Automation Conference in 1982. Wearing cardboard computer terminals on their heads and carrying slogans such as "IBM: Intensely Boring Machines" and "Office Automation Is for Office Automatons," they tried to enlist the sympathy of attendees—including John C. Whitmarsh, editor of the enemy tabloid *Computerworld*.

Don't leave home without it. Banks call them automated teller machines, but after ATMs, what? APMs, that's what. The Southland Corporation, which runs the well-known 7-Eleven convenience stores, is planning to install automated gas-pumping machines across the country. And why not? Southland is the largest independent retail gas pumper, one billion gallons through the hoses in 1982. You just stick your credit card in, fill 'er up, and get the bill on your next statement. Why didn't Exxon think of that?
Actually, a company called Athena Systems, based in the Boston area, thought of a similar idea in 1970. The company intended to mount computerized card readers near gas pumps to record transactions; alas, Athena's financing dried up during a recession, the company went under, and the concept went into hibernation.

A penny for your electronic pulses. George Wittmeier of Kirkland, Washington, has a right to be mad at a computer. Somehow he underpaid his income tax by one penny; the computer toted up interest and fines totaling $159.58 and sent him a dunning letter. An IRS spokesman said charac-

Anticomputer protestor (note digital wristwatch) attempts to convert *Computerworld* editor Whitmarsh.

Photo courtesy John C. Dvorak

teristically, "Obviously the computer has gone berserk." George was less caustic; said he, "If the computer could prove all taxpayers underpaid by one cent each, we could pay off the national debt just like that, without a tax increase."

The first microprocessor. Also called a computer on a chip, it was developed in 1970. Today there are more microprocessors than there are people on the earth.

"It's impossible to do a twenty-four-hour-a-day, seven-day-a-week news program without a computer," says Rob Barnes of Cable News Network. CNN uses an Onyx computer system, with a network of thirty terminals, with one on each anchor desk to bring late-breaking stories to the newscaster. First accounts of the Mount St. Helens volcano eruption were read to the viewing audience right off the computer terminal's screen—probably at the same moment (less the speed of microwaves) they were being typed in at the other end.

Xerox claims in its advertising that today's office has changed very little from its turn-of-the-century counterpart. So it would seem: Most executives still write their letters in longhand on yellow legal-size pads, secretaries use typewriters with keyboards designed to slow their typing speed—the first typewriters jammed if they went too fast—and tons upon tons of paperwork die the death of the unread in mile after mile of file cabinets. Thus, one of the hottest uses for computers today is office automation. Word processing, teleconferencing, computerized telephone systems, intelligent photocopiers, networks, and executive computers—it's all part of the push for the paperless office.

Will there ever *be* a paperless office?

Ask Amy Wohl, a well-known office automation consultant from Bala Cynwyd, Pennsylvania: "The paperless office will arrive about the same time as the paperless toilet."

Herman Luscher devised a color test that produces a complete psychological profile based on an individual's ranking eight colors in order of preference. Our friend Rick Bennett spent six weeks programming a computer with the Luscher Color Test, which was introduced as a "traffic stopper" at a high-tech personnel show in Woburn, Massachusetts, a few years ago.

Your authors were visiting Rick at his Synapse Computer Corporation office in Milpitas, California, and decided to give it a try. Here's a sampling from one profile:

Seeks affectionate, satisfying and harmonious relationships. Desires an intimate union in which there is love, self-sacrifice, and mutual trust. Imaginative and sensitive; seeking an outlet for these qualities—especially in the company of someone equally sensitive. Interest and enthusiasm readily aroused by the unusual and the adventurous.

Another testee, a 265-pound systems engineer and member of a motorcycle gang, submitted to the computerized Luscher Color Test. The report:

Tries to escape from his problems, difficulties, and tensions by abrupt, headstrong, and ill-considered decisions. Desperately seeking a way of escape, and there is a danger of reckless behavior to the point of self-destruction.

Upon reading the analysis, the engineer-*cum*-biker threw a gallon jug of wine across the room. The jug shattered against the wall. He then ripped the phone out of the wall, twirled the phone like a lariat, proceeded to climb on his chopped Harley and lay a strip of rubber twenty feet long down the hallway. So all right, Herman, we believe you!

FROM THE CACHE:
Whence the Counting Machine

Actually, "cache" is an old word from the French *cacher*, meaning to hide, but in modern computer lingo it refers to a memory storage module. Every time you see "From the Cache" in *The Naked Computer*, it means you've found a memory storage module of historical interest related to the computer.

Computers are simply counting machines; a computer can't even subtract. (Binary arithmetic allows you to subtract by adding.) What's interesting is all the ways we've learned to put these ultrafast counting machines to work for us. If we reach deep down into our cache bag, the first computer we pull out is the abacus, whose origins date back to 500 B.C. in Egypt. The abacus as we know it today came into use in China about A.D. 200; it was called the *saun-pan*, or computing tray; in Japan it is called a *soroban*.

Learning to use an abacus isn't hard, and your skill at arithmetic increases rapidly with its use; the abacus is in daily use throughout the East. In 1946, a contest was staged between Army Private Thomas Wood, the most skilled electronic desk calculator operator in the United States, and Kiyoshi Matsuzaki of the Japanese Ministry of Postal Administration. They were given fifty problems in addition, subtraction, multiplication, and division; Matsuzaki, wielding his *soroban*, won in everything except multiplication. Lee Kaichen, a Chinese professor, beat computers with his abacus in Seattle, New York, and Taipei in 1959. Some abacus experts become so adept at calculating that they eventually set the abacus aside and do it all in their heads.

Another rather interesting counting machine was devised by a Spaniard named Magnus around A.D. 1000, a machine made of brass resembling a human head with figures instead of teeth. The thing looked so diabolical that priests destroyed it with clubs; we'll never know if it worked.

Leonardo da Vinci (1452–1519), the consummate Renaissance man, dabbled in science but was never known to be interested in calculating machines. Yet in 1967, two volumes of his notebooks were discovered in Madrid's National Library of Spain detailing a digit-counting machine. A model, interpreted from his drawings, is at IBM.

Blaise Pascal (1623–62) was a child prodigy. Before he turned thirteen, he had proven the thirty-second proposition of Euclid and discovered an error in René Descartes's geometry. At sixteen, Pascal began preparing to write a study of the entire field of mathematics, but his father required his time to hand-total long columns of numbers. Pascal began designing a calculating machine, which he finally perfected when he was thirty. The Pascaline, a beautiful, hand-crafted brass box about fourteen by five by three inches, the first accurate mechanical calculator, was born. The Pascaline was not a commercial success in Pascal's lifetime; it could do the work of six accountants, and people feared it would create unemployment—not unlike modern sentiments about computers and robots. Pascal was dismayed and disgusted by society's reactions to his machine and completely renounced his interest in science and mathematics, devoting the rest of his life to God. He is best known for his collection of spiritual essays, *Les Pensées*, even though the basic design of the Pascaline lived on in mechanical calculators for over three hundred years. As a counting machine, the Pascaline was not superseded until the invention of the electronic calculating machine. "The arithmetical machine produces effects which approach nearer to thought than all the actions of animals," wrote Pascal in the *Pensées*, "but it does nothing which would enable us to attribute will to it, as to the animals." Pascal, a genius by any measure, died of a massive brain hemorrhage at the age of thirty-nine. In 1968, a programming language was named after him.

One of the most common and useful applications for a personal computer is writing, called *word processing*. The term grew out of *data processing*, which is a computer working with numerical information as opposed to the written language. "Next to liquor, word processing is a writer's best friend," says one writer we know.

We wrote *The Naked Computer* on home computers, using a word processing program called "Benchmark." To make learning Benchmark even more fun, NEC Information Systems, which sells the NEC PC-8000 computer we're writing on, asked Beth Harrington, a free-lance writer in Boston, to pen a story (using the NEC and Benchmark, of course) for a self-paced audio cassette training course for the word processor. Entitled "A Modern Day Romance," it tells the story of how Freeman Buckboard, who has to churn out a report in short order, meets Gertrude Pankhurst, who helps him get the job done on her word processor. They fall in love, of course—that is, Gertrude falls in love with Freeman, and Freeman falls in love with the computer.

For the past four years, *Computerworld* has hosted the Ridiculous Button Contest, wherein readers submit their favorite clichés and turns of phrase in the hopes of these being chosen to become a CW button. A sampling of some past winners:

- Kiss My Bits
- Micros Are Thinker Toys
- Pardon Me, Modem
- Floppy Now, Hard Later
- Garbage In, Gospel Out

- Bugs Are Sons of Glitches

- King Kong Plays Pong

- Ma Bell Runs a Baudy House

- Someday My Prints Will Come

- Loose Bits Sink Chips

Along with being dubbed a Certified Funny Person and winning a hand-held computer gem, the winners share the knowledge that their witty gem will find its way into thousands of pockets across the country; *Computerworld* gives away a hundred thousand buttons annually at computer trade shows.

Gene Primoff, vice-president at Worldwide Computer Services in Wayne, New Jersey, has announced that his firm will award $25,000 to the first person who can prove or disprove the twin prime conjecture that "there are an infinite number of twin prime pairs." Euclid (c. 300 B.C.) proved there are an infinite number of prime numbers—those that are divisible only by themselves and 1. Computers have permitted calculating prime numbers in ways difficult or impossible in the past; in 1979, the largest known prime number was $2^{21,701}$. One mathematician postulates that the chance of two numbers both being prime is about the same as getting heads on two successive flips of a coin.

If the computer age has been good for anything, it's been good for finding prime numbers. What it's *not* been good at is telling us what prime numbers are good for!

On the track of a killer. For nearly two years, Atlanta, Georgia, was a city gripped by fear and terror, watching twenty-eight black children disappear and die. Wayne Williams was tracked down and convicted for murder in the case with the aid of a special computer system developed by Samit Roy, director of data processing for the city of Atlanta.

Using a sophisticated IBM data base organizer called STAIRS (Storage and Information Retrieval System) and powerful IBM computers, Roy and his staff entered every scrap of data the police and investigators from ten separate agencies could find. The disparate pieces of information were threaded together by the various STAIRS programs to find reoccurrences and similarities. Williams's downfall was when he was spotted at the bridge; once information about him, including the kind of vehicle he drove, a physical description, employment, and such were entered, the evidence mounted. By the use of two action verbs, "known" and "seen," Williams's activities and whereabouts were tracked. Using these techniques, "In ten minutes we were able to compile a forty-page history," declares Roy.

The computer's activities didn't cease with arrest; once prosecution began, the big IBM tracked the defense's testimony against prior statements from witnesses, then used the results during cross-examination.

Wayne Williams is safely behind bars now, the children of Atlanta sleep better at night, and Samit Roy's computer system is available to law-enforcement agencies across the United States.

Benched by a computer. Hank Stram, former head coach of the Kansas City Chiefs, thinks the "sideline computer" will be standard field equipment in football by the end of the decade. "Game analysis is extremely detailed and gives a competitive edge," says he. "The computer is fed all the offensive and defensive plays of an opponent's last three or four games, then analyzes the information and comes up with the opponent's tendencies in specific situations." Stram, who is now a sports consultant at MDS Quantel, a computer firm, says computer analysis helped the Chiefs put the Minnesota Vikings away in Super Bowl IV. And Dallas Cowboys coach Tom Landry gives it credit for helping him call a crucial play in a game against Miami last year. And *both* Super Bowl teams were computerized this year. Gee, if the idea really catches on, maybe they can play the whole game as a computer simulation and save us from the boredom.

Taming the Green Monster. Computers have helped sports in many ways. In 1975, for instance, a computer helped prove that pitchers had been right—the left-field wall at Boston's Fenway Park is actually 9 feet shorter than the posted 315 feet from home plate at the foul line. It took an aerial photograph, a computer, some basic trigonometry, and World War II mapping lenses to solve the mystery. Officials decided not to move the wall.

Bread and circuses, computer-style. Dayton's Department Store in Minneapolis has taken the drudgery out of filling out credit-card applications with the Touch 'n' Talk computer from Information Dialogues, Inc. The customer touches squares on the screen to activate the computer, which displays questions while asking them in a soft voice at the same time. Once the application is completed, it is printed out on paper, which the customer takes to a salesperson and—*voilà!* $300 in instant credit.

Dayton's says credit-card applications have risen 38 percent since the Touch 'n' Talk computer was installed.

Elliot Nestle of Synapse Computers tells the story of how a Dr. Schlumwasser at UCLA landed a government grant for a study on the sexual habits of sea slugs. His premise was that their sexuality varied according to water temperature—the hotter they got, the hotter they got, so to speak.

Dr. Schlumwasser bought Interdata's first computer to monitor the heating coils that regulated the water temperature in the tanks he kept the sea

Drawing by Tim Eagan

slugs in. The experiment proceeded, but upon returning from a rather long lunch one day, the good doctor found the computer had gone haywire and boiled the slugs to death. According to Elliot, however, they went with a smile.

CHAPTER 2

THE YOUNG AND THE RESTLESS:

People and Companies That Made Computers Great

The new breed is young, bright, energetic, and infused with a vision—microcomputers stacked miles high, offices awash in binary code, kids welded to computers, sugarplums pierced by microwaves.

The old breed is rich.

Some are the movers and shakers, others are moved and shaken. Some have gone from rags to riches, others from riches to rags. Some are gurus, some are frauds; most are a tantalizing combination. Some were trained in the discipline, while others fell into it from other occupations. A few, it sometimes seems, came from outer space.

Thomas J. Watson, Sr., prime mover of IBM, began his career as a salesman for National Cash Register. After working there for nearly twenty years, he was fired in 1914 by NCR's feisty president, John Patterson. Piqued, Watson accepted the presidency of the Computer-Tabulating-Recording Company, a miniconglomerate that contained the remnants of a company built around Herman Hollerith's inven-

tion of the punched-card tabulator for the Bureau of the Census. Watson began a two-pronged crusade: One prong was to marry punched-card technology with calculating technology; the other was to get even with NCR.

Until his son, Tom Watson, Jr., bet the company on the development of the IBM 360 computer—a minimum $300 million gamble that cost more than the cost for developing the atomic bomb—the company was a midget among giants such as Westinghouse and General Electric, which forsook computers to pursue careers in nuclear reactors, and RCA, which chose to chase after color TV development instead of computers.

Since then, Watson and progeny have watched GE, RCA, and Xerox get out of the computer business; in 1982 IBM earned more than all its computer competitors combined. NCR, its nemesis, didn't turn a profit in computers until 1973, fifty-nine years after Watson senior was canned.

But now the pioneers are dying off. Mauchly, Watson, Sr., Kettering, and Terman are gone—and memories of the early days are fading like so many bits of magnetism on the rusting iron doughnuts that once served most computers as memory cells. By the time the computer industry is bigger than the oil industry—about 2001—who will remember that RCA, GE, and Westinghouse were once in the business? Or that these others were, too: Philco, Xerox, Cincinnati Milacron, Sylvania, Bendix, Packard-Bell, General Mills, Royal McBee, Monroe, ALWAC, North American Aviation, Northrop, Singer, and Pillsbury?

And how many of the new guys—Apple, Grid, Fortune Systems, Spartacus, Trilogy, Magnuson, Apollo—will have come and gone?

What's the average age of a computer person? In 1969 the American Federation of Information Processing Societies surveyed thirty thousand members and came up with an average age of thirty-four. From the results of the survey, it was clear that the survey was biased toward people with longevity—meaning the average age of the computer-jockeying population as a whole was less.

Although these people have aged since that survey, the industry has grown considerably since 1969. In fact, by *The Naked Computer*'s most conservative calculations, enough youngsters have been brought into the fold to make the average age 30.5.

Steve Wozniak, cofounder of Apple Computer, once crashed his private plane after takeoff and suffered amnesia for five weeks. Shaken, he took leave of Apple to return to U.C. Berkeley to finish his degree in computer science—a pursuit he interrupted when he cofounded Apple and became a multimillionaire.

Wozniak, who was a "phone phreak" and guerrilla-theater buff in his first college stint, joined Steve Jobs in 1977 to make computers. The two Steves parlayed a $2,500 investment and facilities in the family garage into a $600 million company, along with personal fortunes of well over $100 million each.

How'd you like to work for a company that throws weekly beer blasts? For the five hundred employees of Tandem Computer, an eight-year-old manufacturer of fail-safe computers, 4:30 P.M. on Friday is a perfect time to chat and chug a beer with President Jim Treybig, who often is attired in a western hat and cowboy boots. The company has jogging paths, an employee swimming pool, day care, male beauty contests, promotion from within, yoga classes, corporate barbecues, and a management manual that says, "You never have the right to screw a person or mistreat them."

Does it work? Tandem grew in seven years to become a $300 million company; it's sure to land in the Fortune 500 within the next seven. The key is tying employees into corporate performance. Everyone gets stock options—$100,000 a head for employees who have been with the company since 1977.

H. Ross Perot, the man who once gave the New York City Police Department twenty Tennessee walking horses and who founded Electronic Data Systems, is eccentric by any measure. His penchant for hiring former Marines and Army Green Berets as staff, however, paid off when two of his employees were taken hostage in Teheran during the Iranian revolution. Receiving no support from the State Department, Perot in February 1979 assembled a strike force of employees, hired ex-Green Beret Col. Arthur (Bull) Simons, an old friend, to lead them, and masterminded their release in a commando raid.

The employees were being held hostage by the revolutionaries to convince EDS to come back and man computers it had left behind during the American evacuation. A $12,750,000 ransom was unpayable because the Iranian banking system had broken down. Perot himself cased the prison when he was allowed to visit the prisoners earlier in the month. The EDS forces arranged for an unruly mob to storm the prison; during the resultant melee the prisoners scrambled over a wall and made their getaway. Jimmy Carter should have done so well.

How did Perot get so rich? In 1962 he founded the company and championed a "cafeteria management" style of data processing. His company would run a customer's computers on a turnkey basis. He landed a big Blue Cross/Blue Shield contract in Texas, and EDS was on its way. When EDS went public, Ross's stock was worth $16 a share. By March 1969 it had climbed to $169. By May it was back down to $29, and Perot had set a Wall Street record for the largest paper loss ever.

When Ken Olsen was working at MIT's Digital Computer Laboratory, his boss, Norman Taylor, asked him to build a small computer to test the memory they planned to install in the Air Defense Command's SAGE computer they were building. It had to be an under-the-table project; money wasn't formally allocated. In addition, it had to be completed in ten months to perform its task. Olsen was a hardworking but odd kind of guy; one of his colleagues said of him, "He's a nerd. He'll never go anywhere." Ken looked the project over, then told Taylor it couldn't be done in ten months. "Then do it in nine, and I'll buy you a case of Scotch." Olsen doesn't drink, but he loved the challenge, so he did it. That machine provided the conceptual foundation for Olsen's Programmed Data Processor—or the minicomputer, the product with which he founded Digital Equipment Corporation, the world's second largest computer company.

THE TOP COMPUTER MILLIONAIRES

NAME	COMPANY	WORTH ($M)	COMMENTS
David Packard	Hewlett-Packard	$1,000	Cofounded H-P in garage in 1938. First high-tech denizen of Silicon Valley. $538 investment grew to shares worth $1 billion.
William Hewlett	Hewlett-Packard	$650	Other cofounder with Packard.
H. Ross Perot	Electronic Data Systems	$325	Founded EDS in 1962. Owns 52 percent. Estimated worth today: $325 million.
An Wang and family	Wang Labs	$620	Emigrated from China, 1945; U.S. citizen, 1954. Invented magnetic core memory. Founded Wang Labs with $15,000 in 1951. Own share,

			$200 million; wife's, $120 million; childrens', $300 million.
Mandel brothers	Newark Electronics	$250	Brothers Jack, Joseph, Morton bought distributor in 1968 for over $20 million. Each worth $75 million.
Max Palevsky	Scientific Data Systems	$200	Son of a house painter. Started SDS in 1961 with investment of $100,000 shared by another, and $900,000 venture capital. Sold to Xerox in 1969 for $1 billion. Palevsky walked away with $100 million, since grown to $200 million.
Ken Olsen	Digital Equipment	$157	Left MIT to start DEC in 1957. Venture capital investment: $70,000, cashed in later for $350 million.
Pat McGovern	International Data	$150	Founded newsletter and data base of computer sites in 1964 for $3,000. Launched *Computerworld* in 1967. The only major stockholder.
Howard Vollum	Tektronix	$135	Started appliance shop after World War II. Built oscilloscopes, started business in 1946. Company revenues over $1 billion.
Saul Steinberg	Leasco, Reliance Group	$130	Founded computer leasing business 1961. Acquired Reliance in 1968. Wealth includes immediate family.
Gordon Moore	Intel	$125	Left Caltech to join William Shockley in 1956. Cofounded Fairchild Semiconductor in 1957. Started Intel 1968.
Virginia Binger	Honeywell, 3M	$100	Inheritance. Daughter of 3M founder, wife of Honeywell chief executive officer.

THE TOP COMPUTER MILLIONAIRES

NAME	COMPANY	WORTH ($M)	COMMENTS
Steven Jobs	Apple Computer	$100	With Steven Wozniak began in family garage in 1976 with $1,300 from sale of VW Microbus. Owns 13.6 percent of Apple.
Henry Singleton	Teledyne	$100	Left Litton in 1960, started Teledyne with $225,000 and venture money.
Armas Cliff Markkula	Apple Computer	$91	Invested $91,000 in Apple, left Intel to be chairman of the board.

Source: Forbes 400.

Tale of a technological gunslinger. Neil Lincoln, a senior engineer at Control Data Corporation, defines a supercomputer as "a computer that is only one generation behind the user's needs." Since it takes considerable time to design and build the world's fastest, most sophisticated, and most expensive computers (they start at $4 million and often cost as much as $20 million)—used at such places as Los Alamos and Lawrence Livermore Scientific Laboratories, the National Center for Atmospheric Research, and the Department of Defense—there just aren't too many around. Seymour Cray used to work with Neil Lincoln and was CDC's top designer. A complete recluse and workaholic, Cray demanded in 1962—during the Cuban missile crisis—that CDC, headquartered in Minneapolis, allow him to move his lab to his hometown of Chippewa Falls, Wisconsin, far from any possible nuclear hubbub. CDC acceded, but in 1972 Cray resigned and formed his own supercomputer company, Cray Research, Inc., and went into head-on competition with CDC.

It took Cray four years to deliver his first computer, the Cray-1, but it was the fastest computer on earth. Installing a Cray-1 is no simple task. A Cray team goes to the site months in advance to install a false floor strong enough to support the computer; several thousand dollars' worth of special Freon plumbing, to cool the thousands of circuits, must be installed underneath. The Cray-1 is tested for months, then mounted on a platform and moved by truck to the site. In the case of certain Defense Department installations, the truck stops in a deserted location, the drivers lock it up and leave, and military drivers take the Cray to its secret location. Otherwise, Cray delivers the machine complete with two engineers to maintain and upgrade it—forever.

By the summer of 1982, about forty Cray-1's had been installed, and it was still the fastest computer. Yet for the past two years there were two projects under way to develop a computer ten times faster. One project was in Mendota Heights, a suburb of Minneapolis and Cray Research headquarters, and was conducted by a group of bright young engineers; the other was in Chippewa Falls and was Seymour's very own. Both projects were completed at about the same time; the first was an improvement over the Cray-1 and was dubbed the X-MP. The other was an entirely new computer that achieves its speed by supercooling—in this case the entire computer is immersed in a tank of subzero fluorocarbon fluid; the computer was called the Cray-2.

John Vincent Atanasoff devised the first real electronic digital computer in 1937, but he lives today virtually unrecognized by his peers or society. Atanasoff discovered the four basic principles for a digital computer in an interesting epiphany on a dark and cold winter night; he jumped in his car in front of his Iowa house to think things over for a bit and ended up drinking in an Illinois roadhouse four hours later, with all the details worked out in his mind.

J. Presper Eckert and his partner John Mauchly "borrowed" from Atanasoff's unpatented work, went on to build ENIAC, and today are generally proclaimed fathers of the modern computer. Meanwhile, George Stibitz built the Complex Number Calculator at Bell Labs in 1939; Bell says that was the first digital computer. And that's not the end of the controversy.

Photo courtesy of Sperry Corporation

J. Presper Eckert stands before ENIAC at the Moore School of Engineering, University of Pennsylvania, 1946.

What's in a name? Some are suggestive, such as Synapse Computer; others are mundane, such as International Business Machines. Some seek to institutionalize a founder's name, such as Amdahl, Hewlett-Packard, Magnuson, and Osborne.

The most esoteric: Atari is a warning to one's opponent in the Japanese game Go.

The hippiest: Apple reflects its owners' concern with health foods and clean living (the original name was Apple Fruit Packers). Lotus Software represents founder Mitchell Kapor's hippie-radical-1960s-TM-organic-substance background. (Lotus makes a data-base program for the IBM personal computer.)

The juiciest: Georgia's favorite fruit, peaches, came to be the name of Atlanta's successful Peachtree Software.

The most stalwart: Broderbund, the German word for brother bond, was founded by Doug and Gary Carlston.

The most misinterpreted: Pickles and Trout conjures up all kinds of ideas; turns out these were the owners' last names.

The most backward: Sorcim suggests magic, sorcery, and images of power; it's actually Micros spelled backward.

The most roundabout: Tandy/Radio Shack began as a firm selling leathermaking hobby kits—you know, the billfold that you sewed together with plastic cord—started by Dave Tandy. He's since sold off everything except consumer electronics.

Who really *invented the computer?* Conrad Zuse was an early pioneer in the computer field. Born in Berlin, Zuse took a degree in civil engineering, but his interest in mathematics stimulated him to build a machine made of electromechanical relays that would perform complex equations. He built his first computer in his parents' living room and called it the V-1. When World War II broke out and the Germans began launching the V-1 and V-2 rockets, Zuse renumbered his computers with a Z-designation; Wernher von Braun helped him escape from Berlin in 1945 with his best machine, the Z-4, hidden in a wagon, and Zuse went into hiding in the Swiss Alps.

He was a man with many innovative ideas; he hired blind programmers with a talent for mathematics who were very proficient. He did work for IBM and Remington Rand (which became Sperry Rand/Univac) and later sold his interests to the German computer firm Siemens. Semiretired, in his seventies, he lives today in the village of Hunfeld, Germany, within walking distance of a high school bearing his name.

But Time and Chance Happeneth to Them All Department. Ever wonder how IBM came up with the idea of the type ball for the Selectric typewriter? It wasn't intentional; in fact, it was the by-product of a new computer language. In 1964, Ken Iverson and Adin Falkoff were trying to design a character set for Iverson's new, easy-to-use notation, called APL (A Programming Language). It was a series of symbols, and it seemed there was no easy way to transfer the idea to a standard typewriter, so they had to do it themselves. In the process, they found the easiest way to create the symbols was if they configured them around a ball. IBM liked the idea so much it employed it for all its typewriters in 1971.

Biggest publishing success. Your respectful authors call him Chairman Pat, but to the world at large he's Patrick J. McGovern, head of the world's most prestigious and influential computer publication, newspaper, and re-search organization. When he sold his car nineteen years ago to launch a newsletter on the computer industry with the $3,000 proceeds, even *he* probably didn't know the heights to which the industry would carry him. In 1967 he launched *Computerworld* to generate leads for his data files. The newsletter, nicknamed "The Gray Sheet," still exists, but *Computerworld* is the success story: It's the number one trade publication in the country, with over a hundred thousand paid subscribers (and four times that number of pass-around readers). Today Chairman Pat has an empire that spans the globe and is worth over $120 million.

His most recent summit-level conference was his marriage to Lore Harp, founder of Vector Graphic.

For a honeymoon, McGovern and Harp journeyed to Nepal. McGovern tells the story of visiting a monastery where handwritten sacred documents are stored on thick stone shelves. He discussed their importance to other monks with a lama, who said it was difficult for monks from faraway monas-teries to traverse the vast distances to read them. Hence, said the lama, they had plans of copying the tablets. "By hand?" asked McGovern, imagining scribes at work for hundreds of years. "Oh, no," replied the lama, "we use a Xerox 9200."

Burroughs, like many other computer firms, began business life peddling calculating machines. International though it was in scope, it was not an aggressive, innovative firm; management was imbued with caution and con-servatism. Perhaps the best-known and most innovative Burroughs was Wil-liam, the old man's grandson, who wrote *Naked Lunch*.

William C. Norris is a maverick. Raised on a farm near Red Bluff, Nebraska, after World War II, Norris formed Engineering Research Associ-ates, which was bought by Sperry Rand in 1952. In 1957 he left Sperry Rand and formed Control Data Corporation, one of the two top supercom-puter makers in the world and a major force in computer services. When Control Data had to face what Norris felt was unethical competition from IBM, he brought suit—and won.

Norris believes that computers can contribute to solving social problems:

He developed a health-care program for the Rosebud Sioux of South Da-
kota, and he created a computerized education program called PLATO,
now available in over a hundred cities across the nation. Since 1962, Control Data has sunk over $900 million into PLATO without ever showing a
profit—personal computers, such as the Apple, have had much more success in the schools, mostly because they are much less expensive.

Norris has said he wants to be remembered not as an entrepreneur who
started one of the world's most successful computer companies but as someone who helped solve the nation's social problems with business techniques.
Perhaps testing the waters, Control Data established the Wheels Program,
which financed used cars for paroled ex-convicts to help them land and keep
jobs. Unfortunately, some of the ex-cons took the wheels and split—to the
tune of $137,000.

In the midst of high-tech endeavors, Bill Norris hasn't lost touch with
his roots. He encourages his employees in Minneapolis to raise vegetables in
the huge garden adjoining CDC headquarters. And should anyone doubt
his sincerity, the old windmill from his father's farm stands tall on the lawn,
where Norris can see it from his office.

THE BILLION-DOLLAR CLUB
(COMPANIES WITH OVER $1 BILLION REVENUE FROM
INFORMATION-PROCESSING INDUSTRY)

COMPANY	1982 REVENUES*	HISTORY
IBM	$28,934,000,000	Founded as miniconglomerate Computing-Tabulating-Recording Company in early 1900s. Included The Tabulating Company, formed in 1890 by Herman Hollerith, inventor of punched-card equipment used by Census Bureau. Thomas J. Watson, Sr., installed as president in 1914. Name changed to IBM in 1924. First computer shipped in 1952.
Sperry	$2,950,000,000	1946 inventors Eckert-Mauchly of ENIAC leave the University of Pennsylvania over patent dispute to form Electronic Controls Corp., later Eckert-Mauchly Corp. Plan and start building Universal Automatic Computer (Univac); 40 percent stock sold in 1948 to American Totalizer, racetrack scoreboard company,

		rest to Remington Rand in 1950. Rand ships first Univac 1 in 1951. In 1955 Rand merges with Sperry Corp. First computer profit in 1966. Sperry drops Univac division name in 1982.
Honeywell	$1,685,000,000	Raytheon's computer division, after miserable development efforts, joins Minneapolis Honeywell Corporation, a maker of thermostats. Buys Computer Controls Corp. (CCC) in 1965; GE installed base in 1970.
Burroughs	$4,186,000,000	Begun as adding-machine company, bought into business in 1948.
NCR	$3,526,000,000	Longtime cash register company, bought Computer Research Corp., a Northrop spin-off, in 1952. First computer profit in 1973.
CDC	$3,301,000,000	Engineering Research Associates, formed out of disbanded Navy group after World War II and headed by William Norris, bought by Rand in 1952. Norris leaves in 1957 and founds Control Data Corp.
Hewlett-Packard	$2,168,000,000	Founded by David Packard and William Hewlett in garage in 1939 to make electronic equipment.
Digital Equipment	$3,881,000,000	Founded by Ken Olsen, MIT scientist working on SAGE computer, in 1957; $70,000 in venture capital start-up. Cash in for venture firm in 1972 at $350 million.

*Includes only revenues related to computers, data processing services, software, or peripherals. Not listed are Wang ($1.159 billion) and Storage Technology Corporation ($1,072 billion), since primary revenues come from word processing (Wang) or peripherals (STC), not computers.

The world's first programmer. "She was thoroughly original, and her genius, for genius she possessed, was not poetic, but metaphysical and mathematical," said the *London Examiner.* She? The first programmer was Lady Augusta Ada Lovelace (1816–52), daughter of the poet Lord Byron and for eight years mentor to Charles Babbage. Babbage spent most of his life trying to perfect a calculating machine; the first was called the Difference Engine, the second the Analytical Engine. "We may say most aptly that the Analytical Engine weaves algebraical patterns just as the Jacquard-loom weaves flowers and leaves," wrote Ada. "Here, it seems to us, resides much more of originality that the Difference Engine can be fairly entitled to claim." (For more on the Jacquard Loom and Babbage's Engines, see "From the Cache.")

Ada bore a gift for writing similar to her father's, and in 1843 she began a translation of a famous paper on the Analytical Engine. Her insights were such that her notes grew to three times the length of the original article and were accepted for publication in a book entitled *Taylor's Scientific Memoirs*. Babbage tried to persuade her to redraft the material and publish another book on the engine, which she agreed to begin work on but that never progressed beyond notes.

Ada did not lack the ability; to quote from the *Examiner* again,

> With an understanding thoroughly masculine in solidity, grasp and firmness, Lady Lovelace had all the delicacies of the most refined female character. Her manners, her tastes, her accomplishments, were feminine in the nicest sense of the word; and the superficial observer would never have divined the strength and the knowledge that lay hidden under the womanly graces. Proportionate to her distaste for the frivolous and commonplace was her enjoyment of true intellectual society. Eagerly she sought the acquaintance of all who were distinguished in science, art and literature.

Ada helped correct some errors and fallacies in Babbage's work but developed on her own the notion of repeating one set of instructions over and over while making a large calculation—what we term today a "loop" or "subroutine." It would be another hundred years before her idea was implemented.

Ada's interest extended well beyond science; she loved to bet the horses and became deeply indebted as a result. She was known to take opium as well as alcohol. There are tales of her liaisons with Babbage and other scientists, which may or may not have led to her untimely death, due to cancer of the womb, at thirty-six—the same age as her father when he died. Today the Department of Defense has a special programming language called ADA, to honor the world's first programmer.

The world's second programmer. It would be a hundred years before women became involved with computers again. By that time, technology had progressed beyond gear-driven calculators to devices employing electricity, vacuum tubes, and relays.

Babbage's machine was reborn at Harvard University in 1944 as a machine called the Mark I, or Automatic Sequence Controlled Calculator. Babbage's twentieth-century counterpart was Howard Aiken; Lady Lovelace's was a woman named Grace Murray Hopper, a math teacher at Vassar and Barnard, then a lieutenant in the Navy, who programmed the Mark I for Aiken in 1943.

It was Grace Murray Hopper who saved the Mark I project—"tamed the beast," as one staffer said—by writing the complex instructions that made it work.

And Grace Murray Hopper said, "It was all so obvious. Why start from scratch with every single program you write? Develop one that would do a lot of the basic work over and over again for you." This planted the seeds for COBOL (Common Business-Oriented Language).

Grace worked with the Eckert-Mauchly Computer Corporation while UNIVAC I was being built, and she stayed on as the company passed on to Remington Rand and the Sperry Corporation until retiring in 1971. She has won nearly every award in the computer industry, and in 1971 Sperry established a Grace Murray Hopper Award. She is a captain in the Naval Reserve, travels worldwide giving speeches, and expects to celebrate "the party to end all New Year's Eve parties" in 1999—the year she will be ninety-four years old.

In 1982, the DeVry Institute of Technology conducted a study in Chicago that showed the number of women entering data processing jobs had increased 20 percent over the previous year. A *Computerworld* survey the same year indicated that two thirds of U.S. companies have more men in data processing management positions than women.

He's called "The DP Doctor," and he's an outspoken critic of the status quo in business. Joseph A. Izzo is head of a small but prestigious consulting firm called the JAI Group in Santa Monica, California, whose staff performs "turnaround management," a nice way to say they go into a data processing department that is serious trouble and get things operating normally again. "We're hard-core implementers," says Joe; all his people are DP pros, with an average of eighteen years in the business. The job, if the JAI Group SWAT team does it well, is over in twelve months; the cost: $350,000 to $1.2 million.

"The Mad Poet of Computerdom" is how *Playgirl* dubbed Ted Nelson, their choice for top bachelor and sex symbol of computing. Ted earned a place in *The American Bachelors Register*, published in 1982 by The Playgirl Press and Simon and Schuster. Ted, once editor of *Creative Computing* magazine and author of three books (*Computer Lib*, *The Home Computer Revolution*, and *Literary Machines*), now spends his time on his life work, Project Xanadu. The Xanadu Hypertext system is a library system

for "hyperintellectuals" that "in a proper world of the future will be all of us. Intellectual boundaries are artificial," says Ted. "The natural and normal human condition is to be interested in everything, but most people are lobotomized by school. School ruins things for us, course by course, and the last thing to be ruined determines your profession." On Xanadu, any portion of text, graphics, music, or other data can be retrieved instantly on your home computer. Ted plans to make the Xanadu archives available through satellite links and is accepting reservations from interested parties at a hundred bucks a pop. By the way, his imaginary dream-playgirl is a brilliant young novelist-scientist named Esmerelda Huxley. Says he: "If she wants to talk philosophy, she will murmur, 'syncretistic eschatology.' If she wants to make love to my body for hours while I recite poetry, she will say, 'plinth.' If she wants to be rejected, she will say, 'tennis.'"

A total of 4,360 people with a minimum net worth of at least $100,000 invested $55 million in 1981 to become limited partners in Trilogy Systems' venture to build a monumental computer: an IBM-compatible supercomputer built with very large-scale integration (VLSI) circuits, the most advanced computer of its kind today. Why all the interest? Trilogy was started by Gene Amdahl, one of IBM's hottest designers. In the course of trying to solve a hypothesis in college, Gene designed his own computer, the Wisconsin Integrally Synchronized Computer (WISC), more sophisticated than IBM's best. He later went to work at IBM as chief planner and project engineer, then director of experimental computing machines. He was responsible for the IBM System 360 computer architecture, the machine that defined computer technology from 1964 to the present. Amdahl left IBM in 1970 to form Amdahl Corporation, then left his own company to form Trilogy Systems, whose first computer will be announced in 1984. The Trilogy computer, says Gene, will be twice as fast as anything in existence.

Taking stock in America. In 1982, the top hundred computer firms grew four times faster than the U.S. economy as a whole. Warner Communications' Atari group showed a 475 percent increase over 1981. It's no secret that computer stocks are hot. If you had invested $10,000 in the following computer firms in 1974, your stock would have been worth this in 1980:

Commodore International (personal computers)	$1,715,520
Computervision (graphics systems)	335,780
M/A Com (telecommunications)	331,240
Prime (minicomputers)	557,430
Rolm (switchboards, militarized computers)	274,390

| Tandy (TRS-80 personal computers) | 478,000 |
| Wang Labs (word processors) | 328,000 |

When IBM announced its Model 4300 computer in 1978, demand was so hot that customers put in orders they never expected to pay for, simply to get a good delivery position. Until IBM switched to a lottery system over a first-come, first-served basis, a brisk scalping trade ensued in selling delivery positions.

Rivalry makes the world go round. Digital Equipment Corporation's PDP-8 (Programmed Data Processor), introduced in 1964, was the first mass-produced minicomputer, and at a price of under $20,000, was an incredible buy. DEC sold thousands of them and built its fortune and reputation in the process; unfortunately, someone forgot to give Edson D. deCastro, the chief engineer on the PDP-8 project, the credit he deserved. And when Ed designed his next machine in 1968, management wasn't interested in it. So Ed resigned and started Data General, competing head-on with Digital. With the designs he created at Digital? Some think so. Whether it was or not, Ken Olsen felt betrayed: "What they did was so bad we're still upset about it," he said ten years afterward.

The two companies were characterized in a *Fortune* magazine article as "The upstarts" and "The gentlemen," the latter referring to Digital, of course. Today, Data General is called "The Darth Vader of the computer industry."

Digital had a reputation for being nice guys—the salespeople worked on salary, not commission—and Data General wanted to be known as hustlers and go-getters. An excerpt from an *unpublished* ad:

"They say IBM's entry into minicomputers will legitimize the business. The bastards say, Welcome."

It's little wonder that when Keronix, a company making computers that aped DG's, mysteriously lost its factory to a fire one night in the early 1970s, many thought Data General had torched it. And DG did little to discourage the myth, seeming almost to get a kick out of the notoriety. Nobody ever found a shred of evidence that DG had anything to do with the Keronix fire.

How to sink your own ship. Charlie Day was chief of data processing operations in a federal antipoverty agency within the Department of Health and Human Services that got the ax with the Reagan administration's budget cuts. Day decided that wasn't fair—especially since he had to log only one more year to qualify for retirement at full pay—so he helped labor attorneys file a class-action suit on behalf of his fellow workers and himself. They won, and the judge said they should receive hiring preference for any vacant jobs in Health and Human Services. Charlie was offered a "computer-related" job but turned his nose up at it—it was beneath his previous job classification of GS-14. So they found him a GS-14 job, which old Charlie was obliged to take—cleaning animal cages. Day, still pulling in nearly fifty grand at the menial task, is waiting to be reassigned to a position, in the words of an HHS spokesman, "more commensurate with his skills."

The best way to amass a fortune in computers, of course, is to have a grandmother who bought a hundred shares of IBM in 1945. They'd have cost her $18,500 then. Today they'd be worth $3.8 million.

FROM THE CACHE:
Before Hardware or Software . . . Thoughtware

He was a philosopher who developed the theorem of optimism, "Everything is for the best in this best of all possible worlds." He was a mathematician who worked out the fundamental theorem of calculus at the same time Sir Isaac Newton was developing his theories, with neither knowing of the other's work, and his mathematical forms for calculus have come to be universally preferred. He wrote an essay when he was twenty years old that formed the basis of symbolic logic nearly two hundred years later. He built a calculating machine superior to the Pascaline and that became the first general-purpose calculator for bookkeepers and mathematicians in 1673.

Who was this remarkable man? Gottfried Wilhelm von Leibniz (1646–1716), son of a philosopher and one of the greatest German Renaissance thinkers. It was Leibniz who said, "It is unworthy of excellent men to lose hours like slaves in the labor of calculation which could safely be relegated to anyone else if machines were used." Leibniz practiced what he preached: He worked incessantly, eating not at regular hours but only when he became hungry, slept little, studied, wrote, and thought incessantly, often working in his study armchair for days at a time. He established two rules by which he conducted his life—to strive for clarity and definition and to make everything serve an end—and as a result he saw the advantage in using binary arithmetic (1's and 0's) in simplifying mathematical properties and laws.

Leibniz's interest in binary numbers, however, was as much religious and spiritual as it was mathematical. Pierre-Simon de Laplace, a French mathematician, wrote of Leibniz, "He imagined that the unity (1) represented God and zero (0) the void; that the Supreme Being drew all beings from the void, just as unity and zero express all numbers in the system of numeration."

Leibniz was a statesman, founded the Prussian Academy of Science, invented calculating machines too complex to be manufactured in the seventeenth century, and gave mankind a great deal to think about.

"That the symbolic processes of algebra, invented as tools of numerical calculation, should be competent to express every act of thought, and to furnish the grammar and dictionary of an all-containing system of logic, would not have been believed until it was proved in [George Boole's] *Laws of Thought*," wrote Augustus De Morgan, a nineteenth-century mathematician. Boole's landmark book, whose full title is *An Investigation of the Laws of Thought, on Which Are Founded the Mathematical Theories of Logic and Probabilities*, formed the foundation for Boolean algebra, without which we would not have today's computer.

George Boole (1815–64) was a self-taught mathematician who by virtue of his lack of formal training saw mathematics in new ways. When he was seventeen, he experienced a moment of revelation while walking across a field. He believed that knowledge is gained not only from direct observation but also from an undefinable and invisible force, which his wife, Mary Boole, was to term "the unconscious" in a book entitled *Boole's Psychology*, written after his death. Boole discovered *invariants* early in his studies, a concept that proved central to the theory of relativity.

But it was Boolean algebra, which proved that logic could be reduced to simple algebraic systems, that we remember him for. And it was not until Alfred North Whitehead and Bertrand Russell acknowledged his contribution in their three-volume *Principia Mathematica* (1910–13) that mathematicians began studying his work seriously.

CHAPTER 3

STREETS PAVED IN SILICON:

The Mystique of the Computer Chip

Today's computer brain lives in a city of transistors, resistors, capacitors, and connectors—where city limits stretch only a quarter inch and the distance between streets, or wires, is only 2.5 microns, five thousand times smaller than the thickness of a human hair. Blow those streets up to normal size, and a typical computer chip would be as large as Los Angeles. Or shrink the earth, as scientists have shrunk computer circuits, and New York would be two feet from San Francisco.

Making chips is deadly serious alchemy, turning beach sand into brainpower. Silicon, extracted from sand, is grown into crystalline rods, which are then sliced by diamonds or lasers into skinny wafers about three inches across. The chips are fabricated on the wafers in rows, with circuits imprinted by a photographic etching process. As many as thirty layers of etching may be required to construct a single chip.

The chip is the handiwork of man as he mimics God. But it's also the frontier where man meets quantum mechanics—and he comes away awed. God, of course, invented quantum mechanics.

The limiting factor of how fast a chip works—and thus how fast a computer built around it works—is the speed of electrons as they flow across conduits only a few electrons wide. Semiconductor devices have been made that can actually detect the impact of a single photon— the smallest "quantum" of light—against a surface.

Chips are getting so complicated, in fact, that only computers can trace their complexities. Only computers can tell if a chip designer is inadvertently building a blind alley where an open byway should exist, or leaving open manholes around to trap electrons on their busy path toward the next junction.

But as chips are built by imperfect humans—aided by imperfect machines made by imperfect humans—someday they too will be obsolete. Adam, after all, was built of mud; chips are only made of sand.

Someday the chip will be made useless and graceless by God's handiwork again—the DNA molecule. Already scientists are studying the complex helix to see if its ability to remember genetic code can be used for computer memory.

What, then, will the chip makers have wrought?

Let there be light. Chips today are miniature arrangements of gates, streets, and storage tanks for electron charges. Signals coming into a chip— thanks to the properties of semiconducting materials—can be switched, stored, reversed, or otherwise varied in thousands of ways before exiting the chip. But scientists are now experimenting with chips that do the same for light. This is no easy task, since light has different properties from electricity. Optical chips would have to have tiny lenses, mirrors, and prisms on them and would be able to transmit information significantly faster than today's electrical circuits.

Grace Hopper's recipe for a nanosecond. Take a wire and cut it 10.8 inches long. Electricity will travel that far in a nanosecond, which is one billionth of a second. For a picosecond, or a thousandth of a nanosecond, chop up the wire in a pepper grinder. There are computers now that can perform instructions in a few nanoseconds; soon there will be picosecond computers.

Intel and Texas Instruments pioneered the "computer on a chip." It was essentially enough electronics crammed onto one piece of silicon to enable the resulting device to perform the computations that computers of the day could and do them at a thousandth the cost. These chip-computers typically shunted data around eight pulses at a time and thus were called eight-bit computers. Today, Intel is selling an eight-bit computer chip for $2.00.

The densest man-made memory contains a half million transistors in a space the size of a pinky nail; in a typical chip it can take longer for a signal to get across the chip than for the chip to perform a multiplication. A complex chip may have twenty-four miles of communications pathways etched on it.

Chip miniaturization is limited by the photographic etching—you can't make parts smaller than a light wave since you can't see them, even with a microscope. The solution: Make chips using X rays. When the "light wave" limit is met, a state-of-the-art chip will be as complex as an urban street grid the size of North America.

A single computer chip can take tens of man-years and $1 million to design; produced in quantity, they sell for less than $10 each.

The scientists at Bell Labs have won the world race to produce the first super memory chip. Dubbed the 256K RAM (random-access memory), it can hold 256,000 1's or 0's and is so small an ant can hold it in its jaws. Yet it can store as many phone numbers as a four-hundred-page telephone directory.
    Japan will most likely win the next race: Due soon is the one-megabit—or million-bit—RAM, over four times the memory of Bell's superchip. Nippon Electric Company already says that it has developed fabrication techniques that will allow ten to twelve million transistors to be jammed onto a chip smaller than a contact lens.
    How is such miniaturization achieved? First you shake the magic powder over the transistors, then you . . .

Today's computer would be impossible to design without computers; researchers at Carnegie-Mellon and MIT are developing computers to design chips without human help.
    Most chips made don't work—the key to making money in the business is to make sure that at least 10 percent of any manufacturing run will work. Errors can be caused by imperfections in the silicon, misalignments in etching successive layers on the chip, faulty design, or introduction of foreign material. An employee at one of the major labs was once fired for having dandruff.

The Cray-1 supercomputer has sixteen hundred circuit boards in it, each with up to two hundred chips. It's a monolith, seven feet tall and six feet across, displacing only a hundred cubic feet. It can perform a million more calculations per second than ENIAC in a space a thousand times smaller.

Dick Tracy meets the cowpoke. Laying a hot branding iron to a cow's rump has been the traditional method ranchers use for identifying cattle. But now a company called Identronix has taken the heat off with a new chip, implanted under the cow's hide, which responds to a radio signal. The chip is so rugged it can be found under two inches of concrete or when it's moving 125 miles per hour. Other uses have sprouted: General Motors uses them to help robots identify what kind of task to perform on a car as it passes down the assembly line. The chips act as the eyes for each robot station, telling it what color paint, what body style to weld, and other important information. While there is little resemblance between an auto factory and the open range, the job of riding herd is still important.

Computer technology is generally characterized by generations. Generation number three (read the rest of *The Naked Computer* to find out about numbers one, two, four, and five) debuted with the Intel 4004 microprocessor chip, developed for a Japanese client, Busicom, which wanted to use integrated circuits in programmable calculators.

In 1969, Marcian E. "Ted" Hoff, an engineer at Intel, was assigned to the project. He studied existing minicomputer design and concluded that if he could reduce the circuit complexity of the chip he could make a very small, inexpensive information processor. He designed a four-chip circuit: a central processor chip (which was eventually termed microprocessor), a preprogrammed ROM memory chip, a storage RAM chip, and a shift register chip.

Dr. Federico Faggin and Masatoshi Shima (from Busicom) became involved in the design in 1970, soon after the 4004 was completed. Busicom went bankrupt, and at first Intel couldn't decide whether to put the 4004 on the market. They did, of course, and the rest is history.

The 4004 was a four-bit chip, and even while it was being refined, Intel was working on an eight-bit chip, the 8008. It was introduced a year later and spurred many other firms, such as Fairchild Semiconductor, RCA, and Texas Instruments, to compete in the infant microprocessor industry. By 1974, over nineteen different microprocessors were available.

That same year, Intel introduced the sixteen-bit 8080, which was designed by Shima. It was ten times faster than the 8008, had four times the memory capacity, and required only six support chips (the 8008 required twenty). This chip literally founded the personal computer industry.

Photo courtesy of Intel

Intel's 8088, a sixteen-bit chip, successor to the eight-bit chip.

Shima left Intel to work for Dr. Faggin, who had started his own firm called Zilog, Inc. There Shima designed the second most popular microprocessor, the Z-80. Shima's work ranks him as one of the industry's most influential engineers. He later returned to Intel to head its Japan Design Center.

Intel's latest notable is the iAPX 432, a fourth-generation "mainframe microprocessor" utilizing very large-scale integration (VLSI)—that is, lots more circuits on a chip. Where only ten years ago the 4004 chip held the equivalent of 2,300 transistors, the iAPX 432, in its three-chip system, contains the equivalent of 225,000. It operates at two million instructions per second (MIPS), ranking it among the world's faster computers.

Fact: The chip in your digital watch contains the equivalent of five thousand transistors.

Fact: Most chips contain about thirty thousand transistors.

Fact: Vacuum tubes sent a signal through a circuit in thousandths of a second; chips do it in millionths of a second.

Fact: By 1990 we will have chips that contain over a million transistors and that work at near the speed of light. Your digital watch will have the computing power of ENIAC.

How silicon wafers are made. Life begins, as in nature, with a seed—in this case a tuber, a thin, square rod of silicon about a quarter inch in diameter and three inches long. The rods are lowered into a vat of molten silicon so pure that, as *National Geographic* put it in its issue on chips, if contaminants were redheads, there'd be but fifteen on earth. The primordial silicon soup is maintained at a temperature that cannot vary more than one degree, while the rod is rotated in the molten goo. The rod begins to grow in diameter. Within a day it's almost two feet long and over three inches in diameter.

After it cools and its electrical properties are checked; the rod is sliced into wafers. (A wafer-slicing machine that produces a hundred wafers an hour can cost $750,000.) The wafers then go to a polishing machine; some are polished on one side, some on both, according to the customer's requirements; those polished on both sides cost a great deal more. During this process, the wafer is measured for thickness a number of times on electronic micrometers capable of detecting differences of a micron, or one thirty-nine-millionth of an inch. The more uniform the wafer's thickness, the more usable integrated circuits it will produce.

When the wafer is polished to spec, it goes to places such as IBM's Thomas J. Watson Research Center, where it is photographically etched. The air in such a lab, or "clean room," is exceedingly pure: There are fewer than a hundred particles of dust or contaminants per cubic foot of air. (A normal office might have three hundred thousand.) The stenciling begins. Certain areas on the wafer are masked, while acid etches other areas and forms the circuits. This is done layer upon layer, building what are called "windows." Then a metal, usually aluminum or tungsten, is condensed on the wafer to fill the etched areas and create electrical paths.

There may be hundreds of chips on a single wafer; each chip is worth from a few dollars to $50,000, depending on its complexity. The wafer is then diced up with a diamond saw, and each chip is embedded in a beetlelike case with its legs the contacts to the outside world. It is now ready to go to work.

Dr. Michael Isaacson at Cornell University, using an electron beam, has etched letters into salt crystals so tiny that a thirty-volume encyclopedia could reside on one the size of a half dollar.

From prunes to 'puters. Twenty-five years ago a hundred-square-mile valley southeast of San Francisco was lush with orchards, a hundred thousand acres of plums, pears, and half the world's prunes. To the natives of Santa Clara County, their paradise was aptly named the Valley of Hearts Delight.

Today it's called Silicon Valley—Silicon Gulch by some—an insiders' moniker until Don Hoefler, a trade journalist, made it famous in an article in 1971. And though you still find fruit and vegetable stands as you drive through places like Morgan Hill and Gilroy, all the agriculture has been pushed south of San Jose to make room for high tech. Nine tenths of the orchards are gone. Bayshore Freeway, Highway 101, has become a nightmare for commuters, spewing 850 tons of carbon monoxide into the air every day. Competitors to valley companies lure high-tech brains away by broadcasting, Hanoi Sally style, as engineers and designers sit stuck in traffic jams that rival any in the Northeast.

The marquee change from "Hearts Delight" to "Silicon" began in the eucalyptus groves that surround Stanford University in Palo Alto and was at the instigation of Frederick E. Terman, who passed away at the age of eighty-two while we were writing this book. Terman, whose father, Lewis, devised the Stanford-Binet IQ test, took his degrees in chemical engineering but moved into radio and radar studies once he began teaching at Stanford in 1925.

Terman encouraged his students to start their own businesses when they had an idea, and first and most notable of those who heeded his advice was William Hewlett. In 1939, Terman helped him lure David Packard away from General Electric to start work on something called a resistance-tuned audio oscillator. With $1,000 loaned by the Crocker National Bank, Hewlett and Packard built the device in Packard's garage. Today they are both listed in the Forbes 400 list of richest Americans.

Terman's concept of business and academia working together in the traces of technological advancement led to the founding of the Stanford Industrial Park. Despite high-tech concentrations around Boston, Dallas, and Raleigh-Durham, as the satellite looks down, Silicon Valley still has the highest concentration of high-tech industry anywhere in the world. (Without it, there'd be no satellites to look down.)

As company after company followed the Hewlett-Packard model, the transubstantiation of the valley took place. Today the most lucrative crops are the silicon chips: Eighty companies make them and account for 20 percent of the world's $16 billion semiconductor market. Some of the more notable Silicon Valley corporate inhabitants are Fairchild Instrument, Intel, National Semiconductor, Advanced Micro Devices, Hewlett-Packard, and Varian.

Patty Bell finds fun in "nerds," money in techies with plastic pocket protectors and thick glasses. She's the writer and producer of the record "Silicon Valley Guy." Performed by the mythical group Don Data and the

Rez-Tones, the record jacket sports pictures of the Guy, replete with beeper.
Some lyrics:

> *I scanned the new program down in Word*
> *Processing,*
> *The one with the huge mammary banks*
> *Yeh, Julie! punch my code I am certain!*
> *When I first saw her I thought*
> *Whoa! give me a microsecond*
> *Could I trip her Kipp relay or what*
> *She sorta smiles at me and I'm thinking*
> *I have got to access this chick*
> *But should I go subroutine or main program,*
> *y'know?*
> *So I just subtly invade her spatial arena*
> *And introduce myself for starts.*
> *Hi, I'm Ray FiFo. . . .*

Frederick Emmons Terman, what hath you wrought?

Valley of the armpit's delight. Some things to keep in mind about Silicon Valley:

- *People.* Doubled in population in fifteen years from 1960 to 1975,
  growing to 1.2 million people in 1976. Still growing. A total of
  250,000 people directly dependent on high tech for jobs. Plenty of
  ethnics—45,000 Southeast Asian refugees alone.

- *Housing.* Scarce. Rental vacancy at an unbelievably low .4 percent;
  one housing study showed that expansion plans would add 500,000
  jobs to Santa Clara County but only 170,000 housing units. San Jose
  grew from 95,000 to 660,000 in thirty years, spread from 22 square
  miles to 140. Average house prices in one year, 1976, increased 40
  percent. Prices in general increased over 200 percent in the 1970s,
  double the national average. Between 1970 and 1976, while median
  income grew 42 percent, median housing prices grew 150 percent.
  Average home price was over $100,000.

- *Commuting.* Forty percent of all county travel is commuting. The
  average commute is twenty-two miles.

- *Pollution.* Worst in the Bay Area, especially along Bayshore Freeway.
  Besides the 850 tons a day of carbon monoxide, 240 tons of organic
  pollutants are spewed out of exhaust pipes. One out of five days the
  CO_2 level exceeds the federal standard; one out of ten days the oxidant

level is exceeded. *TNC* eyewitness account: yukkie. Almost as bad as L.A.

- *Job scene.* Nice for geniuses. Median income over $24,000 per year. Plenty of millionaires. For 130,000 blue-collar workers and many nonnative Americans, layoffs and threats from offshore assembly are realities.

No wonder so many companies are starting to move to Arizona. The conditions are better. And remember, silicon is just another form of sand.

"Recognizing a good idea when it came by." This is how Robert Noyce characterizes his success in the semiconductor business. Success, indeed. Noyce was hired by William Shockley when he started Shockley Semiconductor Laboratories in Palo Alto, where he met Gordon Moore. (Shockley must have been a gem to work for: Eight leading officials left the same year the company was started.) A group of Shockley employees, including Noyce and Moore, left to form Fairchild Semiconductor, where the first commercial integrated circuits were introduced in 1959. In 1964, Gordon Moore made a statement that was to become known as Moore's Law: Chip complexity, or the number of individual circuits on a chip, would double every year. Between 1960 and 1982, there has been no significant deviation from his prediction.

Moore also made this prediction, in 1974: There would be twenty million computers in operation by the year 1984. This was an utterly astounding pronouncement at a time when only two hundred thousand computers existed. It perturbed many, including IBM, but what Gordon Moore saw was how Intel's microprocessor-on-a-chip would revolutionize the way people conceived of a computer. At the time even Intel, which had ascertained there were at least twenty-five thousand different applications for the microcomputer, didn't see the chip's potential in the consumer market. And, according to International Data Corporation, Moore will hit his prediction in 1985, only one year late.

Chip off the old cellblock. Werner Bruchhausen boasts over sixty federal indictments pending court action against him. The charge: smuggling over $8 million in illegally obtained chips and high-tech electronic components out of the United States to East Germany and the Soviet Union through no fewer than nineteen European front companies. Among his customers: Siemens AG, West Germany's number one high-tech firm, for Intel chips it couldn't possibly get through legitimate channels.

Bruchhausen is not the only professional high-tech smuggler. Richard Mueller and his firm, Semitronik AG of Zug, Switzerland, were banned from trading with the United States until May 31, 2001, for exporting computerized drafting equipment to the Soviet Union. No one knows with any certainty how many chips are stolen—Albert Williams was charged with smuggling over $1 million in chips out of Intel in the lining of his coat— but the Department of Commerce *is* certain we see only the tip of a very large iceberg. John Jackson, one of the alleged middlemen in the Intel-Siemens heists, fared well until he was caught; his share, delivered in stacks of $100 bills, was usually $350,000, $400,000, perhaps more—he couldn't remember for sure, because nobody kept records.

High-tech smuggling and illegal exportation carry sentences of up to $100,000 and a jail sentence of up to ten years. The only person ever sentenced for such activities under the Export Control Act was Walter J. Spawr, convicted of selling laser mirrors to the U.S.S.R.; he was fined the maximum and sentenced to only six months in jail. So it's no wonder that people like Jackson, who has a criminal record, and Mueller, who has a history of implications in illegal commerce, return to high-tech smuggling. The fine is a pittance of what they haul in, and most jail sentences are suspended.

It's unlikely that Bruchhausen, who has been indicted for conspiracy by a grand jury in Los Angeles, will ever be prosecuted; most European countries do not extradite on violations of export laws. He was last seen romping in Monaco.

Colder than an ice chip. In 1962, Brian Josephson, a physicist at Oxford University, developed the fastest electronic circuit in the world, dubbed the Josephson Junction. The circuit takes advantage of a weird property electrons have when they get very cold—they tunnel through obstacles they couldn't ordinarily surmount and don't leave a trace. Even today research, primarily at IBM and Bell Labs, goes on to perfect the junction, which is similar to an integrated circuit that has been cooled to superconducting temperature. The Josephson Junction uses one ten-thousandth the energy of its regular counterpart and operates at speeds ten to a hundred times faster than the fastest computer on earth. A Josephson computer may be a reality by the end of the century.

BIOLOGICAL COMPUTERS
by Anton Schwartz

Nature's greatest technological wonder is the DNA molecule. For many years we have been able to determine the base sequences—the manner in which chemicals join—in DNA strands. By taking DNA strands out of animals and inserting them into bacteria, we can observe the proteins produced and thus determine which proteins the DNA strands give instructions to. The proteins understand the DNA in the same way computers understand the bits and bytes of coding that tell them what to do. As we begin to identify all these structural functions, an entirely new world will open up to us.

Computers will then be able to determine the genetic code of any animal from a sample cell, analyze the code, and graphically display the coding for the proteins. Conversely, given the three-dimensional structure or chemical function of a protein we would like to produce (whether it exists or not), computers will be able to develop the bases for a new DNA strand, then implant it in bacteria and grow vast amounts of the desired protein.

The first proteins grown this way will be simple structures, such as molecular diodes or memory elements mounted on our computers. But in time we will be able to produce large protein networks to make the ultimate computers. These "biological computers" will not only be many orders of magnitude more powerful than our current machines, but might possibly make our own brains obsolete.

The biocomputer will be able to use the software to alter itself. It will be able to improve itself, to adapt itself to a changing environment, and finally, by using the genetic engineering techniques employed to create it, will be able to reproduce itself. Ostensibly, this means of self-improvement and reproduction seems very similar to Darwinian evolution.

Since computers will improve themselves to meet society's needs better [we hope], they will be logical enough to modify themselves only for the better; none will die out because of unfavorable mutations. This means their evolution will proceed millions of times faster than Darwinian evolution. In the biocomputer's evolution, Lamarck's Law of Acquired Characteristics, which does not apply to animals or humans, will hold true: Computers will be able to improve themselves by altering their genetic codes to improve their "offspring."

[About the author: Anton Schwartz was a fifteen-year-old computer hacker when he wrote this piece for *TNC*. He used a TRS-80 as a word processor and the biocomputer atop his neck to choose the words to process.]

Chip amnesia? In recent years, a strange glitch has reared its ugly head—the "soft fail," which makes the computer choke on a binary bit or cough when it's putting stuff into memory. In some cases, a soft fail brings the computer to a dead stop. It turns out that little alpha particles emitted by radium and thorium present in the ceramic backing of memory chips trigger the circuits to flip when they should flop. Alpha particles thrown off from cosmic rays can cause soft fails, too. The two main causes of cosmic rays: solar flares and nuclear Armageddon.

High-tech teens. Apparently some kids aren't interested in computers just for fun and honest profit. Witness the sting operation in San Jose that netted four teenagers for conspiring to buy stolen chips. At least one or two of them were part of a larger teenage theft ring that pulled off the largest chip theft in history, $3.2 million from Monolithic Memories on Thanksgiving weekend in 1982. A security guard helped several outsiders steal dozens of crates of programmable chips from a well-protected warehouse in Sunnyvale, California, but a $50,000 reward helped nab the crooks. To date, the chips haven't been found.

Intel introduced the 1K RAM chip in 1970. Simply put, that's a chip with 1,024 bits of information storage on it. Since Boolean algebra dictates increasing circuits by square roots, the next RAM, or memory, chip was the 2K, followed by the 4K, which sold over $145 million in 1977, their peak year. The 4K was replaced by the 16K, whose peak year was 1982—$500 million in sales.

In 1981, the 64K RAM chip was introduced and sold over $100 million; sales are expected to peak in 1985 at $1.5 billion. By then the 256K RAM chip will be in production, with the 1-million-K chip just behind. Gobble, gobble.

Biggest price drop for any Intel chip: The 8080, which cost $360 in 1974 and sells today for $3.70.

Dumbest chip. It's about four inches in diameter, an inch and a half thick, weighs four ounces, and can be purchased from pushcarts on New York City streets for $1.00. It's the Chipwich, a big glop of all-natural ice cream sandwiched between two homemade chocolate-chip cookies. Sales in 1982: 20 million. About a thousandth as much in sales as from silicon chips, but much yummier.

FROM THE CACHE:
The Long Road to Silicon Valley

Among the many people to whom we owe our thanks for the computer, paramount is Benjamin Franklin (1706–90). Kite in a rainstorm and all. When the kite was lowered, he found the lightning had magnetized the key, demonstrating a relationship between electricity and magnetism. A few years later Hans Oersted, a Dane, performed a classroom demonstration with a compass and a charged wire, which proved Franklin's hypothesis. Without these basic principles, we'd still be cranking handles on mechanical calculators.

Michael Faraday, the son of an English blacksmith, is credited with the single greatest discovery of all time—the electrical generator. The device, built in 1831, alternated the north and south poles of a magnetic field to create electricity. During the same period, Joseph Henry, an American, took some of Faraday's ideas and applied them to a switching device that became known as the relay. Appointed executive secretary of the Smithsonian, Henry shared his ideas and inventions freely with others, including Samuel Morse. Morse combined Henry's technology with his own Morse code to perfect telegraphy (no mention of Henry's contribution).

Many other men contributed to the evolution of electronics: Guglielmo Marconi devised the first diode, a device that has an input wire and an output wire and in some way changes the electricity that flows through it. Marconi's diode, called a coherer, was used to receive radio signals, which were sent and received over a long wire called the antenna. His British Marconi Company sent the first wireless telegraph message on December 12, 1901. Meanwhile, Thomas Edison was inventing the electric light, a glowing wire within a glass vacuum—which was, in essence, a diode vacuum tube. His chief engineer, Ambrose Fleming, left for the British Marconi Company and combined some of Edison's ideas with some of Marconi's and invented the first vacuum diode tube for use in radios. It was called the Fleming Valve, since it worked on the same principle as a water faucet.

In 1906 Lee DeForest, an American, invented the first vacuum tube one could adjust. By adding another element, the tube could be used not only to receive signals, but also to amplify them. These two principles, the diode and the amplifier, are in use today in all manner of electronics. Transistors function in the same way as vacuum tubes—they're just smaller and more efficient.

William Shockley began working on the first transistor in 1947, but it wasn't perfected until 1952. Shockley, Walter Brattain, and John Bardeen were awarded the Nobel Prize in Physics in 1956 for their work.

Vladimir Zworykin, a Russian who immigrated to the United States, invented the cathode-ray tube, patented in 1928, but it wasn't until Digital introduced its PDP-1 in 1963 that computers used a video display.

But TNC's favorite forerunning genius is Nikola Tesla, the wild man of electronics. Born on the stroke of midnight July 9–10, 1856, near Belgrade, Yugoslavia, he came to America in 1884 with a letter of introduction to Thomas Edison, who promptly hired him.

Tesla actually was the first to invent wireless radio, and in 1943 the U.S. Supreme Court reversed an initial finding for Marconi on that point. During his work with radio communications, Tesla patented the electrical logic circuits called gates, or switches, which determine whether a plus or a minus signal flows through. Tesla's patents, taken in 1903, prefigured the relay, the vacuum tube, and the transistor.

In the same year he took out patents for, in his own words, an "automatic mechanism controlled through a simple tuned circuit." The patent title was "Method of and Apparatus for Controlling Mechanisms at a Distance." In his first demonstration at an exposition on electricity, Tesla floated a submarine in a tank, then blew up the submarine with a remote radio signal.

Tesla loved the power of electricity and dreamed of a world filled with electric light. Many of his early experiments were with resonance, tuning a circuit to a specific frequency. Later termed an oscillator, this is a primary circuit in radios, televisions, and computers. Tesla designed an oscillator in 1898 that developed half a million volts of power, glowing with a ferocious intensity. He had a theory that by intensifying mechanical resonance, he could "split the earth open like an apple." He left New York to conduct experiments in Colorado Springs, to ensure a degree of safety, with powerful transformers. When he applied voltage to the transformer it created a roar that could be heard ten miles away. A picture shows Tesla sitting reading a book in front of the huge transformer, with several million volts of electric sparks spewing all around.

Tesla lived on a grand scale. He was one of the most eligible bachelors in New York and hobnobbed with the most fashionable people, often throwing parties for members of the New York "400." He was afflicted with various phobias and anxieties—nightmares, hallucinations, a violent aversion to women wearing earrings, and a penchant for calculating the cubic contents of the food on his plate, to name a few.

Drawing by Tim Eagan

In the 1930s, as his death approached, Tesla speculated on the future. He envisioned a machine by the year 2100 that would obviate war, that would "destroy anything, men or machines, approaching within a radius of two hundred miles." Tesla was no warmonger; he felt superior weapons were the only deterrents to war. His machine would "provide a wall of power offering an insuperable obstacle against any effective aggression." The machine he described came to pass somewhat earlier than he anticipated; we call it particle-beam weaponry.

CHAPTER 4

A GREASE MONKEY'S VIEW:

The Naked Computer

Once you realize that computers use computers to design computers out of parts the size of germs, you begin to understand their charm.

People who build computers have to worry about things such as whether dots of magnetism are standing up or lying down, how to overcome the fact that electricity in a copper wire moves only at three tenths the speed of light, and whether anybody in the lab has dandruff.

The building blocks of a computer are simple to understand; how on God's earth they are made to work is something else.

The main brain of a computer, the central processing unit, usually called a CPU, is the place where decisions are made—such as what two and two should equal, or if a ton of feathers is lighter than a ton of bricks.

Part of the brain, or at least connected closely enough that for all practical purposes it seems to be inside the computer's head, is main memory. These days main memory is made out of silicon chips and used to store up to thirty-two million characters of data (the equivalent of two dozen Shoguns). When the CPU needs data with which to make decisions, it sucks in the data from main memory in huge gulps.

(There are also lots of little pockets of memory in a computer system—places such as cache memory or buffer memory, where data are stored temporarily on their way to and from the main units. There's even a technique called "virtual memory," where the system fools the CPU into thinking that data stored on disk are actually in main memory.)

The computer's senses consist of input devices—generally terminals with keyboards or punched-card readers. These devices change human actions into electrical signals that can be accepted by the computers. Occasionally computers are connected to devices that interface with the environment, such as valve actuators, temperature sensors, or computer-controlled subway trains. In all cases, the input to the computers is electricity. It's all computers can eat.

The computer's excrement—and some think of it as just that—is also electrical. But printers, of which there are dozens of types, turn these signals into words (sometimes so many that humans tend to ignore them) on paper.

Depending on the electrical signals going into a computer, the electrical signals coming out may not make sense. This is called garbage in, garbage out, or GIGO. Unless, of course, the nonsensical signals coming out happen to be a mistake that increases your bank balance to $100,000. This is called serendipity.

In aggregate, computers store about a million words, or the equivalent of one volume of the Encyclopaedia Britannica, for each person on the planet.

ENIAC was the subject of a patent controversy for over thirty years. John Atanasoff's original computer was to have been patented by Iowa State University, which funded its development in 1939. Atanasoff shared some of his ideas with J. Presper Eckert, codeveloper of ENIAC, and the rest of the story filled legal briefs for years. It wasn't settled until 1974, when the courts ruled the original patent invalid on technical grounds. By then the statute of limitations had expired, ENIAC had been retired to the Smithsonian, IBM was the leader in computers, and $500 could buy the same computational power as ENIAC.

In 1973, Richard Pavelle spent three months with a calculator and paper and pencil figuring out a calculation pertaining to the theory of relativity. In 1974, he tried it again, this time on a computer running an algebra program called MACSYMA. The program ran in two minutes.

THE WHIRRING WORLD OF DISK AND TAPE

We have our lists and calendars and strings upon our fingers; computers have disk and tape. Since 1953, little smudges of magnetism on fast-moving media have served to store all the stuff the computer doesn't have room for in its main memory. When a computer needs some of this farmed-out information, it gobbles it at up to three million characters a second.

Disks operate somewhat like record players—a read/write head detects signals from a rotating disk underneath; tapes act like the tape decks we're familiar with, except they've been specially tailored for the high-performance work demanded by computers. Tape storage is cheaper than disk storage, but retrieving an item at the opposite end of the tape from the last one can take eons (seconds). Disks provide random access of data and are good if the computer needs to skip around its files.

Consider:

- The first commercial disk drive with moving read/write heads was the IBM 305, introduced in 1957. It could record 2,000 characters in a square inch. Today's disk drives can record 15 million characters per square inch, and the Japanese have concocted laboratory models that can record 350 million characters per square inch. Take two Bibles and inscribe them on a postage stamp and you get the idea.

- The read/write head of a disk drive doesn't lay flat on the spinning platter. It rises on a cushion of air to the vast height of 20 millionths of an inch, or 150th the cross section of a human hair. The head, aerodynamically designed to ride on this bearing made of air, achieves lift-off in $\frac{1}{1000}$th of an inch after the disk begins spinning. In terms of mass and tolerance, it's equivalent to a 747 flying $\frac{1}{4}$ inch off the ground but not touching. Should the head for some reason touch the spinning platter, the consequences, at least to the data living below, would be the same as if a 747 were to crash in downtown Chicago.

- Computer users are buying auxiliary storage faster than they're buying computers. Installed storage more than doubles every three years. It's not uncommon for big companies to have disk farms of fifteen hundred spindles (turntables) and still need more.

- The read/write head of most disks is made of the same material as fireplace brick. Manufacturers, however, are fast reaching the limits to which they can hone ceramic (it gets too fragile), so the newest disk drives have heads fabricated like semiconductor chips in the proper shape and configuration to work as a read/write head.

- The first magnetic tape device produced by IBM was the Model 726, in 1953. It could pack 100 characters per inch and move at 75 inches per second; modern tape drives pack 6,250 characters per inch and move at two-hundred inches per second—almost 200 times better in performance.

- If you lived on a magnetic tape, like a datum does, you might have survived the starts and stops of the tape drive in the early days (25G's); today, no way. Modern tape drives accelerate at more than 500G's.

- Scientists agree that modern tape technology could improve two-hundred-fold again before physical limits are reached; nobody knows if anyone will want tapes that fast, however.

The flexible diskette, otherwise known as the floppy disk, was first introduced in 1971 and was used to feed special operating instructions to the large computers IBM was then making (the 370s). Since then, the floppy disk has become a medium in its own right. Billions have been sold—enough to pave lower Manhattan—since then. *The Naked Computer*, in fact, began life as a series of electronic blips on forty-one floppy disks (twenty masters, twenty backups, one frizzled).

Another, much-experimented-with memory type that is just now reaching commercial potential is bubble memory. Here little bits of magnetism on a semiconductor chip float by a stationary read/write head at the rate of millions per second. Since the only moving parts are ethereal forces rather than real things, bubble memory offers some distinct advantages to rotating memories. Were the cost of traditional storage methods not coming down so fast, bubble memory would have hit the streets sooner. Before long we'll have a bubble memory the size of a sheet of paper with the storage capacity equivalent to a disk drive—at about a thousandth the cost.

Even more experimental: videodisks. Yes, just like the ones you watch movies on at home. The disks and players are relatively inexpensive, but the problem to date has been that you can't erase and rerecord on them—the information is permanently etched into the surface with a laser beam. Now Japan Broadcasting Corp. of Tokyo has a disk using a helium-neon laser that records the information magnetically and can thus be magnetically erased. A drawback to videodisks is the refraction of light—scientists foresee twenty-five thousand characters per square inch as the upper limit of storage density. Current disk drives will surpass that by the mid-1980s.

Seeing is believing. One of the biggest obstacles for the hand-held computer has been the display. Most computers that you stuff into a pocket or briefcase have a small liquid-crystal display upon which letters and numbers merrily chase their way from right to left. But help is on the way: Philips Research of Redhill, England, has announced a cathode-ray tube, or CRT, just like your television tube but that is a mere two inches thick. It has all the attributes and desirable features of a standard CRT and is rugged as well; it doesn't require the high voltages of a standard CRT and will be economical to manufacture. In a few years, the portable television will indeed be portable, and if it's a portable computer as well, you could take your office, your homework, or the Library of Congress along on your picnic.

We've heard of cow flops, but computer flops? Yes. Flop is short for "floating point operations per second" and is a standard way to measure the brainpower of the most powerful computers. These are the systems, such as the Cray-1, that are built to handle problems by working simultaneously on many parts of the problem.

The first computer that could operate at more than 20 million flops (Mflops) was Illiac IV, built by Burroughs for NASA. A Cray-1 can hit a peak speed of 200 Mflops; the CDC 205 allegedly can hit 400 Mflops. Hitachi announced a computer in 1982 that can best both those computers—with a claimed speed of 630 Mflops.

By some counts, Illiac IV still claims the record as the fastest computer—it could handle bigger problems than the Cray or the 205 and maintain a high speed. Illiac IV required a whole building to house it and to contain the air conditioning it needed. A *faster* computer could be built using Josephson Junctions, which operate close to absolute zero. A computer two inches cubed would be able to carry out a billion operations per second.

What these computers can do for us. Thanks to modern-day computers and some better algorithms, computer scientists at Stanford are able to contemplate calculating the value of *pi* to 15 million digits. They have been able to discover, for instance, that starting with the 710,150th digit there is a string of seven 3's. Now, aren't you glad you know that?

Bart Khan used to be an electrical repairman, which probably accounts for the fact that his new "charged packet memory device" is made up of off-the-shelf components. If it works—and he says it does—it's the niftiest little storage machine in the world. Khan and his company, Micro Xeno, of Birmingham, England, are about to announce a memory device "the size of a biscuit tin" that stores more than IBM's most powerful disk drive: 9.9 gigabytes. That's 9.9 thousand million bytes, enough to store the names and addresses of everyone in New York City.

There are a handful of ways to link computers in the same geographical area together electronically. One very effective network scheme is called "token-ring-passing," and a number of companies began making token-passing networks and selling them. Unfortunately, they discovered somewhat belatedly that a Swede named Olaf Soderblom had patented the idea about fifteen years ago while devising the network for banks. Olaf was no oaf; he informed them that they'd have to buy a license from him and pay a royalty on every piece of equipment connected up. IBM has coughed over $7 million to date, but many other companies are trying to fight Olaf in court.

Old Faithful. Burroughs built the Mod I Guidance Computer, the first all-transistor computer, for the U.S. Air Force. The Mod I provided guidance for Atlas ICBMs and helped launch a number of satellites, including Pioneer V, Explorer, and a number of communications satellites. It was in operation for only four years, but during that time it never failed during a launch or mission, a record few computers today could match. The Mod I is on display at the Smithsonian.

JOHN VON NEUMANN AND THE STORED-PROGRAM CONCEPT

"I've met Einstein and Oppenheimer and Teller and a whole bunch of other guys," recalls Professor Leon Harmon of Case-Western Reserve, "and von Neumann was the only genius I ever met. The others were supersmart . . . but von Neumann's mind was all-encompassing."

Born in Budapest, Hungary, on December 23, 1903, von Neumann earned his Ph.D. in physics at the age of twenty-two, and in 1927 he became a scholar and thinker at the University of Berlin. Three years later he left for Princeton University, where he joined the faculty of the Institute for Advanced Study.

Von Neumann ordered his life mathematically; he used game-theory concepts in the more personal aspects of his life and was ever a tactical thinker. His head was filled with so many ideas, and he was so busy, that he allowed himself only five hours a night for sleep. He saw great possibilities for applying abstract concepts, like mathematics, to the affairs of man.

During World War II, von Neumann consulted in weather forecasting, ballistics, and on the atomic bomb (the Manhattan Project) with several governmental agencies, including the Army and the Navy. This work led him to an interest in computers. In 1944, von Neumann learned that the Moore School of Electrical Engineering at the University of Pennsylvania was working on an electronic digital computer, under the direction of J. Presper Eckert, Jr., and John W. Mauchly. Von Neumann became a technical adviser and in 1945 wrote a paper, the result of conversations he'd had with others about a new computer design, entitled "First Draft of a Report on the Edvac."

In this now-famous paper, which was neither revised nor formally published, von Neumann set forth the precepts for computer operation that were to dominate the way computers were built for many years. Simply put, he called for storing the instructions that tell the computer what to do with the data along with the data themselves. To the computer, instructions are thus indistinguishable from data and can be manipulated. Programs can modify themselves, depending on conditions.

This stored-program concept is the premise underlying today's digital computers. And although others may have had the same idea as von Neumann, he's considered the granddaddy of the concept.

Von Neumann went on to find new applications for computers. He helped scientists such as Robert Oppenheimer and Edward Teller at Los Alamos apply computer power to the atomic bomb research as well as other weapons systems. He was present at many bomb testings, defying the dangers of radiation exposure. And he threw his support behind Norbert Wiener's work in cybernetics, the study of the similarity between how computers and organic matter function.

John von Neumann, for all his high-minded scientific zeal, was also a man who loved parties, food, drink, the company of beautiful women, and a good joke. He lived elegantly, which was made possible by his extensive consulting and his high position in the scientific community. At one of the many parties he gave, his wife, Klara, presented him with a replica of the Princeton computer he worked on, carved out of ice.

Von Neumann was a compulsive worker, with more projects than he could ever hope to accomplish. He was appointed chairman of the Atomic Energy Commission in 1955, and shortly thereafter he learned that he had bone cancer—probably caused by exposure to radiation. His belief that he was invulnerable did not permit him to accept the fact that he was dying. He continued to work as though nothing were wrong, even as the pain got worse. His mind remained as alert as ever, and as the end approached, he was hospitalized at Walter Reed Army Hospital. There the Secretary of Defense, the Secretaries of the Army, Navy, and Air Force, and the military Chiefs of Staff gathered to pay him a final tribute. Johnny, as most of his friends called him (Jancsi to his parents), died shortly thereafter on February 8, 1957, at the age of fifty-three.

Accidents will happen. On a big IBM computer a graduate student at UC Berkeley was experimenting with aircraft design to improve lift at low speeds. When he tried to run the simulation, the plane crashed. He played with the program, ran it again, and the plane didn't crash. David Walonick, a computer programmer and consultant in Minneapolis, found that his new IBM personal computer divided 0.1 by 10 and came up with 0.001 instead of 0.01. IBM told him beginning programmers "have problems like that." It wasn't corrected until Walonick told *The New York Times*.

What caused the problems? Most errors of this sort occur because designers can't quite decide how to represent fractions accurately. No matter how you represent the Arabic ⅓ in a decimal fraction, even if it's 0.333333333333333333333333333333333333333, it still isn't as accurate as computers can calculate. It still has to be rounded off. Add to this the problem that computers work in binary arithmetic, where everything is represented as a 1 or a 0. More errors accumulate in translating from decimal to binary. In the case of the IBM PC, the computer calculated correctly in binary; it's just that the decimal display couldn't match it.

The more serious problem is that most computer users have difficulty discerning when there is an inaccurate sum; computers are generally regarded as correct.

Drawing by Rich Tennant

"Shay, aren'tcha sposed to do a shubroutine after that GOTO loop?"

Cool computer. Seymour Cray, maverick genius of supercomputers, has invented the successor to the Cray-1. It's appropriately called the Cray-2, and it's one tenth the size of the industry's fastest machine. Just twenty-six inches high and thirty-eight inches long, the Cray-2 bathes in a tub of pure fluorocarbon liquid, which allows its circuits to work four times faster than its predecessor. The goldfish-bowl phenomenon has side effects: It allows engineers to detect circuits that are overheating, and it produces a beautiful turbulence that is fascinating to view.

Most people think IBM introduced its very first personal computer, the 5100, in the mid-1970s, but did they upstage themselves? Dr. Jerome Weisner, president emeritus of MIT, recalls having a prototype of an IBM personal computer in the 1950s that was supposed to show the uninitiated how a computer worked. The device contained twenty vacuum tubes, and a bunch of wires and plugs that could be connected to perform computations. "I collected a lot of things from different companies back then," recalls Weisner, "although none of them turned out to be anything I could use. They were all too complicated."

Weisner's wife got rid of the early IBM machine, along with a number of other things that had accumulated in the attic, when the family moved in the early 1970s. She gave the IBM machine to the MIT furniture exchange, where it was picked up by Bud Napier for $10. The machine, now part of the Napier Family Trust, was recently valued at $50,000.

Bit-width wisdom. Computers can be classed according to the number of bits of information that can pulse through their arteries at any one time. Usually they can handle eight, sixteen, or thirty-two bits at once. In 1967, Ed deCastro couldn't convince Digital to build a sixteen-bit machine; management thought it too progressive. Personal computers, once thought to be all eight-bit machines, are now reaching a new maturity as devices of sixteen-bit, or, in some cases, both eight- and sixteen-bit, which allows them to use software from the best of either world. Hewlett-Packard has announced a thirty-two-bit desktop computer already.

What does this mean to the average user? It means simpler commands; a computer that works faster (you don't have to sit for awkward minutes and wait while the machine stores your sterling prose on the disk); the ability to change from program to program in an instant (enter your annual mortgage rate, then switch to a bar chart to show its effects vis-à-vis inflation for five years); and great communications capabilities, so that you can talk to other computers as easily as you type words on a keyboard.

AN INTERVIEW WITH ADAM OSBORNE

Adam Osborne is a man who takes his work and his pleasure seriously; he is as much a perfectionist about his espresso coffee as he is about his business. Although he's chairman of the board of Osborne Computer Corporation, for instance, he writes personal letters to users having problems with their Osborne-1 computers.

Born in Thailand, the son of a British history professor and "countermissionary," he immigrated to the United States, where he has gone from being an obscure technical writer to being an entrepreneur of international renown. In 1982, over 125,000 of his $1,795 Osborne-1 computers—what *The New York Times* calls the Volkswagen of computers—were sold. The

industry was quick to latch onto the idea of portable computers, and Osborne competitors abound. *TNC* talked to Adam early in 1983:

TNC: So, Adam, how did you get to be sitting where you are?

OSBORNE: I was mesmerized by America as soon as I came here. I realized I had always been an American and never knew it. I loved the free-flowing vigor of the place—the fact that nothing counted here other than achievement and performance. Brashness was almost encouraged, provided it was backed up with some substance.

I was working for M. W. Kellogg in chemical engineering and was anxious to do a bit more than that, so I didn't get on very well. I moved from engineering to thermodynamics, where I did better, but decided to get a Ph.D., which led to a job with Shell Development Co. in Emeryville, California. Before long I was back where I was—looking for something more than a job. I was very brash, which didn't sit well in a large corporation. I decided to work for myself instead, and I hit the sidewalks.

TNC: What did you plan to do?

OSBORNE: Originally, my idea was to be a programming consultant. But that was the summer of 1970 during the most grinding recession this industry has ever seen. There were programmers committing suicide; and for six months I couldn't find a job. I became a technical writer.

Lo and behold, I realized very quickly that technical writing was the armpit of the industry. Writers were paid slave wages and treated with scorn and disdain.

By 1974 I decided I'd go into microprocessor consulting. In order to differentiate myself from all the other microprocessor consultants, I wrote a book called *An Introduction to Microcomputers*, which I intended to self-publish. I put a price of $7.50 on it and figured I'd sell a few and give most away. I printed ten thousand.

Surprise. It was the first and only book on the market, and the copies were just gobbled up. I printed ten thousand more, converted it to Volumes One and Two, and was in the publishing business, which I had pretty much to myself in early 1977. The book sold three hundred thousand copies.

TNC: So you became an industry observer.

OSBORNE: Well, I did get a tremendous amount of input for my weekly newspaper column. I saw what was selling, and I saw what was doing badly. I saw the mainstream of the business develop. I saw companies fold simply because of lousy management.

Within the scenario we saw the emergence of a few well-run companies, like Apple. They had an off-brand product and an idea that was out of the mainstream, which succeeded simply because people wanted something reliable. Radio Shack's product was adequate. Of course, they are a big company. Commodore was a moderately stable company but was selling outside the country.

By 1979, the mainstream of the industry had all but disappeared through bad financial management, and there was nothing left but those on the periphery. Apple, Radio Shack, and Commodore, which did not represent the mainstream, knew little or nothing of where the microcomputer industry had come from. They were now rapidly turning their backs on all the industry concepts and becoming minicomputerlike companies.

For a while I told people what I thought they should build, and nobody did. So I built it. That's the story.

TNC: Some say that in the American way of doing business, people tend to underestimate the importance of the product.

OSBORNE: I think I've noticed that people's minds tend to ossify fairly quickly. The minicomputer fans of the late 1960s weren't nimble-witted enough to see the micro come along. We are seeing the same thing right now with a lot of microcomputer companies afraid to take the next bold step. It's probably the result of the industry's moving so fast that the people and their businesses don't have the time to mature before the next wave comes along. Many of them won't survive, but I think the industry will start to stabilize within five to eight years.

TNC: In your book *Running Wild*, you say there are places we shouldn't use computers.

OSBORNE: Yes. In balloting, for instance, I just feel that the slightest chance of fraud isn't worth it. If we are going to spend a little bit more money for counting or if we have to wait longer, fine. We all know that rigging is possible—it's very easy to do. It's not just the outsiders I'm worried about, it's the people running it.

Electronic funds transfer is the next place where I have a lot of problems because the potential for fraud is so great. I've heard of banks that are doing funds transfer on public-access networks. In 1980 I issued a public challenge to any bank that would guarantee in writing not to prosecute me that I would steal $10 million from them via wire fraud. We weren't actually going to rip off the bank; in fact, we were going to call the bank president and ask him to come and get his money. We'd have a $10 million cashier's check waiting for him. Of course, no bank took me up on the offer.

As for the stock exchange, my God! There has never been an opportunity like that. Who is going to count the shares? Who really knows who owes who what? I think it's madness.

Last year, China finished counting its own. It was the largest census in the recorded history of the earth. The job required twelve times more people than it took to build the Great Wall. The Chinese are using 21 IBM mainframe computers, 170 IBM data-entry machines, and 8 Wang computers to tally the questions and do the nose-counting. The results are due in 1984.

Don't keep a good idea to yourself. Continental Airlines set up one of the best flight-planning and seat-assignment systems ever on its computer. Why, the company reasoned, shouldn't we sell this computer service to other airlines and get more bang for our buck? It did, and they pulled in $9 million in 1982. United and American thought what Continental did was a good idea, so they're planning to offer data processing services, too. The computer department used to be considered a service for the organization; now the emphasis is on producing revenue. Some dirty tricks are also possible. Airlines that have sold their reservations systems to others have been known to favor their own flights over competitors in listings for travel agents.

The computer munchies. The Los Alamos Scientific Laboratory is home to the first Cray-1 and will soon be home to a *fifth* Cray. The lab also has four CDC 7600 supercomputers and fifty Digital VAX-11/780s as well as a few other computers here and there. (It's the biggest stockpile of computers in the world.) Robert Ewald, director of computing at Los Alamos, says they could easily use a hundred more Cray-1's. Los Alamos works on defense and energy projects, highly complex simulations and modeling that take a Cray hundreds of hours to process. "Big science requires big computing," Ewald says. Indeed; the memory banks at Los Alamos house the equivalent of twenty-five million copies of Tolstoy's *War and Peace.*

The computer industry's annual trade show. It's the National Computer Conference, and it's usually a real circus. Like any other vendors, computer companies try to sell their products with a variety of gimmicks. Some of the more interesting ones over the years include:

- Sperry has a woman extolling the virtues of her company's machines to a talking portrait with moving eyes and facial expressions; when she needs reinforcements, a plaster bust "comes to life" to convince the portrait.

- NCR has used basketball star Jerry Lucas to demonstrate how people can improve their memories. Lucas can memorize a page of numbers from a telephone book.

- Data General has used a belly dancer to display the chip on which its MicroNova computer was based. The chip was lodged in her navel.

- Technology Transfer Institute displayed holograms, the most unique of which was of James Martin, an industry guru, in his sorcerer pose.

- NCC characters: a gladiator, various robots, singing twins (female, of course), cowgirls, a Wurlitzer jukebox, hot-air balloons, a karate chopper, the Xerox monk, mime troupes.

Who really won World War II? The Japanese have systematically captured the world market in consumer electronics, automobiles, motorcycles, pianos, and cameras. Can they do it with personal computers? Steve Jobs, president of Apple, thinks not. Says he: "The first wave came and it sort of flopped up on the shore like a dead fish. The second wave (spring, 1983) are about fifteen machines . . . and, in my opinion, they are going to flop up on the shore like dead fish."

Meanwhile, U.S. computer makers are competing furiously with each other. In 1982, approximately 2.5 million personal computers were shipped worldwide. As you read this, the figures will have doubled.

The world's fastest computers. The idea behind supercomputers was to have a dazzlingly fast, prestigious machine used by scientists, educators, or governmental and research agencies, such as the Atomic Energy Commission, the U.S. Weather Bureau, or the Defense Department. In 1955, IBM tried to build a supercomputer called STRETCH, but it was a vacuum tube machine that was made obsolete by transistor technology even as the first machine appeared. Only nine were built, and IBM took a $20 million bath on STRETCH.

Neil Lincoln, an engineer at Control Data Corporation, defines a supercomputer as "a computer that is only one generation behind the problems the customer is presently experiencing." Herewith a gallery of history's hottest machines:

- 1946: ENIAC, brainchild of J. Presper Eckert and John W. Mauchly, built at the Moore School of Engineering at the University of Pennsylvania. It could perform five thousand calculations per second.

- 1951: UNIVAC I, son of ENIAC and the first commercial computer. The first two machines were delivered to the Bureau of the Census, pointing out just how seriously the government took the national nose count. Sperry kept the machine's memory alive in the name of their computer division, Sperry Univac, not renamed until 1982.

- 1953: UDEC, or Unitized Digital Electronic Coomputer, installed at the Wayne State University computation center. UDEC, manufactured by Burroughs (which changed its name that year from Burroughs Adding Machine Company to Burroughs Corporation), was a huge machine. It weighed several tons, contained ten miles of cabling, used three thousand vacuum tubes and seven thousand transistors; its unique characteristic, however, was unitized "building block" construction. Commenting on this when it was installed, Dr. Arvid Jacobsen, director of the computation lab, said, "UDEC may never become obsolete."

- 1954: First commercially owned Univac I delivered to General Electric.

- 1958: Seymour Cray of Control Data builds the first fully transistorized supercomputer, the CDC 1604. It used germanium transistors and was very fast; his next machine would outperform the 1604 by three orders of magnitude. CDC president Norris added the firm's address, 501 Park Avenue, to the nomenclature of the last machine he worked on, the Univac 1103, to give the machine its 1604 designation.

- 1963: The first true supercomputer in that it used silicon transistors, greatly enhancing speed, the Control Data CDC 6600 was shipped to the Lawrence Livermore Labs in California.

- 1967: Burroughs begins work with the Department of Defense and the University of Illinois on the ILLIAC IV, intended for global weather forecasting. When it was completed in 1972, ILLIAC IV went to NASA's Ames Research Center for "complex data processing tasks."

- 1975: Seymour Cray, now out on his own, introduces the Cray-1, the fastest computer on earth. It retains this title until he introduces his next machine. Cray can also be credited with bringing sense and sensibility to numerical designations for computing machines: The Cray-1 was followed by the Cray-2.

- 1980: CDC brings out its competitor for the Cray-1, the CDC Cyber 205. The two operate so fast and perform so closely to each other that tire tread pattern and the size of hood ornaments determine which crosses the finish line first.

FROM THE CACHE:
Evolution of the Species

A computer can do nothing unless data are fed into it and there is a way to see the results; it's called input and output, or I/O. Curiously, the form I/O first took—the punched card—remained unchanged for over seventy years, from the 1880s until the early 1960s. Herman Hollerith, a young American born in 1860 during the nation's eighth census and who worked for the U.S. Bureau of the Census, applied the punched card Joseph Jacquard had used to give weaving instructions to the loom in early nineteenth-century France to the census tabulating machine.

Hollerith devised his statistical tabulating system between 1884 and 1890, when the Census Bureau put it to work for the first time. As a result, the counting took only two-and-a-half years—one third the time it had taken in 1880. A head count of 62,622,250 was represented by 2 billion holes. In the November 11, 1891, issue of *The Electrical Engineer* was written, "This apparatus works as unerringly as the mills of the gods, but beats them hollow as to speed."

The punched card, which was the same size as the dollar bill at the time, was named the Hollerith card. The card had such great potential that Hollerith formed the Tabulating Machine Co. in 1896. Through mergers in 1911, it became known as the Computing-Tabulating-Recording Co., or C-T-R. In 1914 the firm hired a man named Thomas Watson, who quickly rose to president, then chief executive officer; in 1924, Watson renamed the company International Business Machines, Inc. And the Hollerith card became known as the IBM card.

Hollerith's tabulating machine was electromechanical, using some of the technology of the electric telegraph key and counters not unlike the Pascaline. To read the cards, electrical contact was made through the holes when a pin touched a bath of mercury below; it could read between fifty and eighty cards per minute. Operators were known to extract a bit of mercury and deposit it in a spittoon, disabling the machine so they could take a break.

Machines that performed business calculations were beginning to proliferate. Otto Steiger, an inventor from Zurich, Switzerland, invented the first successful calculator, called "The Millionaire"; between 1894 and 1935, 4,655 were sold. William Seward Burroughs (1857–98) perfected the Adding and Listing Machine, which was introduced in 1886. Burroughs, noted for his remark, "Accuracy is truth filed to a sharp point," figured there was a market for 8,000 machines—one for every bank in the United States. By 1900, 972 had been sold, but in the year 1906, the sales force sold 7,804 machines. Two years later, the 50,000th adding machine was manufactured, and in 1926 Burroughs hit 1 million. Earlier, the machine proved so popular that Ford Motor Company produced a special model car with a large rack to carry the adding machine and dubbed it the "Burroughs Special."

By the 1930s, mechanical machines were giving way to electromechanical ones, and George Stibitz of Bell Labs and Conrad Zuse in Germany were designing relay-operated calculators. Stibitz's machine went to work switching telephone calls, and Zuse's machines were used to perform calculations in aerodynamics for the infamous German V-rockets.

Vannevar Bush was another matter. While Stibitz and Zuse were developing circuitry that would lead to the digital computer, Bush, the dean of engineering at MIT, was trying to reinvent Babbage's machine, which Bush called the Differential Analyzer. It used electricity only to power the electric motors that turned shafts, which turned cranks, which turned gears that clanked away solving differential equations and the like. Bush, noted for his remark, "In a scientific war, the scientists should aid in making the plans," ruled governmental committee after committee with an iron fist. As World War II approached, Bush's machines were outclassed by far less pretentious and complex devices, such as the German ENIGMA encryption machine. Science turned to digital, rather than analog, calculating machines, and the Differential Analyzer ended up as a curiosity in the Smithsonian.

The first hybrid calculator/computer was the Mark I, a joint project between Harvard University and IBM. It embodied all the earlier precepts, dating back to Charles Babbage, that defined what an automatic calculating machine should be able to perform: It operated on a universal calculus and performed mathematics in a logical, step-by-step fashion. The Mark I was 51 feet long, 8 feet high, and linked 760,000 electronic components with 500 miles of wire. It could add or subtract two 23-digit numbers in $3/10$ second.

But it was ENIAC that takes the honor of being the first true electronic computer, as it was built with vacuum tubes, not relays, and incorporated the three classical components of a computer: the central processor (CPU), a memory storage, and an input/output device.

ENIAC, however, used decimal arithmetic, which was certainly a step forward from analog, or step-by-step counting, but it was EDVAC that takes the honor of being the first computer to use binary, or digital, mathematics. It was the brainchild of John von Neumann and was completed in 1950.

EDVAC spawned machines called EDSAC, MANIAC, IAS, and JOHN-NIAC. An apocryphal story relates that the name MANIAC was coined to stop the inanity of referring to computers with acronyms, but as we all know, it had little effect.

Another landmark computer was WHIRLWIND, built at MIT in 1951 by Jay Forrester, Ken Olsen, and others. It is considered by some to be the first minicomputer, because it could perform calculations on data in parallel. ENIAC operated in serial; that means it began with the first number and calculated until it completed the last number. WHIRLWIND could calculate numbers in groups, so the answers would appear more or less right away. This was termed *real-time computing*, and it took the computer out of the realm of theoretical mathematics and gave it jobs in the real world, such as helping to land aircraft and tracking missiles. It could do these things because in part it had a magnetic core memory, the first of its kind. Today's minicomputer is about the size of a dishwasher, but WHIRLWIND was a behemoth that filled a two-story building. The WHIRLWIND project defined memory technology for the 1950s and eventually led Ken Olsen to found Digital Equipment Corporation.

Research is moving ahead on many fronts: Governmental, military, and university research labs have developed prototype very-high-speed integrated circuits (VHSIC), and other technologies beyond silicon are being explored. Jack Kilby, who invented the integrated circuit in 1958, says, "Twenty-five years is a long time between drinks in this business. We're about ready for another something big."

CHAPTER 5

MIND OVER MATTER:
The Thoughtful World of Software

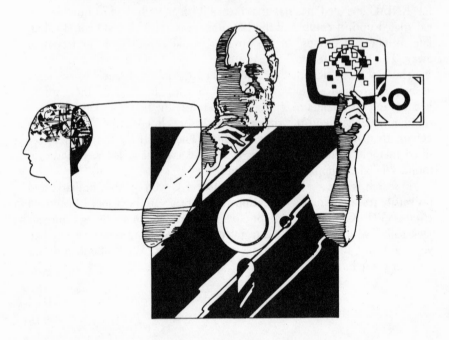

A computer's brainwaves are measured by symmetrical arcs on an oscilloscope, peaks and valleys representing 1's and 0's, the units of computer thought. If a computer's lucky number is 7, it may think "7" but it would tell us "111," which is how "7" is said in a language of only 1's and 0's.

Long ago, if you wanted to converse with a computer you had to talk to it in the 1's and 0's it understood, generally in the form of a punched card where a hole meant "1" and no hole meant "0." Before that it was even worse. You had to throw switches or plug wires into receptacles in the computer to tell it what to do, an activity that took place in the vicinity of several thousand very hot vacuum tubes.

Eventually humans realized they could use the computer to help it talk to itself, and they devised instructions made of 1's and 0's that told the computer what was meant by such stuff as:

IF C$(K) = S$(K) THE 3170
or
ARGUMENT: = DIGITVALUE (NEXTCHAR);

Piles of instructions like these came to be called a program; piles of programs constitute software. By 1960, most computers understood programs. So did a handful of long-haired eccentrics called programmers, who were called systems analysts if they made over $15,000 a year.

Another way to think of programs is this: They're the thoughts that computers have.

There are over two hundred computer languages. The one most used by professionals is COBOL, which stands for Common Business-Oriented Language and was based on an earlier language invented by Grace Murray Hopper. The language familiar to most people is BASIC, or Beginners All-Purpose Symbolic Instruction Code, partly invented by John Kemeny, a Dartmouth mathematician who later became the college's president. The language most used by people who pay for programming is English (French in France, German in Germany, etc.): for swearing when printouts are unreadable, data unworkable, and budgets unmanageable.

The most widely purchased software package. It's VisiCalc, a program for personal computers such as the Apple II or Radio Shack TRS-80 that allows users to alter rows and columns of tables and that keeps track of the results. The program has sold over five hundred thousand copies at $300 each. The most expensive software is that which comes with IBM's large computers: up to half the cost of a $6 million machine.

Although many computer programs are short, a typical "applications" program, such as payroll or inventory control, can have fifty thousand lines of instructions and cost $10 per line to develop. The longest applications program, a total insurance system by Informatics, has over ten million lines of code.

Origin of the word "bug." The word is derived from its antonym, debug, and was coined in the 1940s when an operator discovered a dead moth causing malfunctions in the signal relays of the Mark I Automatic Relay

Calculator at Harvard. From then on, an attempt to fix malfunctions was termed debugging the system.

The original moth, done in by its first encounter with a computer, has achieved immortality in programming jargon. And, according to Grace Murray Hopper, who worked on the Mark I and witnessed the source of this entomological etymology, the moth's carcass can still be viewed. It's taped to a page in a log book housed in a Navy museum in Virginia.

Computers aren't the only thinkers that have "bugs." Psychologist Lauren Resnick of the University of Pittsburgh says that people have them, too. Misunderstandings of how to apply the rules of arithmetic, for instance, can extend into adult life. In a test by two other scientists, John Clement and Jack Lochhead at the University of Massachusetts, eight out of seventeen engineers missed a simple problem by hand. Using a computer, though, all got the correct answer.

Have you ever wanted to figure out if it would be profitable to "lay in" a group of feeder pigs and "finish them out" to market? Then the Agric-Calc Feeder Pig Module is just for you. This software package from Michigan City, Indiana, helps you calculate costs, supplies, and profit margins on your TRS-80, which is just about as popular an item as the tractor on the farm these days. This is no rehashed business program, either; it features such key items as projecting how many pigs you expect to die, calculating price per hundredweight of market hogs times sale weight, and weight gain versus cost of feed. As one reviewer noted, once you've worked with this program you might find it more profitable to take a Florida vacation.

Now you don't have to move to Marin County, California, or sit in an auditorium holding your water all weekend to get self-actualized. All you have to do is slip Avant-Garde Creations' Life Dynamic disk into your home computer and away you go. There are eleven different programs. In "Relatopoly," the monopoly game for relationships, you throw the video dice on the video board and "land" on "relationship episodes," some good and some bad. Or try the poem-writing program "that will have you writing good poems in minutes." Then there's the Aliveness Life Dynamic, where you play in the Primal Oil Field, jangle the Keys to Awareness, and plot your Rationality (your score is 18; you're sometimes rational). The Environment Life Dynamic helps in "identifying positive environmental characteristics, oppressed aspects of yourself, and finding rare individuals who'd be perfect for being part of a truly beautiful life-style/space." There's a game in the Physical Life Dynamic where the media bombard you with "all kinds of ads for unhealthy food and drugs" you must defend yourself against while remaining "open to benevolent elements in your surroundings." The nice folks in Eugene, Oregon, who bring you these Life Dynamics invite you to "communicate" with them about your "experiences."

Want to enliven the bedroom scene tonight? Well, just plunk your computer down between you and punch up "Interlude." The program will ask both you and your mate how you feel tonight and then suggest some sexual adventures and various positions to try. There are 106 "interludes," from gentle and romantic to wild and kinky. If one of you isn't quite into one, you can make second choices. They say "Interlude" (over twenty thousand programs sold) permits people to express their feelings more honestly, since they're talking to a machine, so be careful your mate doesn't kick you out of bed in favor of the computer!

Drawing by Tim Eagan

Other porno programs:

Pornopoly bets your money and your clothes against your trips around the electronic board, visiting such places as Satisfaction Avenue, Kinky Court Place and a great corner stop at Free Necking.

French postcards, bedtime stories, the dirty old man, and comic strips past and present appear on "Animated Sex Cartoons." Not only are the graphics graphic, but they're also accompanied by appropriate sighs, moans, slurps, and such, and you get to write the captions.

Adventure games where you search for gold and treasure are fun, but one that takes place in "Lost Vagueness" in the year 2020, pursuing the favors of three charming ladies, sounds like a real trip. In addition to exploring your sexual prowess, "Softporn Adventure" takes you in and out of casinos and up and down the gutters, where various criminals and thieves are after you incessantly.

"Encounter" is just that: you have to sit and answer a bunch of shrink questions before you get on with matters. But once you answer the seventeen questions, the computer knows your moods and desires and suggests a Lewd for you, and some of them are quite outrageous. If, however, you want to go beyond the limits, this program allows you to enter your own questions and Lewds—in fact, "Encounter" is sort of like a good sex partner, because you can do anything you want.

If you like to combine business with sex, "Whorehouse" is the game for you. This is a game for the guys (Will it replace Monday night football or Friday night poker?); each player strives for the title of King Pimp, and play begins by putting your wife on the sidewalk. However, Jim Miller, the program's author, assures us that if you have a liberated wife, a few quick changes in the program puts her behind the desk and you in the red-velvet room upstairs.

Mike Downing has always been interested in doing sports analysis with a computer, so writing a program to handicap horse racing was not only logical but also fun. All you do is enter four or five values for the horses from the racing form, and PHD-1 (Probability Handicapping Device) does the rest. Mike says that a study showed PHD-1 returned $1.50 for every $1.00 wagered over eighty-five horses chosen. Mike started his own company, Joe Computer, in Woodland Hills, California, and met Ken Perry, who had written a program called Pro Football, which he now markets. It turns out Perry's program won forty-four of sixty bets in 1980—better than the sports services, and, most important, better than the Las Vegas line. "A progressive bettor would have made a fortune," says Mike. The more fainthearted may simply want to pick up a copy of James Jasper's book *Basic Betting* and try a few at home first.

The year is 1952, and John Cullinane is sharpening skates for the Boston Bruins. He decides he needs a real career and begins working on a business degree from Northeastern University. After graduation, he lands a job as a computer programmer. Today, John Cullinane is president of Cullinet (né Cullinane Database Systems), a firm doing $50 million a year in software packages, mostly for IBM computers. How did he do it? He learned that B. F. Goodrich, a tire manufacturer, had a database management system that it thought could be marketed. Cullinane did it and called the system IDMS, to compete with IBM'S IMS. It worked twice as fast as IMS, and Cullinane was off and running.

Bill Gates was playing poker one night in January 1975 in a Harvard dorm when a friend showed him a copy of the now-legendary issue of *Popular Electronics* with a cover story about the Altair personal computer, the first ever, available only in kit form for $397. Gates was excited and got together with his friend Paul Allen, who worked for Honeywell at the time. They began writing a programming language for micros, which they called Microsoft Basic. They've sold nearly a million copies; their firm, now located in Seattle, Washington, is earning over $15 million a year.

About the same time, Gary Kildall was teaching computer science at the Naval Postgraduate College in Monterey, California, and experimenting with an operating system, the program that tells the computer how the software and hardware work together. He called it CP/M—an acronym for control Program/Microcomputers—and offered it to Intel. The company turned him down, so he started his own company, Digital Research, and today CP/M is an industry standard. In 1982, Digital Research netted over $20 million.

Kildall's first attempt at entrepreneurship was in a partnership with Ben Cooper building computerized horoscope machines that were placed in supermarkets and stores in northern California. The several they built were decorated with dazzling astrological designs—but the printer kept jamming up. The machines ended up in a warehouse, but bits and pieces of the computer code that made them work ended up in CP/M.

Most reclusive programmer. Paul Lutus has written some of Apple Computer's best sellers, including Apple Writer, a word processing package. Paul lives in a cabin high up in Oregon's Cascade Mountains—he had to string a thirteen-hundred-foot extension cord just to plug his Apple in. When he has to go to Apple headquarters in Cupertino, California, he hops on his bicycle, rides to the small airport where his personal plane is waiting, and flies to California; then, throwing his backpack on, he tools his bike to Apple. Outside his cabin, just in case he doesn't want to make the trek, is a microwave dish so he can send Apple-to-Apple electronic mail.

Picture Software Arts, a company crammed on one floor in a bank building overlooking Central Square in Cambridge, Massachusetts. An anomaly: high-tech sprawled everywhere while a world hundreds of years old goes on below. On our first visit, Dan Bricklin, chairman of the board, greeted us in a flannel shirt and Levi's; his partner and president, Bob Frankston, was similarly attired. Bob's desk area was covered by no less than four computers, which beeped every so often to signal that some electronic mail had just arrived.

Today, Software Arts, the company Dan and Bob formed to make Visi-Calc an institution, is located in a building built in 1872 in Wellesley, Massachusetts, but which, once you're inside, is the picture of modernity.

Each office has outlets for computers installed in the walls; computers are virtually everywhere. As he walks through the new digs, Dan constantly emphasizes the people-pleasing aspects: day rooms for people to congregate in, kitchens with refrigerators stuffed with snacks and soft drinks, all at the company's expense, and a laid-back atmosphere in which people can create and grow together.

Dan had a dream: "I visualized an electronic blackboard and electronic chalk in a classroom," he says. But Dan was a business major, not a computer programmer, and had his hands full working on his M.B.A. at Harvard. He enlisted the support of Frankston and Steve Lawrence, their first employee, to prepare the program. Dan Fylstra, a buddy living in the same apartment building, was starting a business called Personal Software, which at the time was into both business and game programs for personal computers. He suggested they make it work on an Apple. Dan chose the name VisiCalc, or Visible Calculator, and they started selling the program in January 1979.

Frankston worked all night and slept all day. Bricklin went to school all day and caught up with Fylstra when he could. They began marketing the program, but initial response was unenthusiastic. Then Ben Rosen, who had taken an interest in the industry as an analyst at Morgan Stanley, gave VisiCalc a rave review in an industry newsletter: He called it "the software tail that might wag the personal computer dog." The symbiosis worked: VisiCalc helped sell Apple Computers, Apple computers helped sell VisiCalc.

Many industry insiders credit Fylstra, the marketer, with VisiCalc's success; if you listen to Bricklin and Frankston, however, it's because it's a great program. Otherwise, why would everyone want to imitate it? Yet there's little doubt that Fylstra ran away with the store when he set up VisiCorp in California; now Software Arts is no more than another author on the list at Fylstra's publishing/marketing company. Surely it's just another petty intrigue in the world of business, but it can't help but be felt deeply in an industry only a few years old.

What's in a language? Plenty. The type of software language one uses may affect the ability to produce an outcome. Ask medieval scholars. Only the most assiduous and brightest mathematicians were able to master long division. The reason: The language was Latin, and Roman numerals don't lend themselves to mathematical manipulation.

Code cracking. John Kemeny, the mathematician who coinvented Basic and was president of Dartmouth College from 1970 to 1981, was born in Hungary. In 1942, when he was sixteen, he was still struggling with English when his high school teachers pushed him to take an experimental verbal aptitude test. At the time he could speak only Hungarian and Latin. The test, however, was multiple-choice, and Kemeny discovered there was a pattern to the answer key. He cracked the code, and speaking almost no English, got one of the highest verbal aptitude scores in New York City that year.

The "Wolf Fence" algorithm? This is what Edward J. Gauss of the University of Alaska calls his method of debugging time-sharing programs. It's a way to find out where, in all those thousands of lines of code, an error (the wolf) might have occurred. First you divide the territory (the program) with a fence (a print instruction) and determine in which portion the wolf is howling (the error occurs). You keep partitioning the territory this way until the wolf is isolated in a tight corral of fences. Then you shoot the wolf. The method, says Gauss, evolved from a method he taught years ago. That one was called the "Lions of South Africa" algorithm.

Sixty to 80 percent of a company's programming effort is typically spent "maintaining"—finding errors, updating, revising—old programs. And U.S. companies have spent over $1 trillion (in 1983 dollars) on programming since the computer was invented. In any one year, U.S. companies will spend more money on programming than the entire Gross National Product of Greece.

The first programmed machine. The Jacquard loom, invented in 1801 by Joseph-Marie Charles Jacquard, a French weaver. In the loom, needles connected to the warp (lengthwise) threads butt against punched cards. If a needle hits a hole in the card, its thread is raised and will appear on the top of the fabric. If there is no hole, the thread will remain on the bottom.

Different patterns could be generated by different patterns of holes in the cards, and cards could be fed into the loom in a sequence, allowing many operations to take place automatically—just as in computers that used punched cards.

The Case of the Mysterious Simplex Algorithm. Linear programming is the branch of mathematics that concerns itself with input-output problems of many variables. An oil company, for example, might use linear programming to decide how much of what type of gasoline to blend from the available stock of crude oil—in fact, that's how linear programming was first put to use in the 1950s. Another example: You have so much money to buy liquor at a party and you want everyone to get as drunk as possible. How much beer at $2.05 a six-pack, wine at $6.00 a gallon jug, or tequila at $9.95 a quart should you buy, given that only half the people will drink any one drink? To get the answer requires examining all possible combinations of beer, wine, and tequila evaluated at so many cents per ounce of alcohol (degree of drunkenness), keeping in mind who is likely to drink what. There are lots of combinations, but only one that will maximize the alcohol content in the blood of the most partygoers.

In fact, a relatively simple linear program problem might involve ten variables—which would require looking at over three million combinations and evaluating them for a maximum solution. Most linear programming problems come with many more variables involved than that.

In 1947, a man named George B. Dantzig, now at Stanford University, invented a method called the Simplex Algorithm to short-cut the process of examining all the combinations of variables. With it, complex problems with thousands of constraints and variables can be solved easily (with the help of computers to do the boring stuff).

It's a mystery why the Simplex Algorithm works as well as it does. Mathematicians can come up with no reason why the algorithm should be so efficient at paring linear programs down to size. They have even come up with theoretical problems that can bring the algorithm to its knees. But those problems just never seem to pop up in real life.

Recently, Soviet scientists developed a competitor to the Simplex Algorithm that received front-page press. By theoretical standards, it should work much better than the Simplex Algorithm. It doesn't. In fact, it hardly works at all.

Here's to the Simplex Algorithm. It works, and nobody knows why.

No cure for "infinite loops," or computer programs that, by error of design or coding, never stop. It can be proven mathematically that no computer program can be devised to test another program before it's run and predict whether it will go into an "infinite loop."

The longest computer program. IBM MVS Operating System, 520 million 8-bit characters coded into thirteen million instructions.

THE TEN MOST IMPORTANT COMPUTER LANGUAGES

NAME	DATE	INVENTOR	COMMENTS
Algol	1958	Peter Naur and committee	Designed over a period of years by international group of computer scientists. "Algorithmic Language"; good for scientific uses.
APL	1962	Kenneth Iverson, Harvard, IBM	"A Programming Language"; good for modeling programs.

Design started in 1957 as an adjunct to teaching classes and writing a book. First use begun within IBM.

Basic	1965	John Kemeny and Tom Kurtz (Dartmouth)	"Beginners All-Purpose Symbolic Instruction Code." A Dartmouth decision to provide time-shared computing available to all students led to a need for an easy-to-use programming language. Written with help of students. First application up and running on May 1, 1964, at 4:00 A.M.
Cobol	1959	Committee	"Commercial and Business-Oriented Language." The committee was divided into a short-range group and an intermediate-range group. The intent was to come up with a standard language before each computer manufacturer did (and created programming Babel). The short-range subcommittee came up with an interim language—which has now been in use over twenty years. Grace Hopper is often referred to as the inventor of Cobol because much of it is based on Flow-Matic, an earlier language of her design, and because at DOD she was responsible for developing a compiler that would make Cobol run on most any computer.
Fortran	1954	John Backus, IBM	"Formula Translator." Implementation began after specs became public within

THE TEN MOST IMPORTANT COMPUTER LANGUAGES

NAME	DATE	INVENTOR	COMMENTS
			IBM. Many versions since then; most used for scientific work, some business programs. Widespread usage began in 1957. Having developed rudiments of Fortran in one year, Backus has been spending years since trying to replace it with a better language. An IBM Fellow.
Jovial	1960	Jules Schwartz, System Development Corp.	"Jules' Own Version of the International Algebraic Language." Would have preferred Ovial, but deemed too racy a name. Used in developing air defense computer software. Is still used only in military systems—dead giveaway to enemies that obtain software.
Lisp	1958	John McCarthy, MIT	"List Processor." For artificial-intelligence applications. Based on making connections between lists and tables of data. IBM gave MIT a 704 computer; McCarthy concepts developed, 1956–58; first implementation of Lisp, 1958.
Pascal	1971	Niklaus Wirth, Eidgenossiche Technische Hochschule, Switzerland	Written to show the Algol committee, which Wirth had resigned from, that Wirth's version was superior to the committee's. It was. Named for Blaise Pascal and used for systems development.
PL/1	1964	Bruce Rosenblatt, George	"Programming Language." Secret committee asked by

		Radin, Standard Oil, IBM	IBM to come up with a new programming language for the IBM 360. First named NPL, for New Programming Language, but the National Physics Laboratory in England had a fit, so IBM renamed it Programming Language 1. Business orientation.
Smalltalk	1972	Alan Kay, Xerox's Palo Alto Research Center	Devised a new language for Xerox for communicating with personal computers, especially visually oriented. Basic concept behind new Apple computers.

Note: Dates chosen generally refer to date of first publication of language specs. Since languages evolve, exact starting dates are not meaningful.

One of the earliest specialized programming languages was called APT, for "Automatically Programmed Tools," developed by Douglas Ross at MIT in 1959. The language is used to program robots and numerically controlled machine tools. Its first handiwork was presented at a press conference on February 25, 1959, jointly sponsored by MIT and the Air Materiel Command. It was much ballyhooed, and a *New Yorker* write-up said, "The Air Force announced today it's a machine that can receive instructions in English, figure out how to make whatever is wanted, and teach other machines how to make it."

An Air Force general was quoted as saying the breakthrough would allow the United States "to build a war machine that nobody would want to tackle."

What was the object made by the machine running under APT?

An ashtray.

The word "byte," which today means a collection of eight computer bits (enough to code all the letters and numerals), was coined by Werner Buchholz from IBM during the designing of the IBM STRETCH computer.

How many computer programs are there? According to SOFSEARCH, at the beginning of 1983 there were 27,000 different software packages available in the United States. One out of five was an accounting package of some type. The rest ran the gamut from Actuarial Applications Excluding Valuation (8) to word processing (374). There were 1,106 Comprehensive

Business Management Systems, 1,881 programs related to amusements, 40 adult "mature theme" games, 63 diet programs, 813 finance-related programs, and 3,465 programs that help you write other programs (operating systems, control programs, etc.). By type of computer:

HARDWARE	NUMBER OF PROGRAMS
Mainframe	4,659
Minicomputers	8,551
Microcomputers	13,790

One of 27,000. For $150, Rainbow Computing will sell you a program that computes your weekly bowling score.

Bill England wrote an environmental control program for a client in Washington but had a sneaking suspicion he might not get paid. So he wrote a software time bomb into the program, set to booby-trap if he didn't have his money in thirty days. The client didn't pay, the bomb went off, the client went berserk, and England got paid. England is currently in Moscow, doing God only knows what.

The 1960s live. Andy Fluegelman was an editor on *The Whole Earth Catalog* once upon a time, but these days he's working for *PC World*, which is devoted to the IBM Personal Computer. When Andy got his personal computer, he found some shortcomings in the communications software, so he sat down and began writing a new program. When he got through he called it "PC-Talk," termed it not software but "freeware," and offered it without charge to anyone who sent him a blank diskette. If you like it, you can send him $25; if you don't want to, that's OK, too. "Copy-protection schemes are all going to great efforts to go against a natural tendency," says Andy, who encourages people to make copies of PC-Talk for their friends.

Wanna become a rich and famous software developer? First, buy a copy of Kern Publications' *Software Writer's Market* (yes, just like the writer's *Writer's Market*). Then *caveat emptor.* If you go it on your own, marketing is a hassle. If you sign up as an author for one of the big software, hardware, or publishing houses, you get a small chunk of royalties. (Although a few hotshots make six figures from a single program, most software authors are lucky to make $10,000.) Worst of all, some unscrupulous outfits look at your proposal, turn it down, and write their own in-house. It's a disk-eat-disk world.

Quotations from Chairman Edsgar. Edsgar Dijkstra, who helped found the principles of modern (structured) programming, has his own opinions on the state of the art. A few examples:

"If [the advertisements for seminars and short courses] are prefixed by the words 'in-depth,' you can be sure they are junk."

"The word 'language' is a misnomer—languages are things like Dutch and English. They are for telling jokes in and making love in."

"The use of Cobol cripples the mind; its teaching should, therefore, be regarded as a criminal offense."

"The use of anthropomorphic terminology when dealing with computing systems is a symptom of professional immaturity."

"It is practically impossible to teach good programming to students who've had a prior exposure to Basic; as potential programmers they are mentally mutilated beyond hope of regeneration."

Professor Dr. Dijkstra—as he likes to be known—says there are other, more controversial truths he keeps to himself "for reasons of professional etiquette."

Arf, arf. In some versions of Fortran, when you type certain sequences of characters, called strings, you must precede them with the letter "H." For example, instead of typing DOG, you must type 3HDOG. Why? One programmer's way of honoring Herman Hollerith.

Businesses and governments paid over $7 billion for packaged software in 1983, the equivalent of 280,000 beginning programmers' salaries for a year.

The title of 1982's computer movie, *TRON,* is a command in Basic—it means "turn on trace," which means the printer will print the program line numbers as the program runs. What do you do when you want to shut it off? TROFF, of course. Which is what the box office did: TROFF *TRON.*

GREAT MOMENTS IN SOFTWARE

- June 16, 1951: First programming error at the Bureau of the Census.

- September 20, 1954: Harlan Herrick runs the first successful Fortran program at IBM.

- September 1958: John McCarthy introduces LISP, the first language for working with artificial intelligence. An important feature of LISP is keeping unused information for later use, called garbage collection, fathering the notion of GIGO—garbage in, garbage out.

- November 18, 1963: General Motors produces the first auto part designed completely by a computer: a trunk lid. Owners of 1965 Cadillacs don't know and don't care.

- May 1, 1964: Tom Kurtz and John Kemeny of Dartmouth run the first Basic program at 4:00 A.M. Author Gantz, at Dartmouth in 1964, plays selection number fifty on the fraternity jukebox at the time, oblivious to the winds of history blowing through the night. The song is "Reputation," by Little Anthony.

- June 23, 1969: IBM announces it will no longer sell its hardware and software as a package—the software must be purchased separately. Called unbundling. Overnight, a $3 billion business is born.

- 1970: Jay Forrester runs the "World Dynamics Model" in Dynamo, a simulation and modeling program, to help Boston's Mayor John Collins solve the problems of managing a big city. Discoveries: Aiding the unemployed draws more unemployed to the city, causing social reform to backfire; free public transportation creates more traffic, since people will live farther away from work; and city-funded housing takes up space business and industry could use, hence fewer jobs.

- May 11, 1979: VisiCalc, the first program an inexperienced computer user could really operate, is introduced at the West Coast Computer Faire. Only available for the Apple, it made both Software Arts and Apple a mint. With over five hundred thousand copies sold, it's probably the most influential program since Fortran.

- January 29, 1983: Author Rochester loses seventeen pages of this, the software chapter, due to a disk crash. What's a disk crash? In this case, a scratch in the magnetic coating that wouldn't allow the head to read the seventeen pages of stellar prose. Like when there's a glob of something on a record and the needle sticks. Gimme rewrite!

A CONVERSATION WITH CHARLEY LECHT

"My dream is that with hardware and software systems, we can improve the quality of life. Ultimately—and I don't think it's science fiction—I believe a cure for cancer has a good chance of coming from the computer industry, rather than medicine."

Charles P. Lecht thrives on ideas. He derives nourishment from them. "What if" is his favorite train of thought.

It's his speculative, contemplative nature that propelled him in his career from his first job as a programmer in the early 1950s to the head of

Advanced Computer Techniques and author of five books. Today, Charley has left the bustle of running a large company and spends his days at Lecht Sciences, a think tank specializing in computers and communications (and an occasional game, such as Nerd Alert). We asked him where he thought software was heading.

LECHT: In the 1990s, we'll have massive command and control centers at AT&T, IBM, American Express, and Citibank, like the command control center in the movie *THX 1138*, where software is the neuronal connection in a gigantic brain. In terms of applications development, forget it. In the late 1980s and into the next decade, it will be done by business applications people, and the softwareniks will be relegated to maintaining the old applications environment or changing over to new environments.

It's said that approximately 80 percent of all programs currently in operation are in Cobol. Some say the library of applications approaches $50 billion in Cobol. But no one will be writing applications in Cobol in 1990. It's proven to be a lemon of a language, although it was the best lemon around in its time.

TNC: How will we tell computers what to do?

LECHT: What has prevented natural language from making its debut as the means through which people express computer applications is that computers don't have a powerful enough CPU or enough memory. HAL [in the film 2001: A *Space Odyssey*] was a very realistic computer. It's where we are all going: a bank of devices all running the same program at the same time.

I think what we'll see long before the end of the decade are larger banks of numerous processors. You'll say, "I want to create a general ledger, computer." It'll say, "All right, tell me a little bit about what you want to do." You'll say, "I think the column headings for my general ledger should be the following: dah-dah, dah-dah." The computer will reply, "I understand."

TNC: This is quite a departure from current technology.

LECHT: The clue is that we want a language in which we can express our application in the most natural way, and that language is English for those who speak English. You should be able to speak ambiguously to a machine and let the machine figure out what you meant, then straighten out your ambiguity.

Once the instructions are stored, partly by algorithm, partly by brute force, the process of creating a program will involve a dialog with a virtual superhumanlike being you can talk to. The systems processors will then talk to one another. They'll put the program together and give it back to you. That's the ultimate.

What does natural language mean in programming terms? If you wanted sales figures in a normal query language, your computer screen would look like this:

PRINT LNAME, 82-SEP-ACT-SALES. 82-SEP-EST-SALES.
82-SEP-ACT-SALES—82-SEP-EST-SALES.
(82-SEP-ACT SALES—82-SEP-EST-SALES) / 82-SEP-ACT-SALES

IF   REGION = NEW ENGLAND AND
82-YTD-ACT-SALES < 82-QUOTA

However, if you were to use Intellect, an English-language query system from Artificial Intelligence in Waltham, Massachusetts, you would simply type:

I WONDER HOW ACTUAL SALES FOR LAST MONTH COMPARED TO THE FORECASTS FOR PEOPLE UNDER QUOTA IN NEW ENGLAND.

Why didn't someone think of that before?

FROM THE CACHE:
Conversing with Computers

La Rochefoucauld said, "Everyone complains of his memory, and no one complains of his judgment." If a computer can remember its instructions, judgment is a whiz; because a computer is nothing but on and off switches, it can't make a mistake. Only the people who program or design it can make a mistake, but that's another story.

Early computers understood only 1's and 0's—binary mathematics. Programmers had to write things such as 1001100011 so the computer could perform its functions. Today we credit Claude Shannon for applying Boolean logic—binary arithmetic—to switching circuits. As a student at MIT, he'd worked with Vannevar Bush's clumsy machine and "had to kind of, you know, fix [a complicated relay circuit] from time to time to keep it going." He wrote up his ideas in his master's thesis in 1937, changed the way computers were designed, and got a Nobel Prize for his efforts. (His ideas on information theory have also been useful in genetic engineering and neuroanatomy.)

In the 1950s, things were made easier by assembly language, which allowed certain mnemonic words called microcode to be used instead of 1's and 0's. Every machine had its own, so a program for the ENIAC worked only on an ENIAC. Writing a program in assembly language is almost as dull as writing binary code. (The world's record for marathon assembly language program-writing goes to Carl Alsing of Data General, who in 1980 wrote the microcode for the MV-8000 supermini at home on his "micro-porch" in two weeks.)

Software development for programs and memory storage has paralleled hardware in its growth, almost generation for generation. For example:

GENERATION	HARDWARE	SOFTWARE MEDIUM	SOFTWARE IMPLEMENTATION
First (1946–60)	Vacuum tubes	Switching wires, magnetic drum or mag core memory, punched cards	Manual or media input of machine codes (strings of numbers)
Second (1958–67)	Transistors	Mag tape, hard disks	Procedural languages. More Englishlike commands that were translated by the computer into the number strings it could understand.
Third (1964–77)	Integrated circuits	Floppy disks, bubble memory	Nonprocedural languages: Even more Englishlike. Commands are often in guise of answers to questions computer asks; commands translated into other commands several times before being translated in the numbers computers can understand.
Fourth (1971–)	Microchips	Software-on-a-chip	Extensible and Englishlike language. Capabilities of language change on the fly based on functions invoked. Computer automatically checks instructions for reasonableness. Laypeople can operate computers without learning complex vocabulary.

More promising is the new concept of *firmware*, made possible by large-scale chip integration. If a chip could store the instructions to make it a CPU, engineers reasoned, why couldn't it do the same for programs? Thus was born the PROM, or Programmable Read Only Memory. Most personal computers use PROMs to store their operating system, so when you turn it on you are automatically in, say, Microsoft Basic. It's like flipping on the television with a channel preselected.

In fact, within the next few years we may see all programs and languages in firmware. Your computer may have a switch just like your television's channel selector to choose from several options: Basic, CP/M, word processing, data base management, spreadsheet, and so on. And if you want more built-in programs, all you'll have to do is plug in more chips.

CHAPTER 6

OF CHIPS AND KIDS:

Computerkinder

Eugene Volokh made $480 a week as a computer programmer for 20th Century-Fox in 1982, but he couldn't drive to work. He was only fifteen. John Harris, twenty years old, made $300,000 in royalties last year from video games Mouskattack and Jawbreaker. Greg Christensen, eighteen, pulled in about $100,000, while Thomas McWilliams, Jr., sixteen, earned a measly $60,000.

Cherub meets computer.

A quarter million kids will go to computer camp next summer; most schools have at least one personal computer for kids to play on; dozens of people under twenty-five years of age made $100,000 last year writing software; kids who can't read are maneuvering little video turtles on computer screens and making graphics complicated enough to stymie computer scientists of a decade and a half ago. Kids are teaching adults; kids and computers click.

Social scientists are already cranking up the grant machine to per-

*form studies on the social impact of all this youthful computerism—
with the first question whether the computer age discriminates against
the poor. One study showed that more than half of a hundred private
schools in the United States begin computer instruction in the first
grade. The Japanese are planning to introduce it in kindergarten when
the next generation of computers comes off the line. And elementary
schools seem more advanced in computer studies than secondary
schools—planting an educational time bomb that will go off when the
kinder hit high school and find their teachers don't know the difference
between bit-mapped-graphics and pipelined array processing.*

*And some of the playful antics of the younger generation have
sober side effects—such as a third family income, daytime narcolepsy,
or visits from John Law. For not only have kids taken to the computer
with zeal, they've also brought with them a built-in game-playing
penchant that works as well cracking the computer codes at Ma Bell or
altering their grades in school as it does playing Asteroids or Pac-Man.*

Youngest computer operator. The five-month-old daughter of Corey
Schou, a computer scientist from the University of Central Florida in Or-
lando, who rigged a home computer so the baby could operate it from her
crib. Pushing a button changed designs on a screen near the crib.

Youngest computer programmer. Danny Jacoby, who, in the late sixties
at the age of six, took a five-day intensive programming course at New York
University that was designed for college professors.

The most precocious computer whiz. It may have been Norbert Wiener,
one of the industry's pioneers, born November 25, 1894. When he was
eighteen months old he taught himself the alphabet. By six he had read the
works of Darwin, Ribot, and other scientists. At eleven he enrolled at Tufts
and at fourteen at Harvard's graduate school. At eighteen he had his Ph.D.
in philosophy and mathematics. He went on to become the resident genius
at MIT during the early years of computerdom; he coined the term "cybernetics."

Why we like computers. Studies by psychologists show that babies at six
months can tell the difference between two numbers. Adult chimpanzees,
even after hours of training, can't.

By the age of three, kids have already figured out how to classify sets of
numbers; they can also understand causality, construct order, and deduce.

These and the motor skills to manipulate a keyboard or joystick are all you really need to run a computer.

How addicting are computers? In 1982, when Rensselaer Polytechnic Institute gave entering students computers to see how they'd take to them, it discovered that in a short time they used them as much as kids who had brought their own with them to school. Even the liberal arts weenies.

"I swam, I hiked, I ran a computer." In 1982 *The New York Times* ran its first full page of ads for computer camps. The first computer camp had opened only five years earlier. In 1983 the number of kids attending computer camp surpassed a hundred thousand (mostly day camps, like the YMCA's).

There are already at least two hundred computer camps in the United States at over a thousand locations. They generally have at least 25 percent noncomputer activities and sometimes specialize by type of machine or special student interests. Generally they have to enforce the outdoor activities; the kids would rather be hacking away at their terminals. The Boy Scouts offer a merit badge in computers. Remember when you used to make lanyards in arts and crafts at camp? Now kids are designing video games.

- The first computer camp: Opened by Dr. Michael Zabinski outside Simsbury, Connecticut, in 1977. Catching toads and whittling in the morning, programming in Basic in the afternoon. Zabinski enrolled eighty-four kids for a one-week session.

  In 1983, Zabinski was running the National Computer Camp, with 135 kids from all over the country and England, Germany, Colombia, El Salvador, and a few other foreign lands. That's 135 kids for a week . . . times six weeks.

  "This is the first camp I've been to that's not boring," said sixteen-year-old Chet Dobro. "I mean, I've just been doing high-resolution graphics, and next week I'll be using random-access files. This involves you. This is real fun."

- The first "family" computer camp: Clarkson College's.

- The first computer camp for kids with diabetes: held at the National Computer Camp during the first week of August 1982.

- Age extremes: Computer Camps International offers computer instruction for kids as young as five years old; Elderhostel, Boston, offers computer instruction for kids over fifty-five years old.

- Learning extremes: In the course of a summer camp, kids go from neophytes to pretty good programmers. In the lesson plans for one camp, CompuTime, lesson A-1 begins by telling how to turn on the video monitor by pulling out the volume button. By lesson A-9, it is telling you about such things as character strings ("one-dimensional array or sequence of characters") and concatenation ("the process of adding one string to another").

Whatever happened to the snipe hunt?

In a period of eighteen months, from the fall of 1980 to the spring of 1982, the number of computers in American schools more than tripled— from thirty-one thousand to a hundred thousand. Of course, this is child's play if Apple Computer goes ahead with its plan to give away eighty-three thousand computers to U.S. secondary and elementary schools. (Apple seeks the same breaks computer companies get when they give computers to colleges; last year Congress turned down such a tax-law rewrite.)

The company has already donated sixty-thousand Apple IIe computers to California schools, after legislators relaxed state tax laws. Your esteemed authors think free computers in schools will have far-reaching effects, not the least of which is that author Rochester's ten-year-old, Joshua, can stop selling spices door-to-door to help pay for his school's computer.

Preschool circuit designers? The Learning Company of Portola Valley, California, offers a series of educational courses for kids from three to thirteen that_teach Venn diagrams, Boolean logic, and three-dimensional graphics. Its most amazing program is Rocky's Boots, a game invented by Warren Robinett, thirty-one, the inventor of the popular computer game called Adventure. The subject matter explored by the program is the educational equivalent of a circuit-design class for sophomores at Stanford University.

The Now That the Horse Is Out of the Barn Award. It goes to Digital Equipment Corp., which sent around an internal memo in June 1982, advising DEC personnel to change maintenance passwords on customer computers frequently. What prompted the memo was an incident where a high school student accessed the DEC computer at a major New York bank via an Apple computer hooked to a telephone line. The youth was able to crack the DEC security password—programmed into the customer's computer so service personnel can get into the machine for maintenance—by trial and error. It took six months to catch the culprit, during which time he deleted files, logged out users, locked up the system, and created general mayhem.

How's your CPU, Boris? In the U.S.S.R., computer science students attend colleges and universities without paying any tuition—it's all funded by the state. They usually spend five years studying, and log over five hundred hours of lecture, lab, and practice. During their last three years, students conduct about fifty extra hours of independent research. By contrast, the American computer science student, graduating with a master's degree, has spent less than a hundred hours studying the subject.

Of course, maybe they *have* to work harder. The Soviet Union's best line of homegrown computers, the RYAD series, is almost a circuit-by-circuit copy of the IBM 360, a model outdated by twenty years, more than half the life of the industry.

Day of the turtle. Dan Bobrow sat in his living room in Belmont, Massachusetts, one evening in 1967 with several colleagues from Bolt, Beranek, and Newman who had been trying to develop a computer programming language for kids. With them was Seymour Papert, a mathematician from MIT who had studied child psychology with Jean Piaget. The problem was that there were no languages that were fun. After they broke up, Dan began writing a new language in LISP, the artificial-intelligence language. It used simple words such as PLAY and SENTENCE and, if you want to draw a circle, TO CIRCLE/REPEAT 360/RIGHT/FORWARD/END. Because it used words, it was called Logo, which means "word" in Greek.

What made Logo fun, and what made it want to draw circles? Something called the Terrapin Turtle. The first turtle was a mechanical device with a pen on its belly that drew pictures on paper. The real fun started when MIT developed a graphic picture of the turtle on the video screen. For three-year-olds, Logo and the turtle means an electronic Etch-A-Sketch; to an eight-year-old, it means drawing cars and spaceships. A seventeen-year-old boy with cerebral palsy was unable to write sentences or even hold a pencil; after two and a half years with Logo, he writes college freshman-level papers and majors in computer science. Logo is now offered on most home computers; indeed, it's Apple's third fastest-selling program.

The best thing about Logo is it puts the child in command of the computer, rather than the other way around—which means the kid teaches the computer what to do.

The first turtles, by the way, were built by Dr. W. Grey Walter, a British brain physiologist, in 1948. The toylike tortoises could roll across the floor on their own, moving seemingly of their own volition. They were attracted to light, unless it was too bright, and could travel around corners and out doorways in search of it. The turtles were smart enough to return to their battery charger when they got low on juice.

Job recruiting, Texas style. Texas A&M University, in an attempt to become, in the words of the dean of faculty, Dr. Clinton Phillips, a "world university," offered Dr. Sheldon Glashow, a computer scientist and Nobel Laureate from Harvard, a quarter-million-dollar package deal to join the A&M faculty. Most university profs in Texas take home about a tenth that sum. "We are actively seeking the best and brightest," says Phillips. "There is a chance there to build a large and effective research group," says Glashow, "but there is no indication I'm coming."

He's the dean of computer science education arts and letters. Donald D. Spencer, with a Ph.D. in computer science, has written over ninety books for over a dozen publishers. His books range from coloring books for tots to college texts. We used Spencer's *Illustrated Computer Dictionary* as a reference while writing *TNC*.

Nothin' to it. Steve Grimm and Nikolai Weaver take the honors as youngest computer company founders—as of this writing, at least. They started Plum Software of Los Gatos, California, in 1981, when they were eleven years old. Nick learned Fortran, Pascal, LISP, and Basic on a Tymshare terminal. "Most of it was pretty simple," he says, but "I had a lot of trouble understanding arrays in Basic, because the manual didn't explain them." Steve got his first Apple when he was seven and a half years old, and he wrote Plum's first software, a business program called Filewriter. Both boys say they like to play games on the computer when they're not busy being up-and-coming entrepreneurs.

Drawing by Rich Tennant

Other businesskids of note:

- Jonathan Dubman and Kay Borzsony were fourteen and thirteen, respectively, when they started Aristotle Software to market their own computer games and software.

- Mike Cornelison and Scott Emigh, Del Mar, California, were thirteen when they cofounded Corn Software in 1982 to sell software and games that work on Apple and TI home computers. Corn employs thirty other local teenagers on a royalty basis to write programs. The two have actually toured TI facilities and been hosted by Fred Bucy, president of the company, for an hour-long meeting.

• Software Innovations, Inc., Great Neck, New York, distinguished itself after its founding in 1980 by coming up with a program called Alien Invaders. It was similar to Space Invaders and could run on a Radio Shack TRS-80. It also produced a modified version of Breakout for the TRS-80 and a screen-only Monopoly game. The oldest company executive at the time of founding was fifteen. Top management and 1980 ages: Evan Grossman, fifteen; Roy Niederhoffer, thirteen; Steve Sanders, fifteen; and Tim Binder, fifteen.

A life-size stuffed Great Auk to the designers of the educational program designed to teach kids the alphabet that began by asking the kids (in words on the screen) to log onto the computer by typing their names.

Profile: Jonathan Rotenberg. He's been called "a high-tech impresario" and at nineteen is president of the country's most successful independent computing group, the Boston Computer Society. The BCS held its first meeting in January 1977, when Jonathan was fourteen years old; Jonathan and a friend, a local radio announcer into computers, were present. Jonathan was elected president. (The other member dropped out shortly, shaved his head, and joined a religious commune.) On January 26, 1983, over three thousand people attended the BCS monthly meeting in New England Life Hall for the first public unveiling of Lisa, Apple's state-of-the-art business computer. (When he was fifteen, Rotenberg organized a computer show that had a thousand attendees and forty-eight exhibitors; when he was seventeen, he organized the first Applefest show in Boston, attended by ten thousand people.)

Today, Jonathan is a senior studying economics at Brown University in Providence, Rhode Island, and is what some pundits call in "the second generation of computer whiz kids." He doesn't fit the "computer nerd" or "techie" stereotype that characterized the first wave of adolescent programmers and computer hobbyists. As a matter of fact, he doesn't take any computer courses.

David Needle, managing editor of *InfoWorld* magazine, observes: "The first thing one notices about Rotenberg is his unassuming manner and sense of humor. Onstage before a crowded auditorium of people at the group's monthly general meeting, Rotenberg gave an imitation of a typical Osborne-1 portable-computer user. Rotenberg bent over as if his right arm were straining under a heavy weight, while squinting his eyes trying to read the fine print on the tiny screen. The audience roared its approval.

"What really distinguishes Rotenberg from the average hobbyist, though, is his entrepreneurial orientation. He has been a consultant ($1,500 a day) and has organized some of the major computer shows in the industry's brief history, impressing Apple president Steve Jobs enough that Jobs suggested he leave school and join his company.

"And, of course, his main venture, the Boston Computer Society, which has over fifteen different 'user groups' (people who own Apples, Ataris, Osbornes, IBMs, and the like), a slick bimonthly magazine, *Computer Update* (which scooped the IXO Telecomputer from *Business Week* and *Byte*), and an impressive board of directors, all working on a volunteer basis, that includes executives from the business and computer communities.

"Rotenberg says the Society's main mission is to eliminate 'the aura of elitism' that surrounds much of the industry and to try to become one of the few objective sources of information on computers. He hopes to make the BCS a nationwide organization with chapters from coast to coast. Also in the works, if the BCS can find the funding and right location, is something tentatively called 'The Center for Computer Discovery.' A massive public facility with both permanent and temporary exhibitions, it will offer mainly hands-on, interactive computer experiences; a resource center filled with different personal computers, software, and a library of resource materials; and an auditorium that will serve as a permanent meeting meeting hall for various user groups.

"Once that's in place, Jonathan wants to start a consumer testing facility to provide 'independent, exhaustive evaluations of personal computer products and software.' He could well become the industry's Ralph Nader. Mitch Kapor, president of Lotus Development, a software firm, thinks Jonathan could do just about anything he wants, including inventing a new industry. For Jonathan's part, he says, 'I just hope I don't have a midlife crisis before I graduate from college.'"

Plato lives. Aristotle's protégé, Plato, was responsible for teaching his mentor's philosophy to the people of Athens in the fourth century B.C. The twentieth-century incarnation is Control Data Corporation's Plato, a computer-aided instruction (CAI) system.

There are actually two Platos. One is a network of over a thousand terminals at nearly two hundred locations, connected to a huge, powerful supercomputer at the University of Illinois. These terminals have very sophisticated plasma displays that allow the student to interact with the computer program through touch-sensitive panels on the screen. The disk drives have stored over eight thousand hours of courses on a wide variety of topics, at levels from kindergarten through graduate school.

The new Plato is not a system, but software—programs on floppy disks that run on several popular personal computers. Since it's much cheaper for schools to buy an Apple or an Atari rather than the expensive but more sophisticated terminals, Plato has, to coin a phrase, adapted itself to the language of the land. Alas, no touch-sensitive video screens here; the kids have to type in their answers on the keyboard.

Why did CDC choose the name Plato for its CAI system? It stands for Programmed Logic for Automatic Teaching Operations. Gag me with an acronym!

One-upmanship in the classroom. John Downer and Wayne Walker, first-year law students at Harvard in 1982, may have been the first to psych out their student peers in this manner: They showed up for their exams with computers to write their test papers. Downer used the portable Osborne-1, while Walker lugged an Apple II in. A few students were perturbed by their high-tech classmates. Did using the computer to perform word processing help? "Not much," said Walker. "If my writing continues to improve, I'll go to a typewriter."

Are you computer literate? Educators have used the term "literacy" for some time to define the dimensions of knowledge, but sometimes it comes off as an affront: What's the difference between being stupid and lacking information on a topic?

The Scholastic Aptitude Tests (SATs)* are composed of questions that grow more difficult as you proceed. It's a reductive process. Now, Computerized Adaptive Testing (CAT) promises a more humane approach: First you answer a few questions to determine the appropriate level of difficulty, then you are tested within that range. Educators are wary; many feel everyone should be exposed—or subjected—to the same questions, a democratic free-for-all. Who's going to try it first? The Navy Personnel Research and Development Center.

A computer in every pot—er, dorm room. This fall (1983), a number of colleges began requiring incoming freshmen to purchase a personal computer along with their textbooks and hand-held calculators. It's a movement that took less than a year to seize the imagination of college administrators. Clarkson College in Potsdam, New York, was the first, with students stuffing a Zenith personal computer in their backpacks; the cost is defrayed over four years, and when they graduate, the kids own the machine. Clarkson developed its own word processing package, called Galahad, produced by a campus group called Golden Knights Software. Any guesses what they call the football team?

---

* Speaking of SATs, Krell Software, Stony Brook, New York, says that anyone who can't add seventy points to his combined SAT scores after using Krell's SAT preparation software to study will get his or her money back.

Others:

- Drexel University is following Clarkson's lead with purchase of a personal computer required of all frosh.

- Stevens Institute requires every freshman studying science, systems, or management to spring for an Atari.

- Rochester Institute of Technology has contracted for five thousand Digital Equipment Corp. personal computers, but students can buy them jointly, as they wish. RIT plans to develop an extensive on-campus computer network around the DEC microcomputers.

- Carnegie-Mellon University chose IBM over Digital, with whom it had extensive joint research contracts, to develop the largest computer network in the world—or so they say. Carnegie-Mellon's fifty-five hundred students will be able to tap into extensive research libraries, take tests remotely from computers, send voice messages, and automate most of their reports and other class assignments on the computers. All by 1985.

- Boston University plans to link Digital personal computers with new Digital mainframes over the next few years for use mostly by science students.

- Northeastern University has opened a College of Computer Science, a degree-granting program six hundred students enrolled in last fall. Dean Paul Kalaghan sees the usefulness of personal computers but is concerned over the capital outlay.

What's oddball about all this mandatory buying of computers? The industry is *still* lamenting that the educational institutes are not teaching students the right stuff in their computer science courses. It's like requiring everyone to drive to a class in buggy-making.

Some liabilities of mass computerization:

- At Harvard, students have been known to send "letter bombs" over electronic mail—threats to destroy one another's programs.

- At Dartmouth, where the high school is tied in to the college's computers, students have set up blind dates from their computer terminals and found themselves going out with fourteen-year-olds from the local high school.

- Academics have begun to worry about reuse of previous material. It's much easier to alter someone else's work to make it look like your own if it's on a floppy diskette.

Getting serious. The Saddleback Valley Unified School District in Orange County, California, will require its more than six thousand students to be computer literate beginning in 1986. Juniors and seniors will have to take the semester-long course as a requirement for graduation; it's available now as an elective. The problem is, by 1986 the kids will probably all have their own computers at home, rendering a good idea just another boring class the poor kids have to yawn through.

And then there's the one about the grade school principal who was having an affair with a teacher's aide in the computer room. Apparently it was noticed because teachers and students would frequently find the computer room door locked. There was the usual brouhaha and Mike Royko wrote about it in his column for the *Chicago Sun-Times*. What we liked was that a clipping service in Jackson, Mississippi, sent it to us with a note attached that read, "A STORY ABOUT THE DANGER OF COMPUTERS."

GREAT MOMENTS IN COMPUTER EDUCATION

- 1948: Norbert Wiener's book *Cybernetics* is published by John Wiley & Sons in collaboration with MIT. Wiener defined the term "cybernetics" as "the science of control and communication in the animal and the machine." He also defined the term "feedback" as how animals and machines could examine the consequences of their actions and thus adjust their behavior, improve themselves, in light of that feedback.

- 1949: Edmund C. Berkey publishes *Giant Brains: or Machines That Think*, a work well ahead of its time. Thirty years later Berkey is publishing a newsletter out of a second-floor office in Newton, Massachusetts, without using a single computer in the operation.

- 1958: Karl Karlstrom, dean of computer science book publishing at Prentice-Hall, was a young editor on a business trip. Calling at the University of Buffalo, he met a prof who was writing a manuscript on something called "data processing." Karlstrom reported this to the business books editor at P-H, who wrote him back: "I have traveled the length and breadth of this country, and have talked to the best people in business administration. I can assure you on the highest authority that data processing is a fad and won't last out the year."

- 1961: Daniel D. McCracken's book *Fortran* is published by John Wiley. McCracken has written subsequent works on Fortran that in total have sold over a million copies.

- October 1, 1962: First Ph.D. Department of Computer Science established at Purdue University.

- December 5, 1965: Richard L. Wexelblat awarded first Ph.D. in computer science, at the University of Pennsylvania.

- 1967: Wiley publishes *Basic Programming*, authored by the two Dartmouth profs who invented it, John Kemeny and Thomas Kurtz. Author Gantz, having graduated the year before, was busy purging all thoughts of mathematics from his mind at the time, having taken courses from both Kemeny and Kurtz, and the plot of whose math grades over the previous four years conformed to the mathematical expression $(5-(x+1))/x=y$, where x represented time at Dartmouth measured in years, and y represented grade point measured on a 5.0 scale.

- September 1980: Wang Labs, unable to recruit the caliber of people it needs to develop its technology, opens its own Wang Institute of Software Engineering in Lowell, Massachusetts.

Learning together. Edupro of Palo Alto, California, has introduced hands-on educational games for up to four players, to overcome criticism that computers are antisocial. Players can either compete or cooperate when they play games such as Word-Hunt or Math-Race.

Learning together, encore. San Diego State University has established the Ed Tech People's Message System, the first electronic bulletin board for teachers and trainers to learn the latest in computer education. We gave them a call to see what was happening in education, and we noted in the instructions that we were asked to help keep the system operating "effeciently" (sic).

Learning together, the hard way. Lewis DePayne and three accomplices broke into Pacific Telephone offices in an attempt to steal materials that would help them break into U.S. Leasing Company's computer system. DePayne was found guilty and put on three years' probation; the others turned state's evidence. All are part of a larger group of Los Angeles system hackers who grew out of the "phone phreak" movement.

Remember those computer dating services? In the United States they became a fad in the 1960s; now they're a way of life. But they've always been viewed as somehow suspect.

Not so in Estonia, U.S.S.R. As early as 1970, the Soviet state instituted computerized dating to help agricultural workers meet one another. A "Bureau of Acquaintance" was set up and staffed with psychologists and lawyers. For newlyweds, it also offered the services of a "medical sexologist."

FROM THE CACHE:
Out of the Mouths of Babes

Today's kids are a generation of prodigies, as comfortable swapping game programs over electronic data networks as we were swapping comics in the school yard. But the knowledge of computers is a relatively recent addition to the preadolescent bag of tricks. Just ask Melissa Boey, a teacher of fifth- and sixth-graders in New York City who collected their random thoughts on computers from 1965 to 1975 and which were published in *Computerworld* on June 25, 1975. From the kids:

- If you like to fool around with figures alot become a design engineer. My Uncle Henry is one, and he fools around alot with figures.

- A computer operator puts information into a computer in two ways— by punched cards and by tapes. In the end it comes out like six of one and one for all.

- The programmer can't even make one teeney-weeney mistake, when he feeds the computer. If he does, it can spell a sure Miss Fortune.

- If it wasn't for the ticnickle artist and the ticnickle writer who tell you and show you how to work it, you would really be in a pickle.

- What a "bit" is has a very short memory on my end.

- Remembering eggacly what "binary" means is something that is going to be foreever on my mind.

- When I was reading the library book on computers I knew real good what they do, but since I closed the book, so did my brain.

- Once I saw a machine that looked like a computer. It looked just like a computer should look. And if it could have looked like anything besides a computer, your gas is as good as mine.

- Take a good long look at a computer. Does it have input, output, a bit of binary? No? Then you are not taking a look at a computer.

- I have a bet with my girlfriend Nancy, who shall be nameless that more men do computering than girls. She thinks I'm against girls libbies. Straighten her out for me. I'm not a shove pig, and I hope you not neither! Thanks in advance for proving me. Bye, Harry.

- Could you please send me a real live picture of the big computer called Sage, so I can show the class for my report? If you don't send it by friday, I won't be made. Sinsoily, Gail.

- I want to be in the computer line when I get out of school. How important is math while I'm in the sixth grade? If you say very important, then throw this letter away. I'm not coming to your computer place. OK? Robert.

• From what I can see and think, the computer guys are very excited and thrilled when the computers come up with the right answers. They feel life is a bowl of cherris [sic] then. But just as soon as the are wrong, boy, life is a bowl of worms.

• In the early days of inventing, when they asked how to invent a computer, what do you imagine the person said when they asked him? Yup! He rolled his deep eyes around his brain, twitched up his nose in thought and with a deep throat of gladness he yelled, "ok."

• Where are computers located? On pages 34 through 40.

• From now on, after learning all about computers, I'm going to think wonderful happy-that-you-made-it-so thoughts with a smile in my heart.

And so, we hope, gentle reader, will you, with a deep throat of gladness yelling "ok" when your kid wants to borrow the family computer, which you keep on pages 34 through 40, or wheedles for another pack of floppies. Don't be a shove pig. Let him or her have it. Ask yourself, does it have input, output, a bit of binary? And will this kid of yours, who has become so strange, turtling and microsoft Basic-ing, write the video game hit that will let you quit the rat race and work for the new company that just started in your basement? Sinsoily.

CHAPTER 7

BEATING THE SYSTEM:

Computer Crimes and Capers

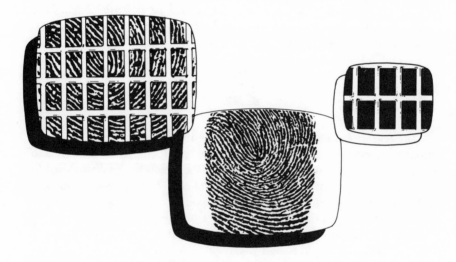

It's a matter of good old "ROI," return on investment. The average armed robbery of a bank nets $15,000; the average embezzlement, $25,000. The average computer-related crime hauls in $500,000.

Unsuccessful perpetrators of gun-and-mask crimes may find themselves putting in up to ten years in the slammer. Their white-collar, computer-savvy counterparts become consultants. Or don't get caught in the first place. Only one out of forty FBI agents has formal training in computer crime, and fewer local gendarmes know the proper stance for frisking a computer.

For lack of devices, only two million Americans were in a position to be tempted by computer crime in 1975; by 1985 over fifty million will have access to computers through some type of keyboard. The U.S. Department of Justice estimates that there are four hundred million automated teller-machine transactions a month in the United

States and that the volume of computerized telephone bill-paying will soon pass $50 million a month.

The opportunities for devil's play increase as the computer wends its way into our daily lives; ironically, it's almost impossible to detect computer theft except through the use of computers—or the frailties of the crime's perpetrators.

And whether it's Stanley Goldblum, the mastermind behind the $2 billion Equity Funding fraud, or the four Manhattan thirteen-year-olds whose electronic joyride through the data banks of a Canadian cement company eradicated ten million bits of data, there's always a thrill in beating the system.

As English salary clerk Henry King said in defense of his 1971 theft of $720 from his company, the computer was a "horrible, impersonal machine." And that was why hedonit.

The biggest known computer crime. The 1973 Equity Funding scandal, also the biggest known white-collar crime, in which computers were used to create fictitious insurance policyholder records, which the company used to bilk funds from companies that reinsure policies. Each year the company had to manufacture many more fictitious policies in order to generate the cash needed to pay premiums on the ones sold in years previous.

The scheme, in which sixty-four thousand out of ninety-seven thousand policyholders were found to be nonexistent, fell apart when disgruntled former employees began leaking information to Wall Street analysts and the New York police.

The lawsuits that exploded out of Equity Funding's collapse are still reverberating through the courts. Of Equity Funding's $3.2 billion in assets, $2.1 billion were fraudulently obtained.

The caper was big enough to include a fraud within a fraud: $140,000 was siphoned to conspirators unknown to the managers masterminding the bigger theft.

The second biggest known computer crime. The OPM Leasing scandal. In this case, the fraud revolved around nonexistent computers rather than computers that performed phony transactions. Beginning in the late 1970s, Myron S. Goodman and Mordecai Weissman, both about thirty at the time, began using fake or altered computer leases, most of them supposedly held by Rockwell Corp., as loans from a variety of banks and other lenders to buy more fake computers. This particular case set the legal community on its ear because of the ethical dilemma of the firm's lawyer, Joseph L.

Hutner, who, on the advice of a law professor who specialized in ethics, didn't turn in OPM when he learned of past frauds. When the frauds continued, Hutner's firm quit OPM but didn't inform the new firm of the scam. Looking back once the case unraveled, it seems ludicrous that the lawyers were so duped by OPM as to be unwitting partners to bogus deals that went down after they suspected fraud.

Goodman, who, during his reign over OPM, had pleaded guilty to a check-kiting scheme in Louisiana and paid a fine of $110,000, was sentenced in 1983 to up to twelve years in jail; Weissman was sentenced to up to ten years. Both claimed the ill-gotten gains had been given to charities in the United States and Israel. Meanwhile, investors were out $200 million (although they got some of it back during OPM's liquidation). Also out were legitimate customers of OPM, who had agreed to lease computers because of favorable clauses in policies written in the contracts. With no business to turn the computers into now, customers could be out anywhere from $100 million to $250 million.

The longest-running computer crime. Double-entry inventory control at Saxon Industries. A Fortune 500 company that reported profits of $7.1 million and $5.3 million in 1979 and 1980, respectively, it went bankrupt in 1982. A bogus inventory record was maintained by computer—and matched against the real inventory by computer—by Saxon's Business Products Division. It was used to inflate the company's annual revenues. The double books were kept for thirteen years, and the crime might never have been revealed if the company had been profitable. Saxon was $53 million in the hole when it went under.

How much money is lost to computer crime? Nobody knows. Various experts have estimated as little as $100 million and as much as $5 billion a year. One sample of 374 cases reported in the early 1970s, compiled by computer crime guru Donn B. Parker of SRI International, formerly Stanford Research Institute, yielded an arithmetic average of $450,000 per incident. It also indicated there were 5 cases reported for every 10,000 computers in use. How much goes unreported? Nobody knows. Certain limited studies have indicated that 85 percent of violent crime goes unreported; but no similar studies for white-collar crime exist. "There are no valid statistics," notes Parker, "since there's obviously no way to tell how much crime goes undetected."

But consider this:

If 85 percent of computer crimes go unreported, and

If each were to result in a $500,000 loss, and

If 5 occurred for every 10,000 computers,

Then annual worldwide losses for 1983 would be $23 billion.

Since most of the computers in use in 1983 were small, such as those made by Radio Shack and Apple, this seems a little high. It's unlikely they could do this much damage.

Of course, nobody knows.

How many computer criminals? One estimate, by Leonard Krauss, vice-president of Data Systems Development Review at Chase Manhattan, is that one out of ten people will be working with computers by middecade and that one out of ten of those will at some time try their hand at cybernetic tomfoolery.

How many burgers? McDonald's cried "Foul!" when twenty-six Cal Tech students followed the rules of a five-county restaurant contest to a "T" but used a computer to help. Programming the school's IBM 370/158 computer to print out entry forms, the pranksters manufactured 1.2 million entries, a third of the total submitted. They won most of $40,000 worth of prizes—but later gave them back. They had, after all, an unfair advantage in free access to Cal Tech's mighty computers.

(Burger King was so impressed by the students' initiative that it gave $3,000 to Cal Tech to use as a scholarship in the name of the students' ringleader.)

Most fitting punishment. When twenty-one-year-old Jerry Neal Schneider was found guilty in 1972 of stealing what may have been over $1 million worth of equipment (only $214,649 worth was proved) from Pacific Tel and Tel through the use of rigged computer instructions, he was given a sentence that resulted in forty days in jail and a settlement of $8,500 ($141.50 a month for five years to Pacific Tel and Tel). Schneider, who had set up a bogus company to funnel the stolen goods, went on to become a consultant in thwarting computer crime.

Schneider obtained the data he needed to beat the system from the company's trash bins, which he walked by on his way to school.

Terms you should know. A *trapdoor* is a set of computer instructions that allows one to bypass the computer's internal-security system. A *Trojan horse* is like a trapdoor, only it lets others in as well as the originator of the trapdoor. *Magic code* is either one of the above that erases all evidence of itself once the foul deed is done. If you know more than this, you're up to no good.

What, me worry? Computer crimestopper Lindsay Baird reports that in only one of thirty recent cases of computer crime he investigated did the clients prosecute. The others buried the losses in "operating expenses."

And one computer vendor reported to the FBI that only 12 percent of the one thousand computer crimes in its files were reported to authorities and that only 18 percent of these led to convictions—that is, 98 percent of the perpetrators walked.

Open Sesame. Biggest password leak: the electronic filching of the password directory of National CSS, a subsidiary of Dun & Bradstreet that provides computer time-sharing. Extent of damage: unknown.

The abuse of disbelief. Poor old UNIVAC I. With a great deal of hoopla, Walter Cronkite announced to the television audience that "an electronic brain" would make its appearance on election-night, November 4, 1952, to predict the new President of the United States. Programmers had labored for months, entering data to help UNIVAC make an intelligent prognostication. Charles Collingwood told the viewers, "A few minutes ago, I asked him [UNIVAC] what his prediction was, and . . . he's not ready yet with the predictions." In fact, UNIVAC had already analyzed the results, with only three million votes counted: a landslide victory, 43 states and 438 electoral votes for Dwight D. Eisenhower. UNIVAC ascertained that Adlai E. Stevenson would only take 5 states. Yet political analysts and pollsters had predicted a very close race; the "electronic brain" must be wrong! Arthur F. Draper, Remington Rand's director in charge of the election-night show, had the program altered not once but twice, in an attempt to bring the computer's predictions more in line with expected results. At midnight, with the Eisenhower landslide going full tilt, Collingwood asked Draper to explain. Said he: "We asked UNIVAC to forget a lot of trend information, assuming that it was wrong . . . but it is now evident we should have had nerve enough to believe the machine in the first place." Draper later said that election night was "one of the worst evenings I ever spent in my life." Eisenhower won, 442 electoral votes to Stevenson's 89.

You can't keep a good man down. Col. David Henry Winthrop, né Norman Henry Hunt, founded a company called DataSync in 1976, offering a computer kit for $298, an awfully tempting price. Turns out the thing never ran, and the terminal was an empty shell. Nor was this Hunt's first swindle. He was brought to trial and given three years in the slammer at Cal State Prison, Chino. Hunt, ever the salesman, convinced prison officials he was a safe bet in minimum security; they fell for it, and Hunt walked out one day. He resettled in Tucson and started World Power Systems, placing big ads for computer equipment in all the major microcomputer magazines. Not only did he bilk customers out of untold thousands, he also beat the mags out of $30,000 in advertising space and suppliers out of over $100,000 in computer gear. He was recaptured and went back to the slammer in California, but in an attempt to lessen his sentence, turned informer, incurring the wrath of fellow inmates. When officials found out there was a contract out on Hunt, they transferred him to the Nevada Correctional Facility in Carson City. There Hunt entered into a deal with a local business-man, Don Fish, to form an enterprise in 1980 named High Sierra Software, offering 102 "serious programs" for the incredibly low sum of $109.95. Hunt had an accomplice, a woman named Diana he claimed was his wife, who kept the books; orders were pouring in, but when Fish started to wonder where the profits were, Diana disappeared.

What's a friendly wager among friends? Three clerk-typists were arrested at Ford Motor Company in Dearborn this year for running an office football pool on the word processor. The football pool, which did $5,000 a week, was part of a larger gambling operation that ran on larger computers and cleared $25,000 a week. It's a classic distributed data processing application.

The federal government's National Bureau of Standards (NBS) worked with some people at IBM, most notably Carl H. Meyer, to design Data Encryption Standards in 1977. DES is intended to protect information and electronic funds while they are going from one place to another. Basically, encryption is like radio scrambling; you garble information at the sending end, and only the proper receiver knows the key to ungarble it. In fact, governmental standards are so low that most hackers can easily unscramble the data. But an inexpensive microcomputer software package called The Protector, from Standard Software in Avon, Massachusetts, provides more protection than the DES. Even if you aren't sending electronic messages, you can still encrypt your data. At the stroke of a key you can turn your Dear Diary into a stream of gibberish no one will want to spend time deciphering.

But was there any heavy breathing? This one may not even be illegal. During a 1971 strike against Honeywell, union members managed to sabotage the computer network of Metropolitan Life. By telephoning a tape recording of the signals used by a central computer to poll remote data stations, they were able to prevent data being printed out at twenty-five local offices. Information flow was blocked for a month. Although the perpetrators were caught by police, the penalty for such an information crime is not particularly robust. The only law against such an event was for "aggravated harassment," the usual statute for prosecuting makers of obscene phone calls.

On May 28, 1982, Albert Franz Kessler was arrested at Los Angeles International Airport with $200,000 worth of stolen advanced electronic defense gear, probably bound for the Soviet Union. As August Bequai, a Washington attorney and security expert, says, "Little companies steal from big companies. Big companies steal from little companies. Everybody steals from everybody." One of your faithful, fun-loving authors was at a party in

Cambridge, Massachusetts, where he met a fellow partygoer who was talking about his world travels. When asked his occupation, the man said he was a courier who rushed packages from place to place, on a moment's notice, for large sums of money. He said that often he wasn't told the contents of the parcel, and in some instances had a briefcase handcuffed to his wrist; the party on the other end would unlock it. He told of one rather furtive, hasty run he had made; your trusty author commented that it must have been a big cocaine deal, but the courier said he figured it was probably stolen computer chips, since Nixdorf Computer Corporation had reported a big theft just a few days earlier.

If you've ever had dreams of being James Bond, here's your chance. All you have to do is pick up the Secret Connection Briefcase. Inside there's a wireless telephone with a built-in scrambler, plus a voice-stress analyzer, so you can determine if the other party is lying; an ordinary-looking pen lights up if there's a surveillance bug planted in the area. Another device detects the presence of a bomb, and a box that looks like a package of cigarettes tells you if someone is tape-recording your conversation. The briefcase is tough; it'll withstand a shot from a .357 Magnum and is primed with its own alarm system. The Secret Connection Briefcase is made by CCS Communication Control, Inc., of New York City. The thing ought to be good; the firm's president, Ben Jamil, was indicted for wiretapping in 1966. The only problem with this $26,000 briefcase is that it's so full of electronic gear that there isn't much room for anything else.

It may just be paranoia, but government sources figure that about thirty of the fifty-two members of the Soviet consulate in San Francisco, just thirty miles from Silicon Valley, are espionage agents of the KGB.

Dave Roberts was no angel. A local boy from Watsonville, California, he'd gotten a job in the warehouse of a Silicon Valley electronics firm and worked his way up to sales rep. He did pretty well for five years, then started job-hopping. Nobody really gave it much thought, but then in 1978, Roberts was nabbed for stealing $100,000 worth of electronic components for a guy named Larry Lowery from Roberts's old employer. He got off on a technicality. The next time he wasn't so lucky. He got ten months at a rehab facility. The third time he got caught—again with Lowery—they both were arrested. The Santa Clara County Sheriff's Department had the goods on them this time: stolen parts, forged documents, the works. Just before Roberts was to go on trial, he was found in a shallow grave on Skyline Drive, murdered execution-style.

GREAT MOMENTS IN CODE-BREAKING

- The Enigma Code, which gave the Allies the information they needed to anticipate the German V-2 rocket launchings during World War II; broken when a German crypto machine was captured and British scientists were able to crack the codes using a new, highly secret device (a computer). The biggest problem for the British was in judicious use of the information: Too much apparent outguessing of German maneuvers would tip off the Germans that their code had been breached.

- The trapdoor knapsack: Adi Shamir, a thirty-year-old mathematician, in 1982 cracked the encryption code developed by Stanford University based on an algorithm called the "trapdoor knapsack." Says Shamir: "I was sitting alone staring at the wallboard on which some equations were written, and suddenly everything fell into place, all the pieces. I saw these missing links and I knew just what to do." Breaking a code this difficult could net a wily hacker a sizable chunk of the $400 billion that courses through the U.S. banking system every day. Shamir's take? He got $100, which the two universities had put up as a bet to anyone who could open the "trapdoor knapsack."

- The public key code: Adi Shamir's own crypto code was cracked by Leonard Adelman, also in 1982. At the Crypto 82 Conference held August 23–25, Adelman used an Apple computer and a program it took him a month to write to crack a crypto code of which Adi Shamir was co-author. It took the computer ten hours.

In fact, many of the crypto programs designed to protect data as they move from one computer to another have been cracked.

Remember the DES encryption standard we mentioned? The one worked on by IBM for the National Bureau of Standards that's supposed to be good for business data encryption? There's a rumor that the Department of Defense and the National Security Agency have embedded a trapdoor into the code so they can crack any DES transmissions they want. They wouldn't do that, would they?

Computer error? In September 1968, Defense Department efficiency expert Ernest Fitzgerald was given a raise and a promotion. In November he testified in Congress that the C5A cargo plane would cost $5 billion, not $3 billion. Within two weeks he was informed that his raise and promotion had been a mistake—a computer error. Within a year he was sent to analyze a bowling alley in Taiwan.

Most everyone is aware of the Unit Pricing Code, or UPC strip, which appears on almost everything we buy. And most everyone has seen the big, white plastic antitheft tags hanging from garments in clothing stores. Now, it seems, the technologies are joining forces to kill two birds with one stone. Two firms, Checkpoint Systems and Sensormatic, are working on stickers and labels that have paper-thin radio circuits glued to them. Most antitheft systems now in use work on magnetic principles: Once you've bought an item, it is passed over a demagnetizer. The problem with these more sophisticated radio circuits is how to deactivate them. Sensormatic has a royal approach: You konk the item with a magic wand, which blows the radio's fuse.

Things Are Tough All Over Department. A Yuba City, California, man, Richard Alexander, twenty-one, was arrested in the summer of 1982 for using a computer to steal parts from his employer, the Auto-Motion Parts Store. The take was $1,287.38. Caught, Alexander was fired, forced to pay the money back, dumped by his girlfriend, and kicked out of the house he was living in. He might have lived in jail, but his sentence was reduced to six days.

Biggest known "salami slice." According to Leonard I. Kraus, a computer consultant, in 1975 a computer programmer was apprehended with $385,000 in ill-gotten securities. He had sliced fractions off each employee's share in a company investment plan and diverted them to his own account.

Just say the word "computer." Thomas Chilcott, of Colorado, ran a commodities trading pool begun in 1977. Chilcott claimed his pool, which had as many as four hundred investors, traded in commodities futures and used a sophisticated computerized trading scheme that consistently produced profits over 45 percent. Chilcott claimed the fund never lost money. Although Chilcott claimed the fund had grown to $53 million in assets, when the FBI stepped in in 1982 it could find only $8 million. The fraud was unearthed when the FBI, checking on a possible land swindle in Florida, traced $1.5 million to an investment in Chilcott. Interest piqued, the FBI began looking into Chilcott's activities.

For his efforts, Chilcott was convicted of fraud in May 1982 and sentenced to twelve years in prison. The judge who sentenced him levied only $1.5 million in fines so there might be some leavings for hapless investors to pick over.

The smallest known computer crime. In 1981, on April Fool's Day, Lloyd Allen of Oakland, California, was nabbed for defrauding Bay Area Rapid Transit (BART) ticket machine number 511 of $0.50. By inserting a

$5.00 bill into the computerized machine, Allen was able to get both a ticket and his $5.00 bill back. When he was taken into custody, Allen ate the $5.00 bill.

Biggest known chip theft. It was $3.4 million worth of advanced memory circuits from Monolithic Memories, Inc., from a room that was supposedly theftproof. Charged in the heist were Ron Washington, thirty, and Abel Urbina, twenty-five, both of Silicon Valley. At the time of the theft, Washington was a guard for a security firm working for Monolithic. A $50,000 reward posted by Monolithic was instrumental in tracing the theft, at one time thought to be part of a black-market ring smuggling chips to the Soviet Union, to the culprits. A later, separate investigation of a $100,000 chip theft masterminded by one Larry Kizer, allegedly a Mafia kingpin, discovered a public storage locker containing $4 million worth of purloined electronics, including memory chips from Monolithic and National Semiconductor, and some IBM and Apple personal computers. A known associate of Kizer was Larry Lowery, whom the reader will remember from the tale of the sad demise of Dave Roberts, chip thief. It is suspected now that Kizer was behind the Monolithic burglary.

The Dalton gang rides again. On April 11, 1980, a man named Kenneth Scott, a consultant working for PepsiCo, discovered that someone was using his telephone number on the Telenet data network to attempt access to computer networks in Canada. He alerted Telenet, and the company was able to trace the call to Manhattan, but no farther—the intruder was bounced out of the system for not having the right password before the trace could get farther.

Scott monitored the rogue calls made on his number for the next several days, then Telenet called on New York Telephone for help. About then Canada Cement LaFarge reported to the Royal Canadian Mounted Police that someone had discovered a valid password and accessed its data banks without permission. In fact, it soon became clear that someone or someones were taking an electronic joyride through the computers of Canada using Scott's telephone codes. Computers hit included those at the University of Waterloo, The University of Concordia, Bell Canada, Honeywell, PepsiCo, Canada Cement LaFarge, and thirteen other corporations.

Over the next several weeks the RCMP and the FBI were able to trace the calls to a particular Manhattan telephone and build a case—but not before Canada Cement LaFarge had had 20 percent of its data files wiped out.

On April 25, the manhunt ended. The Manhattan phone turned out to belong to one of the city's more exclusive private schools—the Dalton School, tuition $4,400 a year—and, bearded in their lair, four thirteen-year-olds confessed to the crime.

A decision was made later not to prosecute—although apprehending the kids and restoring the data cost over $250,000.

Perhaps it was the nature of their quest: They were just trying to order a few cases of Pepsi and have them delivered to the school without being charged.

Once a bunko artist, always a bunko artist. Larry Glassner, on probation for mail fraud since 1977, was an early user of a Radio Shack TRS-80. With it he compiled a list of two million names to which to send false invoices in hopes of payment. He had worked his way through hundreds of government agencies, schools, and orphanages when an eagle-eyed attorney in Texas queried a bill for $750. Glassner refunded the money paid, but not before triggering enough official interest to lead to discovery that his computerized billing scheme had netted him $2 million between 1977 and 1979. Glassner had a sad ending. On July 30, 1979, just before sentencing, he put a .38-caliber revolver to his head and died in the third-floor men's room in the State Supreme Court Building in Hauppauge, New York.

U.S. Leasing may have been the victim of one of the more bizarre computer crimes. Around Christmas 1980, a seventeen-year-old student from Los Angeles, after scanning telephone numbers to find those where computers answered instead of people, managed to pry access codes out of a data center computer operator by feigning that he was a maintenance rep. He was then able to crack into the system at will and for the next several days managed to bring the company practically to its knees by inserting filthy language into the computer's inventory files. Whenever anyone from anywhere in the country accessed the inventory—as salesmen did all the time—foul language would come out instead of part numbers.

During a day and a half the company estimates it lost $60,000. It took another $200,000 to track the culprit down.

The computerized briar patch. On January 16, 1982, Massachusetts State Police found themselves conducting a bizarre two-hundred-trooper raid on the Massachusetts Correctional Institute, a prison. In tracking a drug, gaming, and vehicle theft ring in Boston they had come upon a telephone used at the prison by Con'Puter Systems Programming, a computer service bureau run by inmates with long prison sentences.

Subsequent investigation discovered that income-tax fraud was involved, too. In one three-year period in the late seventies, Con'Puter racked up $160,000 in profits. By the time of the raid, the partners were earning—and not declaring—an average of $24,000 a year.

The inmates began their training under a rehabilitation program started by Honeywell in 1967 to teach data processing techniques. (Con'Puter used computers donated by DEC and Honeywell.) Over the life of the program, recidivism of those who had taken the courses was 3 percent, rather than the nationwide average of 70 percent. But as the program aged and inmates were shifted to institutions of lesser security, the watchful eyes of prison officials drooped. By the time of the January raid, Con'puter had scores of government agencies, schools, and hospitals as clients, including its landlord, the Massachusetts Department of Corrections, for which they did payroll processing. Honeywell decided to find less controversial programs for their computers and withdrew in 1983.

You be the judge. Was he guilty of a crime? Theodore Weg, a programmer for the New York City Board of Education who had legitimate access to the school system's IBM 370/158 computer, used it to keep racehorse genealogy records, print mailing labels for a charity, and update his résumé. Was this a crime? The city thought so, and Weg was arrested in 1982.

Not so fast, said Judge Michael R. Jubiler, who granted a request for dismissal to Weg, upholding his contention that he really hadn't stolen anything. The Board of Education's computer wasn't "for hire," so Weg had deprived the city of no revenue. Weg has even indicated that he plans to sue the city for false arrest, illegal imprisonment, damage to reputation, impaired health, and legal costs. His boss, he says, knew about the racehorse files, which he used to test software, and thought they were "cute."

Most well-traveled Dungeons and Dragons player. Han Shan S. Scott Henderson, an eighteen-year-old student at San Jose State College, who racked up over 45,000 minutes of unauthorized computer time and made over $7,000 worth of unpaid-for telephone calls playing Dungeons and Dragons, Star Trek, and other computer games with students at schools all over California and Nevada and as far away as Missouri, Massachusetts, Sweden, and Taiwan. He was arrested in May 1981 while playing Canyon Bomber.

Sometimes the good guys win. In 1977, Christopher Cossette, thirty-six, of Memphis, Tennessee, was mistakenly issued $110,000 in checks by the government as a result of a computer error. While trying to find somebody who would do something about his "misfortune," Cossette was able to collect enough interest to buy a sports car and a pool.

Closest call. On January 18, 1980, the radar signature of a Soviet Aeroflot jet carrying Ambassador Anatoly Dobrynin was erased from the computerized air traffic control system at New York's Kennedy International Airport by an air traffic controller suspected to be reacting to the taking of American hostages by Iran. The jet flew six miles in crowded skies at the wrong altitude—and was probably lucky not to be hit. No one was arrested; one air traffic controller was dismissed.

Is nothing sacred? It took nineteen months for the IRS and the FBI to track down Jerry Dale Thompson, who embezzled $210,000 from his employer, IBM, by depositing checks from customers in his own accounts and then using IBM computers to alter IBM's home office books to cover the fraud.

The first warrant ever issued to search the storage of a computer was issued on February 19, 1971, by Judge Lloyd C. Doll of San Jose to examine the output and storage of University Computing Corporation's Univac 1108. It was part of an investigation of trade secrets theft from a company called Information Systems Design. (The search was successful; the perpetrator pleaded guilty the next year.)

Take the subway to work? Don't lay your floppy disk on the floor. On some subway trains there is a spot on the floor on which magnetic fields from the power system are strong enough to erase data stored magnetically on computer tapes and disks.

Bunion banging for fun and profit. One of the first innovative users of a personal computer—in this case *very* personal—was Keith Taft, an electronics expert with a penchant for playing blackjack. In the early 1970s Taft designed and built a computer more advanced than most of the day that was battery powered and small enough to be strapped to his body. He programmed it to calculate odds while he played blackjack in Nevada casinos. To input cards that had been dealt, Taft rigged switches, activated by tapping his big toes, that were connected by wires to the computer strapped to his midsection—eight hours of play would take ten thousand toe movements. For readout, he installed tiny lights on the inside of the frames of his eyeglasses.

The system worked, and Taft was able to recoup some of the $50,000 and over two thousand hours he spent on his customized computer. But by the end of 1973, Taft realized that hanging around gambling casinos every weekend always under the threat of being thrown out if he won too much wasn't really much fun. He retired from his gambling career and began to devote time to studying robotics.

The Ten Largest U.S. Computer Crimes

Name	Date	Amount ($M)	1983 Dollars	Comments
Equity Funding	1973	$2,100	$4,851	Computer used to create fictitious policies. Nothing exotic about the computer usage, except manual methods wouldn't have worked for fraud of such magnitude. Pyramid scheme of bilking new investors to pay off old ones. Computer operations people pretty much exonerated.
OPM Leasing	1980	$310	$388	Same computers used as collateral for several loans, fictitious and doctored leases used as collateral. Straightforward bilking, computer involvement relatively little except in provision of returnability in case of technological obsolescence. With OPM gone, computer lessee could lose between $100 million and $250 million on trade-in. Investors defrauded of $210 million.
Boxcars	1971	$110	$280	Two hundred fifty-two Penn Central boxcars worth $11 million were found. DP system used to divert. Total loss of all railroad's boxcars at time estimated by authorities at 2,800 vehicles. Cost estimate is *TNC* estimate. Computerized system must be well understood to effect diversion.

Korean Army	1974	$85	$177	Wholesale defrauding of U.S. military supply system in Korea, estimated in 1977 Congressional testimony to be at least $17 million a year since early 1970s. Use of data processing system to divert materials.
Cenco	1974	$40	$81	Computerized inventory to inflate value of stock.
Chilcott	1977	$45	$77	See text. Bogus computer reports to get investments, inflate assets.
Greenman	1981	$50	$57	See text. Use of computer to razzle-dazzle investors in mutual fund to think Greenman had secret formula for picking stocks. Pyramid scheme.
Saxon	1982	$53	$57	Thirteen-year scam of double inventory, kept to inflate revenues. Fortune 500 company goes bankrupt abruptly.
J. Walter Thompson	1981	$31	$35	Ad bookings fabricated and inserted into computerized financial reporting system.
Wells Fargo	1981	$21	$24	Knowledge of the computer system allowed for routine embezzlement to be hidden. Most famous because main beneficiary of the embezzlement was a sports promoter licensing Muhammad Ali's name. Ali not implicated. A stupid crime.

Note: Times are approximate or average time of actual perpetration, not date of capture.

CHAPTER 8

THE STEEL-COLLAR WORK FORCE:

March of the Robots

Karel Čapek first used the Czech word "robot" to describe a mechanical worker in his 1921 play R.U.R., *and since then metal people have been portrayed as everything from a menace to mankind, as in Fritz Lang's 1926 silent film* Metropolis, *to the comical sidekicks in* Star Wars.

And that may be their most glamorous occupation—screen-star and trade-show freak—for robots won't be the household helpers once envisioned for at least another twenty years.

Instead, they're heavy industry's indentured servants. From the 1950s development of robots by George C. Devol and Joseph F. Engleberger to the peopleless factories in Osaka, robots are drudges. Drudge, drudge, drudge. Theirs is a world pierced by radiation, clogged with paint particles, and smothered in a din of decibels too loud for humans. GM uses them to spray-paint and sort parts, Citibank uses them as mailmen, Westinghouse uses them to stick rods of

130

tungsten into blast furnaces, Siemens uses them for publicity at trade shows. Drudge.

They are also dumb. Dumb, dumb, dumb. The second company to buy a robot, Doehler-Jarvis, in 1961, nicknamed it "Knucklehead." The first mobile robot, developed at Johns Hopkins, was called "The Beast." The first mobile robot with vision, built at Stanford Research Institute in 1969, was named "Shakey." The brightest brains at MIT are struggling to make a robot that can tell the difference between a nut and a bolt, so it can sort six different types of fasteners. Three it can do OK, but six? Jeez, give a guy a break!

Reasons to love robots. When Cincinnati-Milacron installed some of its own robots to weld hydraulic tanks, it discovered they could turn out a product six times as cheaply as humans. This was twice as good as expected.

If GM were to accelerate by one year its plans to install fourteen thousand robots by 1990, says Joseph Engleberger, president of Unimation, it could save $738 million a year. One $50,000 machine doing the work of one person costs $6 an hour to run, where a human costs $19 an hour, including benefits.

Industrial engineers in robotics get paid 50 percent more than the norm; sales engineers in robotics now make $100,000 a year, up from $35,000 four years ago.

A study conducted by the University of Michigan indicates that robots can cut industrial accident rates as much as 11 percent by 1985, 24 percent by 1990, and 41 percent by 1995. What's more, robots don't get workmen's compensation or require expensive retrofitting of the environment to meet OSHA standards.

Reasons to hate robots. The Congressional Budget Office reports that industrial robots may oust one to three million jobs in the near future; perhaps as many as seven million by the year 2000. Another source points out that if robots cost $30,000, 5 percent of the eighty million blue-collar workers in the United States and Western Europe could be replaced. And for all the assembly-line jobs lost, cars may not be much cheaper. Assembly-line labor accounts for only 5 percent of a car's cost.

Another study, by the University of Michigan, determined that those most affected by robots would be production painters, followed by welders, then wrappers and packers.

(But orange-pickers don't need to worry. Experts agree that no robot could match a good picker's average of a fruit a second.)

"The industry is lying through its teeth about robots not eliminating jobs and is conducting a concerted and intentional effort to lull organized labor to sleep on the issue."—Peter de Cicco, president, New England District 2, International Union of Electrical Workers.

"The blame for unemployment has often been placed on machinery, and in times past labor has fought the introduction of machines into industries where hand work has been the rule. Even now there are pessimists who deprecate the increasing use of machinery and lugubriously assert that it is a Frankenstein monster. Their memory is short. Thirty years ago two hundred unskilled workers were required to do the work now done by one steam shovel. In the glass industry one machine takes the place of six hundred skilled glassblowers of a few years ago. From these figures it would seem the pessimists' assumptions are correct. They are not. The number of wage-earners increased 3 percent during the eight years between 1919 and 1927, but our production increased 50 percent! Working hours have been cut down, first from a twelve-hour day to a ten-hour day, then down to an eight-hour day. The workingman's week was cut down from six to five and a half days, and it is now proposed to cut it to five. Better pay and more leisure in which to enjoy the fruits of his work—these are the dividends of machinery to the American wage-earner."—*Scientific American*, September 1930.

MARCH OF THE ROBOTS:
Firsts, Lasts, and In-Betweens

The first successful robot. The Unimate, made by Unimation, and sold to General Motors in 1961. It was used to unload and control two die-casting presses, inspect the castings, and place them in a cooling bath at GM's Ternstedt Division in Trenton, New Jersey. Oddly enough, the robot is now on display at the Henry Ford Museum in Dearborn, Michigan.

The first unsuccessful robot. The Planobot, made by Planet Corporation and introduced in Sweden in 1957.

The first successful robot company. Unimation, formed in 1958 by Joseph Engleberger, then in the aerospace controls business, and called at the time Consolidated Diesel Electric. Initial financing was $600,000, supplied by the Pullman Company, enough to build a prototype in 1959. By 1983, when Unimation was sold to Westinghouse for $107 million, Unimation's revenues were over $70 million.

Unimation didn't show a profit for seventeen years, during which time it worked its way $18 million in the hole. By 1982 it was making $1 million a year profit.

Engleberger claims his vision of providing industrial robots was sparked by science-fiction writer Isaac Asimov.

The second successful robot company. American Machine and Foundry, which unveiled the Versatran loader/unloader robot in 1960. Industrial marketing in 1963. Sold the Versatran line to Prab Conveyors, another robot company, in 1979.

Longest absence in the business. Planet Corporation, creator of the Planobot, which flopped on its 1957 debut, reentered the business in 1980 with the Armax line of robots.

Holder of most robot patents. George C. Devol, an American who has over forty patents in both mechanical and numerically controlled robotic devices. Devol, a self-taught engineer, also invented point-of-sale terminals, photovoltaic cells, magnetic recording for machine controls, electronic countermeasures used in World War II, and those self-opening doors we see at airports and supermarkets. In 1947 he received a patent for the first "teachable machine." In 1961 he received a patent on the Unimate, marketed by the company founded by Joseph Engleberger. Devol holds about 70 percent of all robot patents in the world and gets 2 percent on all robot patent licenses let in the United States (1 percent overseas). Kawasaki Industries, the largest robot-user in Japan, licenses Devol's Unimation patent. "We're letting the Japanese walk away with everything. I get so mad I don't even like to think about it. I think we're crazy; they're being smart and we're being stupid." Devol's latest venture: the totally automated factory that not only saves money but manufactures far superior products as well.

Most ironic development. Although it was a U.S. company that first made industrial robots, a U.S. inventor that cornered the market on patents, and a U.S. company that was the first customer, a Japanese company, Kawasaki, was the first to license Unimation's technology, in 1967. The Japanese now make more robots than any other country and account for two thirds of the installed base—it's one of the reasons they can sell us cars so cheaply.

(This sort of thing has happened before. W. Edwards Deming's post-World War II work in statistical quality control was largely ignored in the United States, but the Japanese snapped up his teachings. Using his methods, they were able to raise their manufacturing standards to where "made in Japan" is a symbol of quality, not tackiness. The most coveted industrial honor in Japan is the Deming Prize.)

The Japanese admit to having been overcome by "robot fever." Seiko uses robots to assemble watches—the first human hand to touch the timepiece is yours. Panasonic has constructed an entire vacuum cleaner factory staffed by robots that work twenty-four hours a day, seven days a week, in total darkness. Hitachi uses robots to detect printed circuit board defects. Yamaha has a totally automated factory—there are more tour guides than workers. And Fujitsu uses robots to assemble robots.

The most expensive robot. The "Underwater Manifold Center," developed by Exxon and Royal Dutch/Shell. The system will roam about the ocean floor and enable ships instead of permanent offshore rigs to drill for oil. It will also manage pumping the oil to the surface or to a master control rig five miles away. Its brain will be a TRW Ferranti subsea computer, and it will use a rebuilt GE robot to help it operate valves, change well functions, and repair broken parts. It works in the Cormorant Field, ninety miles northeast of the Shetlands. Even with a price tag of $677 million, the system will be cheaper than the platforms it replaces.

The cheapest robot. RB5X, twenty-one inches tall, made by RB Robot Corp., Golden, Colorado, and listing at $1,195 (batteries included). Sonar, pulsing light, and extra memory cost more. Looking more like a vacuum cleaner than anything with brains, RB5X is designed for electronics engineers and hobbyists who want to experiment. It can remember walls that it bumped into and can be programmed to zigzag about. It is also smart enough to home in on its battery charger and plug itself in when it gets the robot munchies.

The second cheapest robot. Hero, available in kit form from Heath for $1,500. Another two-foot vacuum cleaner type, Hero can be turned into a security device that can detect an adult fifteen feet away. With the proper attachment—maybe these things aren't too far removed from the vacuum cleaner family, after all—Hero can synthesize speech. (Iowa Precision Machine makes Marvin, a more human-looking but less snazzy robot, also for $1,500.)

The most artistic robot. The Rhino XR-7, which looks like an Erector Set with a pincer arm attached, controlled by a personal computer. The Rhino, which starts at $2,400 and goes up to $9,800 in its deluxe configuration, can write, paint, knit, or weave.

The first kookoo robot. The American Motors robot that began blowing its seals and squirting its own hydraulic fluid about. You guessed it—a loose screw had fallen into its gears.

The most chic place to buy a robot. The Robotorium, 252 Mott Street, New York City. The robots here are toys, many windup, and the collection

Drawing by Tim Eagan

ranges from $3 pocket-size robots to $75 Sir Galaxy. Includes Starman, a three-foot inflatable robot. Proprietress: Debbie "The Roboteer" Huglin, a kinetic sculptress who became fascinated by cybernetics and helped design Armatron, the most popular and sophisticated "toy" robot. "We should be able to work within the cell and change it," says Debbie, a proponent of DNA robotics. "If we did, we could do real cybernetics, the marriage of man and machine. You'd have a 'mechanical' kidney instead of a dialysis machine."

The biggest robot rat. Chuck E. Cheese, the six-foot-tall microprocessor-controlled mascot of the Chuck E. Cheese Pizza Time Restaurants. Chuck has other robot friends, all controlled with computers, including an Elvis-like bear named The King; Dolli Dimples, a hippo; Jasper T. Jowls, Chuck's best friend; and the charming Madame Oink.

The most useless robot. A2W2, a $400,000 contraption made by Alvaro Villa to look like Andy Warhol. It will have preprogrammed speech and fifty-four different body movements. Warhol, you will remember, made his artistic reputation on representations of Campbell's soup cans. Let's see: How many would have to be melted down to make a robot?

Avenues or dark alleys? We all know that robots are good at spray painting and spot welding, but look what else they're being trained and designed to do: chicken plucking, fruit and vegetable harvesting, teaching, sheep shearing, fishing, and long-distance surgery, where a doctor in Boston can operate on a patient in Omaha using remote-controlled hands.

The Royal Canadian Mounties have rigged a robot for defusing bombs; the Japanese have invented "The Claw," a robot arm for ocean-floor mining; and agricultural engineers Truman Surbrook and John Gerrish of Michigan State have made a robot lawn mower. Unimation turned down the opportunity to design robots to work at McDonald's—the fast-food business was too irrational. In 1969 RCA displayed the first—and last—robot stockbroker, with the ability to understand some Wall Street lingo and recognize speech from stock buyers or sellers. The World of Robots Company, Jackson, Michigan, will send you a résumé of Denby, a teeny-bopper-size robot it rents for promotional purposes.

Mousebots. The most entertaining event at the 1979 National Computer Conference was a contest to see who could build a mechanical mouse that could make the best total time running thrice through a maze. The "smartest" mouse, called Moonlight Special, was built by five engineers from Battelle Pacific Northwest Labs over a period of three months. It had the ability to learn. In a fitting tribute of mouse over mind, however, the contest was won by a very dumb but very fast mouse that merely hugged the wall, trying all the corridors, until it got out.

Fishbots. You can now buy a microprocessor-controlled fishing lure that can be programmed to twitch and flip in sixteen different fly-imitating ways. $275.

A honeybee has about a hundred thousand neurons, or circuits, yet can navigate, track, smell, reproduce, and communicate with fellow bees. A robot hooked to the world's largest computer, with many times that number of circuits, would be hard pressed to creep the length of a room without banging into the coffee table.

Once robots get more mobile and more intelligent than honeybees we'll be glad Isaac Asimov gave us the three rules of robotics in his 1940s science-fiction classic, "I Robot":

Rule 1: A robot must never hurt a human or through its action allow one to come to harm.

Rule 2: Robots must obey human orders, unless they conflict with Rule 1.

Rule 3: Robots must never hurt themselves, unless doing so conflicts with Rules 1 and 2.

First reported infraction of Isaac Asimov's Rule 1. Kenji Urada, thirty-seven, was killed in 1981 by a robot while attempting to repair malfunctioning circuits. The robot, a self-propelled guided cart, apparently crushed Urada as he probed a circuit that set the thing back in motion. Guess you have to be careful where you tickle these beasts.

First reported infraction of Isaac Asimov's Rule 2. A robot at American Motors' Toledo Jeep plant went nuts in November 1982. Instead of spot welding a piece of sheet metal under the tailgate, the robot grabbed hold of the car and wouldn't let go. Even when one employee hit it with a wooden plank it refused to let go. The assembly line had to be shut down and the robot's plug pulled to rescue the car.

First reported infraction of Isaac Asimov's Rule 3. In 1980 a $50,000 experimental arm five feet long went berserk in the University of Florida's Center for Intellectual Machines and Robots, wildly grabbing and smashing at things until it grabbed its own support stand and tore itself in half. Harvey Lipkin, a graduate student working in the lab at the time, commented, "We had a hardware failure."

The smartest robot. It may be Cubot. This robot has color vision, has mechanical claws for manipulating, and uses special software to perform "adaptive reasoning." Designed by engineers at Battelle Pacific Northwest Labs, Cubot's sole function in life is to solve Rubik's Cube. Cubot spends about a minute thinking before manipulating the cube, during which time it decides exactly what moves to make, then three minutes making them.

Robots that see. Until robots have the ability to make sense of the visual world, they'll never be very impressive. After all, how else will they be able to tell if they're being klutzy or screwing up? Robots have used optics for inspection for years—in the 1960s the Lawrence Radiation Lab used a computer hooked to a periscope and camera to take pictures of cloud-chamber experiments—but that's not the same as seeing. Seeing means looking at an unfamiliar scene and making sense of it.

Machine Intelligence Corporation makes a $30,000 system that enables the robot to sort parts in a bin if there aren't too many different parts. The whole apparatus costs over $100,000. CGA Corporation makes a system that can take key caps in a bin and put them in position in a simulated keyboard. Hitachi of Japan makes a system that uses seven TV cameras and a touch-sensitive robot hand to pick parts out of a bin; it's still a demonstration device. Other companies make systems that can be trained by showing them pictures; GM makes a system that uses special lighting and controlled parts feed to enable a robot to do assembly. Westinghouse may have the most elaborate system in test—a six-robot system for assembling small-motor end-bells out of seventeen different parts. The system still takes humans to operate and reorient it, and special parts feeding systems. Carnegie-Mellon's Vision Institute has a vision system that can deduce three-dimensional shapes from the two dimensions it senses. Most mobile robots can tell the difference between a doorway and a wall—if the angle's right. Most current vision systems are based on a methodology pioneered by Stanford Research Institute, now SRI International, eighteen years ago that relies on silhouettes. Almost none of these systems can work in a dusty, dimly lit, factory environment. And that's the state of the art.

Robots that feel. Pity the robot. Its world, if not sightless, is dimly lit and confined to a universe of a score of parts silhouettes; it cannot hear, it's largely immobile, and even the one sense that most robots have, touch, is so rudimentary that you couldn't trust one with a soft-boiled egg. Most robot touch-sensitive nervous systems rely on feedback devices that measure forces applied in certain directions. These devices are monitored by a computer that tells the robot what to do based on the force measurements.

The most sophisticated commercially available system with touchie-feelie ability is General Electric's Allegra, made in Italy. Its feelers can be installed on any or all of the robot's arm axes of movement, and thus only as much touch as is needed can be bought. The system is also lightning fast: Odometers with 20 parts have been assembled at a rate of 450 an hour; computer chips have been inserted onto boards at the rate of 1,000 an hour.

One of the most advanced experiments is under way at MIT to develop a robot hand with a sense of touch—or at least the ability to tell the difference between a flat washer and a screw. Unique to the device is the size of the sensors—256 fit on the end of a finger. Each sensor "reads" force applied to it; the sensors are placed on special electrically conductive sheets of rubber, with different layers conducting signals from different sensors. Separating rubber layers is nylon mesh (L'eggs, extra sheer); the whole thing has a skinlike texture. The touch-sensor apparatus is mounted on a tendon-controlled finger (the robot part).

The finger, perhaps the most sensitive robot device in the world, was able to tell the difference between six types of common fasteners based on yes-no choices on three parameters (round or not? bumpy or not? stable or not?). Each object "felt" had to be smaller than a fingertip.

And that's it. That's about how much sensitivity a robot finger has. Which makes you wonder how much Proteus, the super robot, *really* felt when he raped Julie Christie in the movie *Demon Seed*.

Robots that walk. There are plenty that roll but none that rock 'n' roll. Mobile robots generally come equipped with wheels—Denning Systems claims it will soon market a mobile robot security guard—but none walk on legs. Marc Raibert and Ivan Sutherland at Carnegie-Mellon are the farthest along in making machines that could jitterbug. Although there have been walking machines before, they've not been computer-controlled and thus were pretty tough to drive. Raibert and Sutherland have built a six-legged machine that walks like an insect and can carry a human (roach coach?), and a one-legged machine that hops. Their first application—once they can program the machines to find suitable footholds and can turn hopping into more useful motion—will be military. Maybe later, sports.

Robots are taking over what has long been one of the dirtiest and most dangerous tasks of man—mining. The thin-seam miner, or "push-button miner," made by a shipbuilding firm in the Netherlands, mines a seam of coal it sniffs out with its sensor. With only a four-man crew, it can mine 420 tons of coal during an eight-hour shift. Think of those four guys trying to shovel out 105 tons each in the same length of time.

Hey, remember the old joke about the nurse who made the patient without disturbing the bed? Well, you better watch out next time you're off to the hospital: Japan is experimenting with robot nurses, and those mechanical hands can be pretty cold.

Fujitsu Fanuc, a toolmaking company in Japan, has one factory in which ten robots work day and night, with only one person supervising them. Their job: to make more robots. The company has invested $38 million in the factory and can pump out a hundred robots a month. Fujitsu has designed special robots that act as helpers to other robots. But what if someone else wanted that job? Apparently it's not a problem in Japan; they're short almost a million blue-collar workers, so robots make sense. A Nissan Motors plant in Japan now uses over a hundred robots and reports no layoffs—so much for technological displacement.

Most famous artificial human. Joseph Golem, created in 1580 by the high rabbi of Prague, Judah ben Loew. Molded out of clay from the banks of the Moldau—and given life through prayer, incantation, and the inscription of the holy name on his forehead—Golem served as the mute helper and spy to Loew. Somehow only the rabbi was able to order Golem about and get anything meaningful, but even so, Golem eventually turned on his master and had to be destroyed.

Oddly enough, three of the greatest names in modern computer design and artificial intelligence trace their ancestry back to Rabbi Loew: John von Neumann, Marvin Minsky, and Norbert Wiener.

General Electric is gutting a building in Erie, Pennsylvania, that was built in 1910 and making it the factory of the future. It's full of computers and robots that will build railroad locomotive motor frames. Today it takes sixty-eight workers sixteen days to build one; the new plant will turn one out every day. James A. Baker, an executive vice-president at GE, seems sold on automation. Says he: "American business has three choices in the eighties: automate, emigrate, or evaporate."

In the 1800s, workers in Dutch factories protested the intrusion of machines by kicking their wooden shoes, called *sabots*, into the gears and shutting them down. Thus was born the word "sabotage." Apparently things haven't changed much in the lowlands; today, 70 percent of Holland's firms use robots, and the humans try to slow the machines down by feeding them parts that aren't in proper order or by putting sand in the works. Guess management must be on to the old shoe trick.

How many robots are there? We know, for instance, that GM, buyer of the first robot, now has over a thousand and plans to install over fourteen thousand by 1990 (to eliminate thirty thousand jobs). And Ford has two hundred fifty and is shooting for five hundred by 1985. Chrysler has closer to two hundred. And about a third of all robots end up working for automakers. General Electric will have a thousand by 1985; most of the other big manufacturers are gearing up for large orders.

But nobody *really* knows how many there will be out there. In 1970 some market forecasts said robots would be an $8 billion business by 1980. Actually, it was closer to $200 million.

In 1980, Paul Aron, a securities analyst for Daiwa Securities America, Inc., wrote: "Japan has about seventy-five hundred robots, about half of the world's installations, and it is producing annually more robots than the total installed in the United States." A year later in a follow-up report Aron said, "In reexamining the [earlier] conclusions, I basically understated the tempo of growth." In 1982, the Robot Institute of America estimated that in 1985 Japan will have sixteen thousand robots to our seventy-seven hundred but that we'll catch up by 1990.

No matter what, robots are hot business. The Robots VI Conference and Expo, the yearly mecca for tin-man fans, hosted over a hundred vendors and twenty-eight thousand gawkers. At one point crowds were so bad that the fire marshals shut down the convention. The conference the year before attracted only a thousand people; the one before that, five hundred.

Neiman-Marcus, you've done it again! ComRo I, that lovable household robot in the 1982 Christmas catalog, was just the absolute rave of our party! We had ComRo taking out the trash, cleaning up little spills on the carpet, lighting cigarettes, hauling briquettes out to the barbeque, and generally

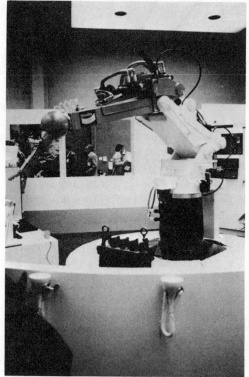

Photo courtesy of Joseph C. Jablonowski

An industrial robot.

entertaining the entire assemblage! Oh, were the Smyth-Joneses upset! Their little Hammacher-Schlemmer thing, what do they call it, Jenus? Well, I mean, you get only what you pay for, and I *know* they didn't pay more than $7,995 for that bucket of bolts! For all it can do, ComRo was an absolute *bargain* at $17,500! (We got the deluxe so we'd get the built-in color TV and stereo AM/FM radio/cassette deck.) Why, we—uh—could have paid for how many housekeepers with that much? Well, of course there is ComRo's robot pet dog, "Wires," who doesn't need to be let outside in the middle of the night. . . .

It's a robot's life. Japanese researchers are developing a robotic dog for the blind and hearing dog they think they'll have ready for duty in about five years. Fido will come equipped with visual and auditory sensors that send messages to microprocessors such as, "Here comes a curb" or "Avoid the car hurtling at us at eighty-five miles an hour." The microprocessor in turn will move limbs and alter directions, as required. This research will, in time, lead to attaching these sensors to the deaf or blind and electronically supplying a form of hearing or sight.

Aaron Fechter is handsome, creative, twenty-eight years old, and rich. He graduated from college with a degree in finance, but dollar signs were the farthest thing from his mind. Rock 'n' roll and inventing things, such as a little car that got ninety miles per gallon, were.

The car didn't go, but his talking animals did. Aaron's firm, Creative Engineering, makes about twelve hundred robots a year, almost all of them peopling Bob Brock's Showbiz Pizza Palaces. More imaginative and technically sophisticated than Chuck E. Cheese and his gang, Aaron's critters include Billy Bob Brockali and a goofy sidekick bird that makes gasohol, and the Rock-Afire Explosion Band—comprised of a gorilla, a mouse, a bear, and a dog—whose performances are rendered by Aaron and his band. For a kid who says, "I don't know anyone nice who has money," he seems to be doing all right.

ROBOTS ON PARADE:
Of Films and Tin Men

With help from Cazar Del Valle, *The Naked Computer* is proud to present the Robot Hall of Film Fame, a chronological listing of some of the more interesting film appearances by robots. Note that only two—*2001: A Space Odyssey* and *Star Wars*—could be considered grade-A movies. The majority were grade Z.

MOVIE	DATE	COMMENTS
Metropolis	1926	First robot movie appearance; director: Fritz Lang; German; plot: rich live above ground, workers below, tending machines. Mad scientist, Rotwang, creates robot look-alike of heroine. Great visually, bad for robot rep.
The Phantom Empire (serial)	1935	Singing cowboy Gene Autry discovers robots on his ranch (underground, living in world called Murania). Tough transition from horse opera to sci-fi.
Undersea Kingdom (serial)	1936	Created Volkite Robots of Atlantis. Longest-lived film robots. Ray "Crash" Corrigan discovers lost colony of

		Atlantis. First robots with pincer hands, no ears, slits for eyes.
The Phantom Creeps (serial)	1939	Introduction of the Universal Studios robot, with zombielike facial features. Stars Bela Lugosi.
Mysterious Dr. Satan (serial)	1940	Used Volkite robots. Republic Studios.
Flash Gordon Conquers the Universe	1940	Robots as electrically charged walking bombs. Robots not used in 1936 Flash Gordon films.
The Monster and the Ape	1945	Robot is monster, called Metalogen Man, and is terrible actor. Ape no better.
Captain Video— Master of the Stratosphere	1951	Miserable attempt to cash in on TV show. Columbia Pictures.
The Day the Earth Stood Still	1951	Introduces Gort, member of an interplanetary robot police force, as companion to Michael Rennie, outer-space emissary. Gort had a death ray in place of a face. Played by Lock Martin, the doorman at Grauman's Chinese Theater.
Zombies of the Stratosphere (serial)	1952	Volkite robots again. Outer-space zombies plan to blow up Earth. Zombie named Narab was played by Leonard Nimoy (who later became Mr. Spock of *Star Trek*).
Robot Monster	1953	Robots may have been gorillas in space helmets blowing bubbles. Perhaps the worst robot/sci-fi movie ever.
Gog	1954	3-D movie. First with a computerized robot.
Earth vs. the Flying Saucers	1956	Robots at the saucer controls.
Forbidden Planet	1956	Reworking of Shakespeare's *Tempest*. Robby the Robot = Ariel. Other actors of note: Leslie Nielsen, Walter Pidgeon,

Movie	Date	Comments
		Anne Francis. Robby stole the show but never made another hit film.
Kronos	1957	The dregs. Giant box crawls across the land.
Robot	1960	Yugoslavian. Male robot builds female robot, have kid robots. Ozzie and Harriet plot.
Sex Kittens Go to College	1960	Tuesday Weld and Mamie Van Doren (yum) meet Thinko, a robot invented by a mad professor.
The Robot vs. the Aztec Mummy	1962	Return of the sheet-metal robot. Used by a mad scientist to violate the tomb of the living mummy Popoca. Most ridiculous plot ever.
Planet of the Storms	1962	First Soviet robot film. Odd life-forms, dinosaurs, and lovable robot George.
Dr. Breedlove	1964	Typical Russ Meyer soft-core porn. Scantily clad female robots.
Dr. Goldfoot and the Bikini Machine	1965	More near-nude female robots. Vincent Price and Frankie Avalon. Music by Sam and the Ape Man.
Sins of the Fleshapoids	1965	Robot survivors of nuke war program themselves to make baby robots.
King Kong Escapes	1967	Best (or worst?) of the Japanese genre. Giant ape fights metal counterpart.
Terror of Mecha-Godzilla	1967	See above. Substitute "Godzilla" for "ape."
He's Called Robert	1967	Another Soviet filmsky. Handsome human-looking robot takes owner's place. Gets confused by societal conventions.
Voyage to the Planet of Prehistoric Women	1968	Soviet robot George, borrowed for this Peter Bogdanovitch special, is worshiped by amphibian women led by Mamie Van Doren (yum).

2001: A Space Odyssey	1968	Great sci-fi flick. Whole spaceship becomes a deranged robot when HAL, a computer, runs amok. More to the movie than that.
Silent Running	1971	Bruce Dern struggles to keep Earth plants alive on space station. Only companions are programmable robots. First use of amputees inside drones.
THX-1138	1971	George Lucas's first film. Androids as police force. Johnny Weissmuller, Jr.
Westworld	1973	Robots help humans act out fantasies. One robot, played by Yul Brynner, goes amok and starts shooting humans. Director: Michael Crichton.
The Stepford Wives	1975	Suburban husbands replace wives with more compliant androids.
Demon Seed	1977	Robot couples with Julie Christie to produce chip off the old blonde.
Star Wars	1978	R2D2, C3PO. Need we say more?
The Empire Strikes Back	1980	Sequel to *Star Wars*. More R2D2, C3PO.
Looker	1981	Electronic preservation of beautiful models inside computers. Director: Michael Crichton.
Heartbeeps	1981	Romantic comedy with entire cast of androids. Andy Kaufman, Bernadette Peters.

The most profitable robot may have been the Robby the Robot (based on the character in *Forbidden Planet*) that New York toy shop owner Robert Wiseman bought in the 1970s for $12. It had no hands. In May 1980 he sold it for $950.

The earliest robot toy was Atomic Robot Man, made in Japan after World War II of shell casings and tin cans discarded by GI's. A five-inch-tall windup. The most sought-after toy is twenty-eight-inch Mr. Atomic, designed by Cragstan. One could easily bring $5,000—more than many functional home-brew robots.

Why NASA loves robots. Having determined that the labor costs of astronauts working in space or on the moon run about $10,000 an hour, the agency is looking for alternatives in the homesteading of outer space. Millions have already been spent determining the feasibility of various colonization plans, and one of NASA's favorites is the establishment of a self-replicating factory on the moon. Consultant-scientists have estimated that for an investment of $1 billion (assuming no cost overruns) such a factory could produce solar cells, out of moon rocks, usable by satellites. If the factory were also able to grow on its own accord—reproduce—the payback could be in as little as twenty years. Of course, if a factory *couldn't* be designed that could build itself out of moon rocks, the scientists estimate that the payback period would be six thousand years. Which is scarier, factories building other factories without human intervention, or NASA embarked on a six-thousand-year project?

FROM THE CACHE:
Why Robots Should Have the Right to Work

Some Jobs Are Fit Only for Robots
by Craig Waters

I remember my father's body and I remember my father's stories. When I was young, my father, Jacob Waters, would come home each evening from the New York Shipbuilding Corp. in Camden, N.J., where he was a welder. He would peel off his work shirt and, occasionally, when he was changing for dinner, would remove his insulated undershirt as well. Then I would see the burns. At the time, the burns made no sense to me; half a dozen might run down his chest in what was nearly a straight line; three or four might be clustered in a circle on his stomach. Later, I understood: Hot slag from the welding iron burnt through his clothing and trickled down his chest, or, if it struck lower, bounced around in one confined area as he tried to free himself from the pain.

And my father told me stories. He told me about welding inside the gun turrets on battleships and cruisers during World War II. It was summer, and the temperature outside was in the 90s, but the turrets were electrically heated to more than 200 degrees (F.) to keep the metal at the proper temperature. Inside, his welding iron blazing, my father slaved in hell. He talked about working inside of tiny heated compartments in the bowels of atomic submarines where the metal was so hot he had to cover the four-foot by four-foot floor with layers of asbestos and lumber before he could sit, his legs folded up beneath him, to weld. When his knees began to hurt him so badly that he could hardly walk, a doctor explained that the intense heat was burning off the fluid in his kneecaps.

Some of the spaces were so small that he couldn't wear a visor; dark glasses protected his eyes, but his face grew fiery with arc burn. Sometimes slag found its way around a lens, and a bit of molten metal would fall onto the surface of his eye and adhere to it until it was plucked off by the company doctor. Once, while he was welding on a yardarm, slag dropped into the top of his boot—his hands filled with equipment, his legs grasping the yardarm, my father was unable to do anything about it. The slag burnt a half-inch hole in the top of his foot.

But the worst job, my father said, was one requiring him to hang by his feet through a small hole in a metal plate and weld while hanging upside down, the red-hot iron inches from his face.

At New York Ship, my father had been burned and blinded and poisoned by what he did for a living. There were other jobs with other companies that yielded similar stories. The one that terrified me most had to do with an automobile-chassis line. When my father went to work for the Budd Co., in Philadelphia, he found that the welders who had been there for more than a short while *screamed*. The pace was so inhuman that, in order to relieve the incredible tension, they screamed for several hours each evening; the night-shift foreman told my father not to let it bother him. It was one of the few jobs my father ever quit.

Now robots work on many automobile manufacturing and assembly lines, and recently they've been designed to weld in the bottoms of ships. As the robots have moved into the factories and shipyards, labor leaders, workers, sociologists, and others have become increasingly concerned about their impact on people: How many workers will be displaced? How many will lose jobs? What human skills will eventually be lost to posterity? The questions are all legitimate and need to be addressed. Those who favor the use of robots frequently suggest that they should be added within attrition levels, and that displaced workers should be retrained for better jobs. They also point out that there are many jobs that people simply should not be performing.

My father would understand what they mean.

CHAPTER 9

VIDEOTS:

Computer Games

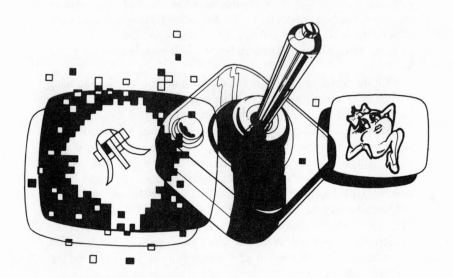

Computer games: friends or foes?

These bleeping, blorking, even talking machines in arcades and homes will suck $4 billion out of teenage pockets this year—the equivalent of a stack of quarters thirty thousand miles high! For our money, what do we get? A generation of videots, whose attention span is measured in microseconds and whose concept of distance is in parsecs. Video games are banned in Boston, the Surgeon General has pronounced them bad for our health, and the kids can't get enough of them.

The contagion seems hard to control. Beefsteak Charlie's Restaurant in New York now lets you play free. Charlie's says it's just like big-screen TV to them; you don't even have to buy a beer. Other restaurants experimenting with the idea are a bit more mercenary: They give you a few free tokens with your food, then hope you'll empty your pockets once you're hooked. Coke is even putting free (?) games in *its vending machines. And adults who should know better are experimenting with video game lottery devices—connect from anywhere to the master computer that picks winners. The next step will be direct connection to your bank and direct deposit into the lottery.*

In the 1950s Elvis struck fear in the hearts of parents; in the 1960s, it was the Beatles. In the 1970s it was drugs, sex, and rock 'n' roll. In the 1980s, the video game is the villain.

You know why, of course. The same reason as always. It's not the epileptic seizures video games have been known to bring on, the lapsed grades of the true joystick freaks, or the small change scarfed off the bureau. It's the secret of it, the cult culture itself. It's enough to scare the bejeezus out of an adult. It's don't touch, be careful, watch out vs. kablaam, blooie, and zappereeno. The real aliens aren't on the screen, they're playing it. Who are these kids anyway?

First videogame death. Peter Bukowski. An eighteen-year-old from Calumet, Illinois, he collapsed in a video arcade last year. The doctor diagnosed heart failure brought on by the tension of the game. He had been playing Berserk.

Video vignette. Meet Mr. Success. Three-piece suit, looks like an up-and-coming young exec or lawyer. Mid-twenties. What's he doing here? Guy like that should be picking up a foxy lady in a fern bar, not playing Donkey Kong in a hamburger joint.

Oh, well. Ten-year-old son Joshua wants to play. Enact the time-honored ritual. Place quarter on the machine, claiming rights to the next round. Mr. Success done, kerplunk goes Josh's quarter. Cripes, is the game over so soon?

Mr. Success back. His quarter up now. Joshua watching Donkey Kong a little closer, getting excited. Getting into it, actually. Plenty of ooh-ahh-ow-wow-watch-out outbursts as Mr. Success plays. Goofy game guy climbs higher and higher, leaping barrels to reach girl held prisoner by Kong.

Get quarter back up. Mr. Success almost done. He finishes. Has un-grown-uplike look on his face as he turns to Josh and says, snarling, "All your noise made me blow the game." Huh? Whole place is a din. Four other machines beeping, whistling, blowing up. Kids and parents milling around, talking; not far away, a large-screen TV blaring. Total decibel level from agglomeration of nearby tables, around 115. Joshua looks up and shrugs. Puts quarter in machine.

Ed Milkow, the sixteen-year-old *Wunderkind* who helped make this book possible, was telling us one day about all the other kids who had written games and made their bundle. There was a seventeen-year-old guy in California who made $200,000 last year; Jonathan Rotenberg, head of the Boston Computer Society; and some others. Ed sighed: "I'm just afraid that if I don't invent something great by the time I'm nineteen, I'll be over the hill."

COMPUTER GAME FIRSTS

- First hand-held computer toy: Merlin, a red robot with a belly full of flashing LEDs (light-emitting diodes). You could play tic-tac-toe and blackjack, program songs that Merlin would play back, and learn the precepts of logic, memory, and chance. Over a million and a half have been sold since its introduction in 1978.

- First computer game: Space War, a shoot-'em-up developed at MIT by students at the computer center and played on a Digital PDP-8. Nolan Bushnell, one of the students, wanted to make it available to the public but realized it would be too expensive to do on the Digital machine. He redesigned it, sold it to Bill Nutting Associates, and it became the arcade game Computer Wars. Bushnell made only $500 in royalties on it, but with that money he started Atari.

- First Atari arcade game: Pong, born on November 29, 1972. Bushnell tried to sell it to Nutting again, but the company scoffed. Too bad. Pong was an enormous hit, making Atari, not Nutting, a household word. It was followed by Space Race and Pong Doubles, the first sequel game in video history. Subsequent sequels: Quadrapong, Pin-Pong, and Doctor Pong (alias Puppy Pong, put in a cabinet that looked like Snoopy's doghouse—not a smashing success). Atari introduced the first video maze game, Gotcha, in 1973.

- Movies that became video games:
  Superman
  Raiders of the Lost Ark
  TRON
  The Empire Strikes Back
  Jaws
  Conan the Barbarian
  The China Syndrome
  King Kong
  Beauty and the Beast

- Stupidest game: Skeet Shoot, where you launch a skeet and try to shoot it down. The graphics are abominable.

- Weirdest game: Lost Luggage, where you're standing at the airport luggage conveyor, trying to retrieve your bags before they burst open and spill your unmentionables all over the place.

- First adventure game: Adventure (of course), based on the board game Dungeons and Dragons, written by Willy Crowther and Don Woods at Stanford in 1977. Adventure placed you in a situation of crawling into an underground realm where you encountered trolls, dragons, and assorted challenges to obtaining a variety of treasures. Your task: to escape with the treasures without being killed or maimed. You typed in commands such as "Go north" or "Take sword" to move through the game. Next adventure game: Zork, written by Marc Blank and friends at MIT, which allowed you to say things such as "Go upstairs and take the knife." Digital Equipment Corporation liked the game so much it used it to debug programs and made it available under the name Dungeon to every purchaser of a VAX computer—thus ranking it as one of the most popular games in history. The title, Zork, was a nonsense word that Marc picked out of the air.

- Most widely played game: DECWARS, available on the CompuServe information network. Dozens of people all across the country can play together at the same time.

- Funniest game: Kaboom!, where a strange man throws bombs at you that you have to catch. If you catch the bombs, he frowns; if you miss them, he smiles. If you win, he gets a shocked expression on his face.

- Longest game: Time Zone, where you travel through time to any of six continents through ten time periods as the hero, interacting with hundreds of characters. You can go from prehistoric times to the days of the Roman Empire to the Wild West, acting out your fantasies on a screen full of full-color pictures. Time Zone fills six disks with over a million and a half instructions and takes more than a year to finish playing.

- Most widely distributed game: Combat, which everyone who buys an Atari video computer system (VCS) gets free. Most disliked game: Combat, because it's boring and hard to move the tanks around to shoot at one another.

- Most disappointing games that began as arcade games and were turned into home computer games: Pac-Man and Asteroids. They were hard to play and the graphics were inferior to those of the arcade games. K. C. Munchkin, the Pac-Man ripoff that was driven off the market by Atari lawyers, was far superior.

- Most reviled game: Custer's Revenge, an X-rated game involving rape and dodging arrows. It was sick enough to be immediately banned from most trade conventions; *Infoworld*, which has been known to review pornographic software, refused even to describe the play.

- **The Arcade Hall of Fame:**
  Computer War (the first ever battle in space)
  Pong (who can forget it?)
  Space Invaders (the first game you couldn't possibly win)
  Asteroids (the Japanese hated it; wasn't cute enough)
  Galaxian (first Space Invaders game where you couldn't predict the next attack)
  Pac-Man (the most successful game ever—the only game to inspire a TV show)
  Defender (the most complicated game ever—you need four hands and twenty thumbs to master it)
  Venture (the first arcade adventure game)
  Tempest (the first vector, or line game—all the others are dot games; it's also the most complex—ninety-nine levels of play)
  Zaxxon (the first 3-D game)

In 1978 the makers of coin-operated video games had themselves a $50 million business selling machines to arcades. Then Bally introduced Space Invaders, licensed from the Japanese, and by 1981 led a $900 million industry. Pretty high score, huh?

Infocom is the thinking man's computer games company. It specializes in adventure-type games—"interactive fiction"—that create scenarios in which you are a principal actor, moving through a series of, well, adventures, which become increasingly interesting and complex. The company was formed by Joel Berez and Marc Blank.

Infocom's games are neatly packaged. Deadline, a detective game with a murder to solve, comes with police interrogations, court exhibits, lab reports, and a map, all in a manila folder. Starcross, an outer-space game, comes inside a flying saucer. This is clearly stuff for the serious computer game player. Zork I is the biggie: Forty thousand copies have been sold. You can play for hours on end, tracing your way through the maze, getting lost in the forest, fighting the troll, and trying to unlock the mysteries of the maintenance room at the underground dam. It's become a cult—there's even a Zork User Group. And Infocom has released Zork II, which picks up where Zork I left off, and Zork III, which, among other things, allows you to travel in time back to the previous games.

Infocom has a unique distribution channel. Games are first written on a large DECSystem 20 computer in a high-level language, then coded to run on the popular personal computers.

It's so simple to write the games that the writer doesn't need to be a programmer. A case in point: Michael Berlyn, a sci-fi author who has written four novels, including *The Integrated Man*, is writing games. "Our development system allows people like Michael to concentrate on the story, making the computer a simple tool in the process—which is what it should be," says Marc.

Infocom plans even better games to come. John Gardner, who picked up the James Bond series where Ian Fleming left off, has expressed an interest, for instance, in being in the Infocom stable of writers. Budding novelists who have knocked heads with the New York literary establishment may have a new lease on life.

A poop scoop for Koop. Dr. C. Everett Koop, the U.S. Surgeon General, chose a conference of psychiatrists and public-health officials to denounce video games as hazardous to the nation's youth. He was talking not about bruised button thumbs, *grand mal* seizures, or sprained trigger fingers, but about family violence in general. Violence on TV, video games, and poor economic conditions were the problems.

Although he mentioned video games only in passing, the industry and the players were appalled. Leading journals immediately called on their own batch of headshrinkers to prove that video games were safe. At any rate, there hasn't been enough time for clinical studies to tote up the number of raving maniacs per thousand produced by video games.

What would you do with the dough? Young Manuel Rodriguez, eighteen, from Stockton, California, worked hard for his $25,000. When Mattel announced that it was hosting the highest-paying video game shootoff ever held, Rodriguez immediately bought an Intellivision and a cartridge of Astrosmash, the game of the contest. For seven months he trained like a demon—on the machine from 10 A.M. to 10 P.M. He quit work at his father's business to practice; he gave up his friends.

Finally, in the fall of 1982, despite having sprained a thumb in the first round, Rodriguez bested a youth from Elmira, New York. It had been worth it. What would Rodriguez do with the money? Buy a new Trans Am, with everything on it.

Don't mess with Ben. Judge Ben J. Miller sentenced eighteen-year-old Eric McGill of Griffin, Georgia, to ten years' abstention from playing video games. It seems Eric was upset that his family wanted to move to a new house, precluding him from frequenting his favorite video arcade. So he set the new house on fire, not once but twice. Eric, who had dropped out of school to take up a career as a professional Pac-Man player, was apprehended after witnesses saw him buy matches and take a cab to the new residence. Oh, yes: The judge thought Eric should look into psychiatric counseling while he cooled his thumbs.

I smell a grud. Tom McWilliams, seventeen, of Orinda, California, goes to high school, but he is also on the payroll at Sirius Software, designing Apple II computer games for $60,000 a year. His latest hit is Outpost, a place in space under attack by Kamicosmic gruds. He's also written a program for his high school to help it keep track of who's in school and where they should be at any time. Who could like a grud like that?

Fantastic Voyage *revisited.* In Microsurgeon, an Intellivision game, a tiny robot (you) navigates through a critically ill body, "outmaneuvering white blood cells that attempt to destroy you," while you try to "eliminate brain tumors, cholesterol in the arteries, cleanse the intestinal tract of tapeworms," and other fun, gory things.

Guess what? Pac-Man's fifty-eight years old! The familiar gobbler was recently discovered munching away in Tallahassee, Florida, part of the design of a quilt made in 1925.

And nuts to you, Pac-Man. Cornuts, which sells thirty-eight million pounds of toasted corn snacks a year, has used a little munching face remarkably similar to Pac-Man as its logo since 1965. Everything's fine, says Cornuts, as long as Pac-Man keeps his puss off competing snack-food packages.

New game cartridges are coming out so fast that monthly magazines devoted to video games can't keep up with them. There are nearly ten million home video games in America, averaging at least seven or eight game cartridges for each kid; in 1982 alone, thirty million cartridges were sold. That's enough money to buy seventy-five thousand fully equipped Porsche 911 Cabriolet convertibles. By 1990, industry analysts expect the home *computer* market to be at the same level as the video game market is today, and all the video game action on floppy disks.

Worth it. Malibu Fun Centers in California reward kids for good grades: Every A on the report card is good for five game tokens; a B gets you two. Malibu asks only that you not redeem your tokens during school hours.

The thinking man's video game. TC-7 Air Traffic Controller boasts no blinking lights or screeching sounds, just a very realistic experience in landing and launching aircraft from a very busy airport. No joysticks or bomb buttons, either—just a touch-sensitive panel to control altitude, airspeed, and other commands a real air traffic controller would issue. Author Rochester, who served as an air traffic control radar technician for Uncle Sam's Air Force, gives this one his seal of approval.

Oh, I see . . . that is, I think I see. . . . Inhabitants of an alien planet have written a game called ⌇⍒⍝⍬⍊⌇ you can play on your Apple II. Unfortunately, the disk was garbled during its interplanetary trip, so the game now is to try to figure out the instructions for it. If you're interested in translating intergalactic jargon, contact Southwestern Data Systems in Santee, California, for details.

Adventures of the PROM programmers. Bob and Holly Doyle are phenomenal people, just like you and me. They met at Harvard, where they were both studying for their Ph.D.'s in astrophysics, fell in love, got married and had some kids. Holly experimented with solar magnetic fields, and Bob worked on Skylab in Houston until the program was defunded. Bob came home to Cambridge and designed a tape recorder that made a synchronized sound track for Super-8 home movies.

By now it was the mid-seventies, and microchips caught Bob and Holly's fancy. "We saw what was happening with hand-held calculators and thought of a technology transfer of the MIT-Harvard-IBM-Bell Labs computer games," says Bob. They built a few prototypes and tried them out on their sons, Derek and Robert, but none of the game companies seemed interested. In a letter to Parker Bros. in January 1975, Bob predicted a $100 million business in electronic games. "We were wrong," he says today. "It was a billion-dollar business."

One day Bob and Holly walked into Parker Bros. in nearby Salem with a Samsonite briefcase. In it was a game called Code Name: Sector, one of the first semiconductor-based games. Parker Bros. introduced it in 1977, and today it's still available.

Next came Merlin, the first hand-held electronic game. It was red, looked something like a Princess telephone handset, and had eleven blinking red buttons. You could play games on Merlin and even tap in tunes, which it would play back for you.

Merlin's magic came from a PROM, or Programmable Read Only Memory chip. Bob and Holly used an Intel computer/debugger/emulator to program the chip that is Merlin's heart. First they write the program that comprises Merlin's functions. Then they hook it up to the Intel and run the program to make sure there aren't any mistakes, a process called debugging. Then they make the program mimic, or emulate, an actual chip that's temporarily programmable (an EPROM, the E standing for Erasable) to see if it works. If it does, they unplug the EPROM chip and stick it into the socket on the board in their briefcase, and off they go to Parker Bros. with a new game, whether it's Merlin or one of the many others they invented.

Developing games this way allowed Bob and Holly to prototype a game in weeks rather than the months it would take actually to etch and cast a new chip. "It allowed us to implement changes Parker Bros. asked for within twenty-four hours. We would take our briefcase home and have the game ready for them again the next morning," says Bob.

Merlin was introduced in 1978, at the same time as Simon from Milton Bradley. The games were similar in that they used microprocessor chips, but Simon did only one thing, while Merlin did eight. To date, Merlin has outsold every other toy in history in number of units and dollar revenues. You can find Merlin in fifteen foreign countries. Merlin made over two million kids happy. Merlin made Bob and Holly Doyle $5 million happy and launched an industry.

Merlin led to another interesting invention. One evening, a friend who was playing with Merlin observed that the sounds it made sounded like the sounds a Touch-Tone telephone makes. In fact, by holding Merlin to the mouthpiece and pressing its buttons, you could dial a number. The upshot was the IXO Telecomputer, a hand-held communications terminal. This little gem, which costs under $500, can connect you to any computer communications system—and will automatically dial the number in the bargain. It was designed by Michael Suchoff, who, while at ARP, designed the microprocessor-controlled music synthesizer in the alien spaceship in the movie *Close Encounters of the Third Kind*.

No more cliff-hangers. Robert Best has invented a computerized video-disk system with a voice-recognition system for participative movies on TV. Initially the films will be cartoons, but you'll be able to help decide the character's fate. Say the hero is stuck on a cliff; he turns to you and says, "What should we do?" and gives you several options. You sing out your answer. But what if you don't? He says, "I'm waiting for your answer." If you're still silent, he says, "OK, if you don't want to tell me what to do, I'll just jump off the cliff"—or something like that.

Pinstripes, drag pipes, and spinner hubcaps. Two ex-Atari employees, Bob Brown and Craig Nelson, have developed the Supercharger, which adds another microchip to the low-budget Atari VCS for high-quality graphics and sound effects, as well as state-of-the-art playing fields. Plug the Supercharger in the cartridge slot, hook it up to a cassette deck, load the game Communist Mutants from Outer Space, wield your superswift Wico joystick or the freehand LeStick, and it's hyperspace all the way.

So What? Department. Atari was the official game of the last Summer Olympics. Odyssey was named the official game of the Knoxville World's Fair. Next thing you know, Armor Attack will be the official game of the Army.

Oh, boy, just what I always wanted. Richard Ross of Jacksonville, Florida, won the nationwide competition as best TRON player. He won a year's supply of free tokens and a TRON arcade machine.

Sounds fishy. Pat Roper, president of Games by Apollo, had to rename his Shark Attack cartridge game because Universal Pictures felt it might be confused with their *Jaws* movies. In Lochjaw, as the game is now called, a diver is menaced by sharks while trying to recover sunken treasure from a buried ship. Just watch and see if some dentist doesn't hassle them now.

Speed Queen Laundromat, Columbus, Ohio. Taking matters too seriously, eleven-year-old Sheven Jones stabbed Charles Moore, fourteen, in the heart when he wouldn't stop teasing her while she played Krazy Kong. She was charged with a delinquency count of murder.

Can I change into my Superman suit, too? Playtime International of Richmond, Virginia, has introduced the video outpost, a telephonelike booth with two coin-operated video games inside. Not to be confused with transporter booths. Beam me up, Scotty!

And now Las Vegas. Video games tailored to the gambling crowd are making big bucks for the casinos. You can bet on a horse race, play poker with a talking machine, watch the roulette wheel spin on the video screen, and play blackjack with a screen that flashes the message "Grab my knob and pull." The reasoning is that if kids grow up on Pac-Man and Defender, they'll naturally gravitate toward video gambling. Must be so; International Game Technology, which builds the machines, went from $300,000 to $14 million in revenue in just five years. Next: New Jersey is experimenting with electronic lottery games in bars and liquor stores. And we thought the *kids* were being exploited.

An arcade games phylogeny. Video game families come in two types: violent and nonviolent. The warrior games are shoot, shoot, shoot; the pacifists' delights are getting out of a dilemma. Brute force vs. strategy. The feisty games originated in America; the maze-and-mayhem games come from Japan. Herewith the fathers and their offspring:

WARRIOR GAMES	STRATEGY GAMES
Space Invaders	Pac-Man
Asteroids	Frogger
Astro Blaster	Donkey Kong

Warrior Games	Strategy Games
Galaxian	Centipede
Astro Fighter	Make Trax
Moon Cresta	Mouse Trap
Gorf	Lock'N Chase
Phoenix	Turtles
Pleiades	Berserk

Walter Day runs the Twin Galaxy Arcade in Ottumwa, Iowa, and keeps track of the top arcade game scores of the Video Game National Scoreboard, which is published in several popular video game magazines. Scores must be verified by the local arcade owner, witnessed by two other joystick jockeys, and officially mailed to Walter by the owner. As we finished *TNC* in early 1983, these were the top scores:

Robotron	252,114,340
Defender	75,865,375
StarGate	70,283,000
Centipede	15,207,353
Pac-Man	9,980,420
Burger Time	4,163,250
TRON	4,036,171
Donkey Kong	3,165,300
Millipede	1,371,507
Donkey Kong, Jr.	951,100

Hats off to Eddie O'Neil of Durham, North Carolina, who spent fifty-two hours at the helm of Robotron to be the number one ace in the country.

What does it take to be a winner? Doug Nelson, who's the top Pac-Man player, estimates he spent between four thousand and five thousand quarters—the equivalent of the cost of 765 Big Macs—developing his skill. Guess Doug must have Big Pac attacks.

Laws, laws, trouble with the laws. A St. Louis firm was caught distributing Donkey Kong look-alikes called Crazy Kong and Congorilla. Worst of all, according to some, are the software pirates, those individuals who make copies of floppy disk programs used in personal computers.

Copying programs is a fact of life; the wise computer user makes a "backup" copy, just in case the disk is damaged (see Chapter 5). What you're *not* supposed to do is give—or sell—a copy to a friend. Some pundits say it's OK to give copies away but not to sell them for a profit. As Judge Learned Hand once remarked, "Wherever the line is drawn will seem arbitrary."

There are pirates and then there are pirates; that line is arbitrary, too. The teenager swapping games with the kid next door probably is no more a pirate than if he were swapping comic books. For our purposes, pirates fall into two categories:

1. Robin Hoods, who steal from the publisher and give to those who can't afford the often exorbitant prices.
2. Don Corleones, who sell bootleg copies of anything they can get their hands on, at whatever price they can get.

"Red Rebel is my CB handle. I chose it because I have red hair, enjoy red clothing, and have a red car. I want to be known as a cracker, not a pirate," says Red, a graduate of MIT who's been involved with computers for over fifteen years and who used to own his own software development company. He sold the business and subsequently had his first encounter with an Apple in 1981.

Red became a pirate, or program cracker, because "I needed five printouts a day on the information for my business. The program, however, was only capable of producing one per command. So I had to break the code and modify the program.

"There is a great need for information about the Apple. When we first started out, we couldn't learn the answer to a question we posed to our Apple dealer. This one of the main reasons Pirate's Harbor came into existence."

Pirate's Harbor is an electronic bulletin board where people exchange news, tips, and programs. "The Harbor started out as a communications program," says Red. "We needed to find out how it worked. We promoted the idea of a Pirate's forum, including an ongoing debate, pro and con, about pirating." One of the subscribers was the author of Wizardry, a popular game, who was attempting to learn if his program was being pirated.

"I don't mind if a program is copy-protected," he says. "As a businessman I can understand the need for it. The best way for a young programmer to learn how to program is by reading the program of a master. There are basically no good books on programming on the market today. Piracy is necessary for stimulation and the exchange of ideas. Bozo [another famous pirate] started cracking so he could learn machine language.

"Piracy is one of the industry's growing pains. Pirating will also force manufacturers to lower their prices. This is good for the consumer and will ultimately be good for the business. If a small company just starting out would put out low-cost, high-quality software, it could conceivably revolutionize the business."

CHAPTER 10

CYBERNETIC CÉZANNES:

Computers and the Arts

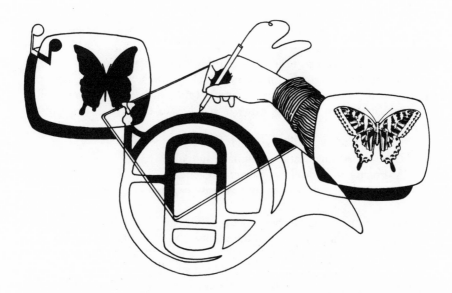

You begin. You sit at the controls while your guests find comfortable seats. You cut in the audiotape, load a floppy disk into your personal computer, turn on the laser disk drive. Flanking your large-screen TV are two concert-hall speakers connected to your stereo. The music begins, and an image appears on the screen. You hit a few keys and it dissolves into a vortex of light and movement, regenerates as a view of the cosmos in time to the cadences of Gustav Holst's tone poem, "The Planets." The music fades to Beethoven's "Pastoral Symphony" as a scene from Dionysian Greece appears and nymphs dance merrily. An overdub of The Moody Blues singing "Nights in White Satin" begins, and the scene changes once again, to lovers and the setting sun. . . .

The Moody Blues and dancing nymphs? It might not be art, but this scene could be played in a living room today.

Early experiments in producing artistic works using computers were so bad that even the artists winced. Wrote critic Thomas B. Hess in ArtNews *in December 1970: "The big point in Art and Technology manifestations in the last ten years has been that none of the technology works." But by the 1980s, artists had come to realize that computers could be used not to supplant traditional art, but to enhance it. Like mixing The Moody Blues with Beethoven. See, the computer isn't always insensitive.*

Byron, roll over. One of the first poets to use a computer to produce original—and not imitative—verse was Jackson MacLow. During a two-month gig in 1971 as "artist in residence" at Information International, a Los Angeles computerized graphic-arts firm, MacLow produced nineteen poems. Since MacLow was into "chance poetry" at the time, the computer's ability to produce random numbers came in handy. An example of some of the works:

"Dazzling biologists diagrammed donnbunny expressions."
"Determined pigs feathered linnaen linterils."
"A director filed dead Schnauzers hysterically."
"A duck distinguished peanuts daintily in Jersey."

Maybe not so original, but more rigorous, were the poems produced by Dr. Louis T. Milic, chairman of the English Department at Cleveland State University in 1969. In an effort begun in the late 1950s at Columbia, Milic began using computers to analyze mathematically the prose and verse of great writers. As a logical next step, he programmed the school's large IBM 360 computers—using the Snobol language—to produce poems in the style of authors analyzed. This one from the computer's mimicry of William Blake:

> *You were happy with your foe*
> *And your puny job did glow*
> *Your foe relived your joy*
> *And you renewed the foolish ploy*
>
> *We were angry at our foe*
> *And our holy wrath did flow*
> *Our foe received our wrath*
> *And we returned the foolish math*
>
> *We were angry at our host*
> *And our noble wrath did coast*

Our host reviewed our wrath
And we reviewed the foolish math

They were gay with their foe
But their holy gaiety did grow
Their foe rejoined their gaiety
And they relived the foolish laity.

As a result of his efforts, Milic concluded that computers may be useful in learning heuristics, but they aren't likely to produce literature of any interest.

Of course, this was before Jackson MacLow's poems were published.

Casio has a new line of electric keyboards that can scan music transcribed not in the usual notation but in bar codes, like those on Campbell's soup cans. Once the scanning is done, the keyboard will play the music back. The player—or is it operator?—can vary timbre, tone, pitch, and rhythm, selecting from a library of twenty different musical "voices" and ten rhythm backgrounds. Lights go on above the keys associated with the melody—for easy learning—and the keyboard can be run using batteries and with headphones (good on planes). Tidbit: It's the only kind of keyboard Gladys Knight of Gladys Knight and the Pips can play.

"Daisy" was the first tune a computer played, at Bell Labs in 1932. Arthur C. Clarke put it on the Computer Hit Parade when HAL sang it while having his memory banks unplugged in the 1968 film *2001: A Space Odyssey*. Bill Gates made it an underground classic in 1975 when he programmed the Altair microcomputer for the first time in Basic to croon the tune.

George Bowley, an engineer-guitarist at Dynamic Systems of McLean, Virginia, has invented a guitar that uses optical fibers rather than traditional metal strings. As the musician's fingers pluck the string, the amount of light flowing through the strand modulates the signal flowing to the amplifier. The system is immune to feedback and electrical distortion, so we should see a decrease in the number of musicians who are electrocuted on stage— unless, of course, that's part of their act. One neat side benefit: The strings glow an iridescent blue.

Walt Disney Studios' $21 million movie *TRON*, released on July 9, 1982, and in which the main characters live inside a computer, ride light cycles across electronic grids, and evade "grid bugs" or "logic probes," may be the most impressive use of computers in art yet. In over half of the movie, fifty-three minutes out of ninety-six, are computer animation and special effects; in much of the rest of the movie, computers provided the backdrops. Four different studios participated in the computer graphics: Information International, MAGI, Digital Effects, and Robert Abel and Associates. Writer/director Steven Lisberger was suitably young—thirty-one—for such a computer-age film.

Although the Disney Studios expected to make over $400 million from this siliconic extravaganza, our source at *Variety* tells us that its North American rentals were $15 million and estimated total gross, $30 million. The arcade game TRON, made by Bally, grossed more. Which just goes to show that plot and characterization still have something to do with a movie's success.

Disney's other greatest technical success was the animated film *Snow White and the Seven Dwarfs*, released in 1937. That movie required over a million hand-drawn, hand-painted frames, three quarters of which were discarded. No wonder computers now do most of the legwork in animation.

Max V. Mathews, Bell Labs, and F. Richard Moore, University of California, have invented an electronic violin that they claim sounds as good as a Stradivarius, the most coveted instrument in the world. Using tiny microphones and integrated circuits to pick up the vibrations of the strings and then amplify and modify them so they sound as if they were played on an acoustic violin, the device sounds exactly like the real thing. Yet it is made of steel.

Stradivari, who told no one the secret of his beautiful sound before he died in 1737, is probably turning over in his grave. But a production model of the Mathews/Moore fiddle might cost as little as $1,000. A Stradivarius costs more than $250,000.

Mathews of course is often referred to as the Father of Computer Music. (You knew that; you just forgot.) He was the first to take computer binary voltages and turn them into sound (1957), he developed an editing program that allowed musicians to work with computers without requiring a Ph.D. in computer science, and he invented the building blocks of computer music, "unit generators," discrete subprograms that contain the code needed to make the computer produce various sounds.

Almost as good as X-ray specs. One of the by-products of a military grant for the study of computer graphics paid to Dave Evans and Ivan Sutherland of the University of Utah was a pair of 3-D glasses. In 1970 the two displayed a contraption that sat on a viewer's head and connected to a computer. Two items of the device were in the headpiece—a mechanical head-position sensor, and a pair of tiny CRT (TV) screens right in front of the eyes. Computer-generated images would be directed to the tiny screens. With proper presentation of the CRT images the wearer could be fooled into seeing himself inside a 3-D image. When the person's head moved, the image would change (as a result of the positioning sensor telling the computer that the viewer's perception was changing). The viewer, however, could *not* be fooled into thinking he or she looked cute wearing a headpiece attached to a position monitoring arm.

Music by computer, computer by music. Severo Ornstein and John Maxwell at Xerox developed a program called Mockingbird that allows a composer to sit at an electric piano and compose music, which then appears on the computer screen just like sheet music. As you write, the notes appear; if you want to change to a different key, the computer will rewrite the score. Then you play the program back through a synthesizer and see—er, hear—what it sounds like.

And now Yamaha has a variation on that same theme. The Yamaha system, available only in Japan, is, in reality, a piano control system. Sensors and solenoids are attached to a panel underneath the keyboard and determine from the pressure of the pianist's ivory tinklings just what note, complete with dynamics, is being played. (A special proprietary chip does all this instant figuring.)

Notes are displayed on a computer screen and can be printed out, both clefs represented. The notes can also be edited from the computer keyboard, then stored on floppy disk. Compositions can be played back from the disk—the sensors and solenoids activate the keys in reverse, like a player piano. The system works only on Yamaha upright pianos. Cost: the yen equivalent of $6,000, not counting $100 installation charge.

Computers and music are a natural together. Musicians, whose job it is to give sound to mathematical form, started playing with computers almost as soon as they were available in the 1950s. Most of us think of computer music as horrible, for one of two reasons: (1) Early analog computers replicated true instruments very poorly, or (2) some computer music was all bleeks, blorks, and burps on purpose. Proponents of random or "aleatory" composition, the most famous of whom is John Cage, were the first to latch onto computers—the best source of the day for random numbers, which were used compositionally to provide the highest degree of chance. (Mozart used dice.)

It was Morton Subotnick who brought us the first truly lovely computer composition, "Silver Apples of the Moon," in 1967, the result of an amazing instrument called the Electric Music Box, created by Donald Buchla. It utilized digital computer technology and could sound just about like any instrument—or other sound, for that matter.

We listen to a lot more computer music than we think. The Moogs, synthesizers, and electronified guitars are all around us, creating new music and influencing the rest. One band, The Human League, chose to play synthesizers because they had no musical training. Vangelis, who scored the movie *Chariots of Fire,* can't read music.

In fact, over the past ten years, the number of people in the United States who claim to play a musical instrument has grown from 31.5 million to 50 million—primarily as a result of synthesizers and electronic keyboards. Hope everybody is having fun. . . .

Put this *on a silicon chip, boys.* In 1906, Canadian Thaddeus Cahill demonstrated probably the most colossal automated musicmaking device the planet has yet seen—a two-hundred-ton contraption of rotating wheels that produced sound as a result of spinning in an electromagnetic field. He called it a "telharmonium." A decade earlier he had begun the whole association of music with electricity by demonstrating the "sounding stave," which could control timbre electrically. Shortly after, he tried to get a franchise to place wires in the streets of New York City for the distribution of this electrical sound. And where would Muzak or Manhattan Cable be if he'd succeeded?

A Wurlitzer prize to Marvin Lautzenheiser, president of a computer software firm and member of the American Organ Society, who, in 1975, hooked a fifty-eight-year-old one-thousand-pipe Wurlitzer to a machine that read tapes prepared on an IBM 370/158. With no human player, the organ could play a handful of countermelodies all at once. Lautzenheiser began his computerizing in 1966 but soon discovered a major problem: The Wurlitzer was too accurate when played by a computer. Notes played on the same beat, because they hit at exactly the same time, produced a ringing. A lot of Lautzenheiser's work consisted of building a certain level of sloppiness into his computer program.

Call 212-925-9645 in 1982 and you could have been in on the establishment of a new art form: telephone art. Artist Mitchell Creedman has scripted and taped conversations/dramas specifically tailored for the intimacy of the telephone medium. As computer types would say, it's point-to-point art.

Sure, it's music. In 1970, as part of a concert at the Guggenheim Museum in New York, Steve Smoller and the Sonic Arts Union presented a concert entitled "Conspiracy 8," in which a computer located at MIT in Cambridge, Massachusetts, formed one third of the orchestra. Smoller, at a terminal linked by telephone lines to the computer, would ask questions of the computer and then narrate the answer to another member of the Sonic Arts Group, who would then modulate sounds that would represent the computer's internal electrical state while it was in the process of answering the questions. These sounds were then piped to the audience over loudspeakers. Sound weird? Not as weird as the music. The other two instruments were a crosscut saw and an organ.

If you saw *Pirates of Penzance* on Broadway, you didn't see a string section in the orchestra pit. It was replaced by a Synclavier synthesizer.

The world's largest work of "conceptual art" requires a computer. It is "Four Corners Project," by David Barr of Northville, Michigan. In 1982 Barr conceived of inscribing a regular tetrahedron—a pyramid with four equilateral sides—inside the Earth. The four points of the tetrahedron would just pierce the Earth's surface. This was the conceptual part of the work. The art part required Barr to place four small pyramids at the precise points on the Earth where the big tetrahedron would poke out of the ground. Two problems necessitated using a computer to plot the points where the pyramids should go. First, most places where a tetrahedron would poke out would be water, since the Earth is only one third dry land. Second, the Earth isn't really a perfect sphere, so finding the *exact* points to place the pyramids was a complex problem in geometry. Barr and his computer did, however, and Barr journeyed to each of them: Greenland, on a mountain; a jungle in New Guinea; a farm in South Africa; and Easter Island.

Maybe this should be called "vacation" art.

One of the seminal computer-art exhibitions was entitled "Software, Information Technology: Its New Meaning for Art," sponsored by American Motors at the Jewish Museum in New York in 1970. One of the works at the exhibit was called "Seek," by Nicholas Negroponte of MIT. On a forty-square-foot platform, a robot arm manipulated and piled five hundred metal cubes into an artistic pattern programmed by a computer. Once the blocks were in place, forty gerbils were let loose, and as they scrambled about the pile, the robot arm would keep repositioning the blocks. If a block was simply nudged by a gerbil, the arm would put the block back in its original position. If it was substantially out of place, the computer would reconfigure and restack the cubes into a new art form.

"Seek" was thus the result of interactions among hardware, software, and gerbilware. The most astounding aspect of the work was the program that ordered the arm about; unfortunately, the arm was plagued with mechanical difficulties, and the gerbils had a habit of defecating on it. So did the critics.

"Rarely have two disciplines joined forces to seemingly bring out the worst in each other as have computers and art."—Nicholas Negroponte.

The first computer-written TV scripts. They were aired on CBS on October 26, 1960, on a show about computers called "The Thinking Machine."

Three Westerns—playlets, actually—written by an MIT computer were acted in pantomime.

The computer, the MIT TX-0, was a work of art in itself. Built in 1956 by MIT's Lincoln Labs, it took up nine thousand feet of floor space and was the first fully transistorized computer. It was built to test transistor logic, not screenwriter logic.

A program called SAGA II, written by Douglas Ross and Harrison Morse, had generated the plots and stage instructions. The computer program was smart enough to reduce a bad guy's chance of shooting a sheriff in a showdown if the bad guy had been drinking, and a swig from a bottle was more incapacitating than a sip from a glass. (The computer did slip up and have the sheriff put his gun into a robber's holster at one point.) It took two months to write SAGA II; it took the computer two minutes to produce the Westerns.

This was also probably the *last* time a computer wrote a screenplay—although it's not always possible to tell that from the quality of modern-day sitcoms.

If you're into the idea of computers writing scripts, Ralph Roberts, a member of the Science Fiction Writers of America and the Mystery Writers of America, has written a horror-story plot generator for personal computers. The program was published in *Popular Computing* in January 1983.

Essentially you pick from a menu of subplots and let the computer generate some randomness in how they go together. The program is modifiable so you can add your own particular twists.

Some sample subplots:

- A.03 A twenty-five-foot alligator steals the legal profession

- A.16 Huge mutant rats eat every third person

- B.15 Slimy creatures from the deep revile assorted national politicians

- C.13 Huge radioactive earthworm outfaces several megasalaried sports stars

Poems for sale. The Foundation for Software Engineering has a program that will write poems on an Osborne computer. For $2.95, the Tempe, Arizona, company will send you one (a poem, not the program).

Kudos to Digital Equipment Corporation for commissioning "Primavera in the Spring," a mural that adorns a wall in the Computer Museum in Marlboro, Massachusetts. Painted by Harold Cohen, the work was designed by computer—a DEC PDP-11/45 running a special program called Aaron, which Cohen devised at Stanford's Artificial Intelligence Lab in the late

1970s. Linked to the computer by a wire is a small device—Cohen calls it a turtle—that does the actual drawing onto large sheets of paper. Cohen fills in the color. Aaron consists of three hundred subroutines that handle various aspects of producing the art—turtle locomotion, shape drawing, line and curve tracing, planning, and mapping.

Cohen doesn't tell Aaron what to draw. Instead the software chooses subroutine combinations at random, but because the subroutines are hierarchical and precise, the resultant drawings do not appear to be random scribblings. One would, in fact, swear they were done by a human; one would swear there was an inner meaning to them.

The real inner meaning may be this: Cohen claims that Aaron can produce enough pretty good stuff in an evening to be the equivalent of a one-man show that took two years to prepare. He has taken Aaron on the road to numerous museum shows, offering visitors the chance to purchase originals—which they can help specify for the computer—for $5.00.

The first to design sculptures with computers. He was Robert Mallary at the University of Massachusetts in 1968. Mallary badgered Amherst student Robert Weiss into writing a computer program to run on an IBM 1130 computer that allowed the computer to pick the shapes to be carved. (Most computer sculptors of the day didn't allow the computer that much artistic license.) The program, called Tran2, read input coordinates (X, Y, Z) for a work from punched cards. Once the beginning coordinates were in the system, they could be changed by the computer mathematically. Once Tran2 was fully sated by the muse, it would print out on a plotter representations of the piece of art it had designed. It could print plots as seen from a variety of angles.

Most importantly, it could print contour slices. Mallary would then photograph the contour and project it onto the medium and construct the piece according to the projection.

Mallary, you will remember, set the art world on its ear at the New York World's Fair in 1964 with his innovative piece, "Cliff-hangers," which was made of plasticized tuxedos.

Take John Swartzwelder. Please. Using a Radio Shack TRS-80, he has written a program to write one-liners. The computer, using random numbers generated inside its funny circuits, has been able to come up with fake headlines, punch lines, and idiotic titles. One headline: SCIENTISTS DISCOVER NEW MOON ORBITING KATE SMITH. Another: STICK FIGURE LEAPS TO DEATH FROM TOP OF STICK. So far the Swartzwelder program has yet to make it to *The Johnny Carson Show.* Said the TRS-80, "I don't get no respect. No respect at all."

Eight Steps to Computer Imaging

1. Obtain a computerized design (CAD) system. It uses a computer to manipulate numbers that will eventually be represented by dots of colors on a screen. These dots are called "pixels," for picture elements, and several hundred pixels per square inch will provide medium resolution (we don't *see* individual dots, but their aggregate). The values of the numbers relate to the color and intensity of any one pixel. Obviously you get all the gizmos and attachments, such as display screen, paper plotters, plug, optional *Star Wars* cassette, etc., that you need to make your CAD system operational.

2. Use your special computer program (it may come with the machine) to call up a library of basic geometric shapes, which you view on your screen. These may produce "wire-frame" drawings as a start. Sooner or later you'll use the computer to flesh them out. Pick some. Combine these geometric shapes into an approximation of the solid you want to depict. (Dr. James Blinn, whose computer simulations of the Voyager spacecraft—the one that went by Saturn, remember?— used 750 polygons to craft the craft.) You may invoke these shapes by entering commands on a keyboard or using a special pen (an important doohickey) to trace them on the machine.

3. Let the computer sand the corners. It can do this mathematically. Let it fill in the wire-frame outlines to make a solid. You need software to do this. See if it came in the carton.

4. If you want, you may now rotate, shrink, or expand your image. The computer can do this automatically by changing the numerical values of all those cute little pixels. Play around, get the feel. Look behind it, see what's there.

5. Invoke the shading routines (this takes heavy-duty software), especially if you're going to go in for metallics or transparencies. You have to figure out where the light is coming from, how far away the viewer is to be, and how intense the light should be. A lot of pixel values get added and subtracted in this particular exercise.

6. Pull in your surface texture software subroutines—as long as you're going to get fancy. If things look at all screwy at this point, call in special software for a final smooth-out.

7. Do you want movement? Tell the computer where the starting and ending points are and how much time this movement should take. Push the button.

8. Film it. You'll want twenty-four frames per second. Each frame can take up to thirty minutes to calculate new pixel values. Let's see. Say

we want a half-hour film. That's eighteen hundred seconds times twenty-four frames, each taking thirty minutes of computer time . . . yipes!

Charles Babbage, the grandfather of the modern computer and avowed enemy of street musicians and organ grinders (too noisy), once proposed a steam-driven musical calculator.

Caruso lives! Charles Dodge, at Brooklyn College, has used electronics to create a piece for piano to be played along with a doctored recording of Enrico Caruso. The song is "Vesti la giubba," which Caruso recorded by singing into an acoustic horn connected to a stylus. Scientists have since used digital recording and storage techniques to remove the distortion of Caruso's voice inherent in the early Gramophone recording. Dodge has taken this "pure" Caruso and altered it and manipulated it at will to produce his composition.

Why did Hee Haw *outlast* Laugh-In? Both were TV shows of the late 1960s and early 1970s, both were "segmented" shows spliced together from separate shots. Well, one was computerized, one was not. Whereas *Laugh-In* used six film editors to pick and sequence shots filmed earlier, *Hee Haw* used one editor and a computer. Shots of a specific nature—barbershop or front-porch scenes—would be shot a hundred to two hundred at a time, then classified under sixty different categories—haystack jokes, grocery-store jokes, etc. In effect, the computer kept an inventory control of thousands of cornball bits. Putting together a show meant calling up certain shots from the computerized inventory, then splicing them together.

Just think. *Hee Haw* is off the air (except in reruns, a revenue stream *Laugh-In* doesn't have), but somewhere lives a computer and that inventory. What trouble would it be to restructure *new* shows using different sequences of old shots? Who'd remember? Recombinant *Hee Haw*. You could name the new show *Yuk Yuk*. Or maybe just plain *Yuk*.

Where giant ants and humans meet. Ever wonder how they actually got King Kong on the same filmstrip as Fay Wray? How they maneuvered the *Them* ants against an L.A. backdrop? The Eggplant against the Chicago skyline?

It's called compositing, and in the old days it meant taking successful pictures of stop-motion dolls (yes, folks, Kong was not the giant ape he pretended to be) and superimposing these frames on the frames used to film the crowd, Fay, or the digestible parts of Chicago. The latter scenes would be filmed against a blue background, the monster filmed in his particular milieu. A matte—or high-contrast black and clear filmstrip—is prepared for each. The background matte will be run with an unexposed film through a filming mechanism—a process called "bipacking"—and the resultant film will show only foreground stuff. (The blue background drops out.) The second matte will be bipacked with the unexposed film during the shooting of the monster sequence. This prevents double exposing the background.

It sounds complicated, but it's really more laborious than anything. A movie may have scores of shots that must be composited. This can represent a certain amount of drudgery.

And who is the avowed foe of drudgery? The computer.

Instead of messing with mattes, the computer (more specifically, the digital film compositor) scans each frame in a scene to be composited and reduces it to pixel number values. (This scanning is not much different from the methods used in an office telecopier.)

To drop out a blue background, the computer need only eliminate any blue pixel values and replace them with the pixel value from the new scene. Composited frames can be viewed on a computer display screen, edited by humans if necessary, and then projected onto film.

Using the new technology, artists and filmmakers can do things that no amount of fussing with mattes would allow. TV antennas and telephone poles (even more unsightly in a 1700s swashbuckler than in real life today) can be removed from frames by erasing with special pens connected to the computer, and other frames can be used to fill in a color. One experimenter, Ralph Weiner of BGA Systems, has been able to color in black and white war footage.

Phenomenal, of course, the idea of King Kong and Godzilla battling it out as warring pixel values. . . .

A NAKED HISTORY OF THE COMPUTER AND THE ARTS

DATE	COMMENTS
1777	Mozart composes "Muzikalische Wuerfelspiel" (K.294d) by using dice to help pick a scale. Most quoted use of random numbers in generating music.
1877	Edison and Berliner invent the phonograph.
1897	Thaddeus Cahill invents electric "sounding stave," first use of electricity to alter timbre.
1906	Thaddeus Cahill demonstrates the two-hundred-ton Telharmonium. Applies to pipe music through wires in the street to New York residents. Plan too kooky.

1908   Arnold Schoenberg develops music theory that diverges from traditional diatonic harmonies. Screech, honk, braat permissible. Key theoretical advance important for computer music fifty years later.

1913   "Noise Music" is invented by Luigi Rossolo, an Italian futurist. Dismissed by critics and listeners as "just so much noise."

1915   Oscillator is invented by Lee DeForest, American. Allows changes in voltages to cause changes in sounds.

1922   Frederick Keisler uses film instead of a backdrop for a Berlin rendition of Karel Capek's play R.U.R.

1929   The Hammond electric organ is invented. Causes stock market crash.

1932   First computer to reproduce music ("Daisy") at Bell Labs.

1948   Pierre Schaefer and Pierre Henry "emancipate" music electronically, demonstrating first totally artificial sounds.

1951   Harry Olsen and Herbert Belar invent a device to generate dual streams of random numbers. Used to produce sound some called music.

        First computer-animated movies made at MIT by taking pictures, frame by frame, of a computer display. The term "flicker" is still used today to describe one attribute of computer displays.

1954   Olsen and Belar's works culminate in RCA 1 synthesizer.

1957   Harry Mathews is first to turn binary code into sound. Computers begin to sing.

        "Illiac Suite for String Quartet" composed by Lejaren Hiller and Leonard Isaacson at the University of Illinois. Random numbers generated, associated with notes, modified by computer. Mozart turns over in his grave.

1960   "The Thinking Machine" airs on CBS. Computer-written screenplay comes up with Westerns. Prelude to the sitcom.

        Jean Tinguely unveils "Homage to New York" at a show at the Museum of Modern Art. It's a room-sized contraption designed to move, whir, and destroy itself.

1961   Iannis Xenakis applies mathematical formula (Markov chains, Poisson distributions, etc.) to creation of music, debuted in piece "ST/10-1, 080262." Finds "Found Music."

A Naked History of the Computer and the Arts

Date	Comments
1966	Artist-in-residence program, sponsored by the Museum of Modern Art, Los Angeles County, begins placing artists in corporations. Most famous alumnus: Andy Warhol, artist at Cowles Communications.
1967	"Silver Apples of the Moon" created by Morton Subotnick on an electric music box invented by Dan Buckla.
	Billy Kluver, engineer, and Robert Rauchenberg, artist, form EAT (Experiences in Art and Technology). Build light-show system for Pepsi-Cola's exhibit at World's Fair in Osaka. Exhibit features largest spherical mirror ever built.
1968	HAL debuts in *2001: A Space Odyssey*. First starring role of consequence by a computer.
	Institute of Contemporary Art, London, hosts first major assemblage of computer art, poetry, music, choreography, painting, drawings, and architecture. Title: "Cybernetic Serendipity."
	Edward Kienholz's "Friendly Grey Computer" sculpture debuts at Museum of Modern Art in New York. Features a computer in a rocking chair. Says Kienholz: "Computers sometimes get fatigued and have nervous breakdowns."
1969	Nam June Paik unveils "TV Bra." Charlotte Moorman plays cello with halter of TV monitors.
1970	EAT (see 1967) is booted out as administrator of Pepsi's pavilion in Osaka.
	The "Software" art show at the Jewish Museum in New York is the first art exhibit with *only* computers and automata in it. Nicholas Negroponte lets forty gerbils loose in his action sculpture. Gerbils make doodoo. Critics say doodoo.
1971	Myron W. Kreuger explores the insides of art with exhibit called "Psychic Space," where viewers enter a room and interact with sounds and visual displays. Funded by government grant. Predicts future physical interaction with electronics, including the "hugaphone."
1974	First Annual International Computer Film Festival held at Evergreen College, Olympia, Washington. A Hewlett-Packard 1000 computer jumps into the pool without software on.

1975	A DEC PDP-11 stars in *Three Days of the Condor* alongside Robert Redford. First case of a computer swooning.
1977	Apple Computer incorporated. First computer to be colored beige.
1982	Walt Disney Studios' *TRON* breaks new computerized graphics ground. Also computer-related plots. Box-office bomb.
1983	*The Naked Computer* is published.

Max Mathews, Bell Labs, once used a computer to blend the songs "When Johnny Comes Marching Home Again" and "The British Grenadiers." One was in the key of F major, the other in E minor; one in 2/4 time, the other in 6/8. The song started out as "Johnny," then evolved into "Grenadiers," then evolved back into "Johnny."

Mathews referred to the piece as "a nauseating musical experience but one not without interest."

FROM THE CACHE:
The Golden Rectangle

That computers are natural helpmeets to the arts is not so strange. Musicians wield applied mathematics when they alter string lengths or vibrating columns of air to modulate sounds (though few would realize they are actually dealing in logarithms when they change octaves or make sounds louder and softer). A canon is, at root, a recursive function. Architects rely on mathematics to provide structural soundness to their designs and the practicality of their constructs (the pieces have to fit together). The painter's palette mimics the rainbow, a godly combine that can be reduced to the equations and formula of the sine waves that make up the discrete frequencies of the electromagnetic spectrum.

It has long been held that beauty is in the eye of the beholder—different people interpret the sum of the analog wave forms art throws off differently.

But is there an absolute beauty? A beauty that is discovered, not created? Intrinsic beauty? A beauty that displays the quality of a tree that *does* make sound in the forest, even if no one's there to hear it?

The ancients thought so.

Beauty, they thought, was a matter of ratio. And the most beautiful of ratios was that in which the two parts were in the same ratio as one part and the whole. It's somewhere between 1/3 and 1/2, and can be represented by the perhaps not-so-beautiful formula $\frac{(\sqrt{5}-1)}{2}$.

The most prominent embodiment of the ratio is in the "golden rectangle" cited by Pythagoras—a Greek of antiquity who made his fame and fortune on theories about triangles, not rectangles—which has sides in the golden ratio. But other geometric shapes can avail themselves of the ratio as well.

Later fans of the golden rectangle include the nameless builders of the Parthenon, who used the ratio in building the temple; Leonardo da Vinci, who used it in his paintings; Johannes Kepler, who felt it was somehow connected to the "music of the spheres" embodied in the movement of the planets; Béla Bartók, who divided his musical scores into segments based on the ratio; and the U.S. military establishment—a pentagon's diagonals form the ratio with themselves.

But nature also favors the golden rectangle. A spiral made by connecting the corners of golden rectangles within golden rectangles forms the same curve generated by a chambered nautilus. Pine cones and the insides of sunflowers also exhibit the ratio.

The direct connection to naked computers is tenuous. So tenuous as to elude these authors. But the indirect connection is not. The machinations of mathematical processes upon numbers find analogue in art. And the goal of art is to capture beauty. That the computer is the ultimate number maker is a given. It follows, then, that artists—some, anyway—will always use it as a tool in their creative process. In some ways it may be a "golden" one.

CHAPTER 11

DARTH VADER:

Military Computers

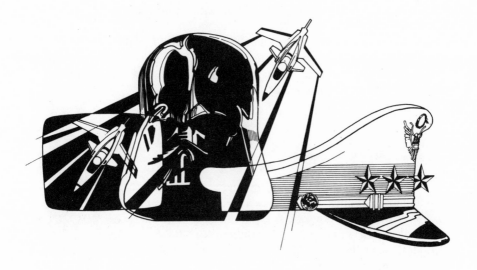

Counting counting they wer all the time. They had iron then and big fire they had towns of parpety. They had machines et numbers up. They fed them numbers and they fractiont out the Power of things. They had the Nos. of the rain bow and the Power of the air all workit out with counting which is how they got boats in the air and picters on the wind. Counting clevverness is what it wer.

—a post-Holocaust shaman in *Riddley Walker* by Russell Hoban

Trace back any computer family tree far enough and you'll find an uncle in the Army; most of the industry's seed money came out of Pentagon granaries. Banks can run on quill pens and ledger books; not so atom-bomb factories.

The first, biggest, and best computers have always been produced

at the behest of brass and braid. Some of the biggest boondoggles, too. One computer for air defense weighed over three hundred tons and, transported in eighteen vans, took three days to unload. The most costly computer ever built was funded by the Navy—and never really worked right. Millions were spent on wiring battlefields in Viet Nam—for naught. In fact, our Naked Estimate says that over $100 million in computer hardware was left in Southeast Asia in 1975. The first job for the first computer was cranking out calculations for the Manhattan Project.

And the generals who coined the term "smart weapons" are now funding "brilliant" ones.

Salute the computers in khaki and gold braid. Salute the glorious and grisly military mind, salute Catch-22 and all the supply officers who, like author Gantz, transposed digits on a stock order and got a ton of toilet paper instead of ten cases of tuna.

The WorldWide Military Command and Control System (WWMCCS, pronounced "Wimex") is the master system of computers and communications by which the Strategic Air Command gets its directives. WWMCCS has cost taxpayers more than $200 million over the years to keep us apprised of hostile activities, yet in 1980 a $1,000 device that connects computers to phone lines caused a bogus full-scale red alert. (Actually, there have been hundreds of bogus alerts caused by hardware and software screw-ups in the WWMCCS system.)

The first ship sunk by a "smart" weapon. Israel's *Elath* was downed by an unmanned, computerized radar-based homing missile in 1967. The *Elath*, launched as the British ship H.M.S. *Zealous* in 1944 and sold to the Israelis in 1956, weighed twenty-five hundred tons and carried two hundred sailors; the Soviet-built Styx missile that sunk it weighed a ton and was only twenty feet long. The *Elath* cost thousands of times the Styx missile.

How smart could they be? During the Okinawa campaign, Japan's *kamikaze* airplanes—"smart" bombs if there ever were ones—either missed their target or were shot down 93 percent of the time.

Homage to Atari. Today's guided missile systems bear remarkable resemblance to the things in arcades. In one model of the air-to-surface Maverick missile, a TV camera mounted in the nose of the missile sends a picture of the target to a TV screen mounted in the cockpit. The pilot picks his prey, gets it in the computer-generated cross hairs, and pushes a button to "lock" the missile onto it. While the missile is zapping the hapless target, the pilot can be picking out new ones. The system also can use infrared or laser light to track a target.

A TOW (tube-launched, optically tracked, wire-guided) antitank missile, which trails a wire after launching and receives tracking signals throughout its flight, costs $7,000. Its primary target is the tank. In one war game in 1972, helicopters launching TOW missiles could knock out an average of eighteen tanks before being knocked out themselves. Almost three hundred thousand TOW missiles have been bought, by thirty-three countries. Yet the military keeps buying tanks—with almost ten thousand on order over the next few years. An M-1 tank costs $2.7 million.

Drawing by Rich Tennant

Battleground or weapons lab? The Soviet smart missile called Swagger had its debut in Viet Nam on April 23, 1972. The U.S. TOW missile saw first combat the very next day.

The first use of television was for experiments in guiding missiles. Commercial use came later.

The first U.S. guided missile. It was the Weary Willie, used in the Kastor campaign starting in 1944. It was a B-17 bomber loaded with twenty tons of explosives and piloted by biped computers (humans) who bailed out twenty miles from the target.

During World War II, both the Germans and the Allies had plans for sophisticated automatic flying bombs. The German V-2's, guided by relay-operated computers developed (unwittingly) by Conrad Zuse, are legendary. Yet B. F. Skinner, a behavioral psychologist, came up with perhaps the most unusual guided missiles. He proposed bombs with a lens mounted in the nose, which reflected the image in front of them as they hurtled through the sky. A pigeon, trained to peck at an image on a screen, would be ensconced inside the bomb to peck away at the target, thus orienting the bomb toward its destination. "Project Pigeon," as Skinner called the scheme, was politely refused by the military.

Why spend the money on "smart" bombs? During World War II over five billion pounds of explosives were dropped by Allied aircraft. Only 20 percent came within a thousand feet of target. The chance that a bomb would hit a target smaller than a factory was about 1 percent. (This was still better than bullets: A hundred thousand bullets were fired for every soldier hit.) There were some reverse economics. The British government calculated that for every $1.00 the Germans spent on V-1 and V-2 rockets, they spent $4.00 to defend against them.

Computer-controlled, laser-guided bombs have a 90 percent chance of hitting target. Conserve TNT; use a computer.

Dr. Strangelove should see us now. The Navy uses the Navstar satellite system—six satellites today, eighteen planned by the year 2000—to track military maneuvers from outer space (Navstar stands for Navigation Satellite Timing and Ranging). Primarily navigational aids, the satellites communicate with each other and with ground stations to keep a lock on their positions. Navstar receivers compare Navstar-transmitted computer signals to matching signals generated in the receiver at the same time. The difference in time multiplied by the speed of light determines the distance to the satellite. From that point on, triangulation is used. With a timing accuracy of one second in three hundred thousand years, Navstar can pinpoint targets on the ground to within ten meters.

Proposed Navstar uses: missile tracking, minesweeping, ambulance, police car and taxi dispatching, iceberg tracking, and (true story) looking for dinosaurs reported to be harassing Pygmy fishermen in Zaire.

And now the silent bomb. Here's a weapon that doesn't kill people, destroy buildings, or even go boom. It's the EMP—the electromagnetic pulse bomb. (A properly rigged nuke could qualify.) Exploded in air, the EMP would blanket the target area—which could be the size of the United States—with gamma rays, which trigger waves of electromagnetic pulses. These pulses could disrupt the normal functioning of the nation's computers, communications systems, TVs, radios, military control systems, and nuclear plant control systems. Even if military systems can be shielded against EMP, the cost to shield all commercial systems—the phone system, electronic banking network, or nuclear power station control systems— would be prohibitive.

Since an EMP bomb has never been detonated, Pentagon planners aren't sure exactly how much damage one would do. But scientists have calculated that a small number of them detonated in the atmosphere would have the same effect on the national power grid as a large lightning bolt hitting every power line in the country. It was two medium-size lightning bolts, to refresh your memory, that caused the 1977 New York City blackout.

Waiting for the big one? Be prepared. Southwest Technical Software Corporation markets a program for Apple computers that will help you design your fallout shelter. The system first determines the level of radiation and thermal blast you can expect, based on location, then tells you how thick to build your shelter walls. Or if one would even do you any good. A joke? The program was written by Bob Karcher, by night a free-lance programmer, by day a designer of nuclear protection systems for Rockwell International.

It's a movie and its name is HUD. But it doesn't star Paul Newman. "Head-Up-Display," or HUD, is the electronic display system featured in both the F-15 and F-16 U.S. fighter planes. Projected onto a sheet of glass between the pilot and the windshield, in green and orange phosphorescence, are plots of up to four enemy aircraft, alarms connected to electronic ears that detect enemy radar signals, and a computer-generated "tracerline," or cross hairs, used to aim machine cannons and missiles at enemy planes.

This, of course, is dark ages technology. The glass of the conventional HUD is mirror enough to reflect the images from a cockpit CRT and transparent enough so the pilot can see out the window. But it's not perfect—the glass blocks some vision, and the pilot must crane his neck to see the whole display.

A holographic projection would work better. With one of these—soon to go in about five hundred F-16 Air Force fighters—the pilot would see the CRT image outside the aircraft seemingly suspended in space.

Commercial aircraft soon will have such displays for providing pilots flight data. Cargo transport companies that lose $150,000 every time a plane is rerouted because pilots can't land for lack of visibility will be glad to shell out $220,000 for commercial HUD displays. HUDs mean a plane can land when visibility is about half what planes can land at now. Holograms are already used to provide the scenery and landscape in fake windows in flight simulators.

Holograms, you will recall, are those eerie images you saw when you went through the Haunted Mansion at Walt Disney World. Why wouldn't they work in the haunted mansions of modern warfare?

First electronic dogfight. The 1982 Israeli/Lebanon war. Score: Israel, ninety-two Russian-made MiGs shot down; Lebanon, two Israeli planes zapped. The key was Israeli use of the U.S. E-2C Hawkeye surveillance plane; variable-sweep F-14 and F-15 ($30 million) fighter planes; specially revamped Sidewinder missiles, which home in on enemy radar pulses; and use of plastic model airplanes beaming radar signals that triggered answering signals from Lebanese ground installations, which gave away the proper frequencies for Israeli jet electronic jamming devices to use.

In fact, the conflict was the first solid support that high-tech weapons enthusiasts found for robot airplanes. Today's drones, or RPVs (remotely piloted vehicles), anchor a $1 billion business. They are slow-flying—the Scout and Mastiff drones made by the Israelis fly at only a hundred miles an hour—but can be programmed to fly in erratic, preset patterns, or piloted by a pilot watching a TV screen at a distant computer. Once the drone finds a suitable target, its coordinates are relayed by the computer to other weapons systems. In some cases, the drones shine a laser light on the target on which missiles can home in. Being small and specially built—exhaust pipes point upward, skins are made of plastic—RPVs are hard to hit.

Only one drone is made by an American company, Lockheed; 50 percent of the market belongs to Canada's Canadair.

First target for a terrain-tracking computer-based guidance system. The Burlington, Vermont, airport. The systems were tested in the mid-1970s by using them in piloted fighter planes flying as simulated Cruise missiles.

The beginning of electronic warfare. Jamming, detection, and masking began in World War II, when U.S. pilots dropped aluminum foil out of their planes to foul up German radar. In 1982 the United States spent $3.4 billion on electronic warfare research and development. This is equivalent to what American teenagers spent that year on video games (equivalent, perhaps, in more ways than just dollars).

The total electronic content of all defense hardware costs over $25 billion a year.

During World War II, ballistics for bullets, cannonballs, and rockets were in need of new study. By then cannonballs were being fired beyond the line of sight, and their spinning and the rotation of the earth underneath them had to be taken into account. The Germans once launched a shell from "Big Bertha," a nine-inch gun, on Paris. It went twice as far as calculated. No wonder both the German and U.S. efforts to build computers were prompted by military desires to improve ballistics accuracy.

The first digital computer, ENIAC, was paid for by the Army's Ordnance Department, which desperately needed new ballistics tables. (The tables told gunners how to aim, given a shell of a certain weight and shape, and given spin, wind, angle, and distance to target.) ENIAC *would have* calculated ballistics tables as its first task except that it was commandeered for calculations associated with nuclear bomb theories being developed at Los Alamos in 1945.

SADARM or sadistic? Consider a system tested in 1979 called Sense-And-Destroy ARMor. The munition starts out as an eight-inch howitzer shell launched from the rear of a battlefield. When it gets over the action, out of it pops a canister on a parachute. As the canister drifts toward the ground, it spins and scans the terrain electronically. Once it identifies a tank, which it is smart enough to do, a warhead inside explodes to form a "kinetic energy" uranium slug traveling at incredible speed that follows the canister sensor's line of sight to blast the tank, wiping everything and every-body out.

It was the ability to understand the inner workings of an exploding war-head via simulation on large computers that permitted scientists to invent this "self-forging" slug.

It ain't the same as the old days, Sarge. The United States' new M-1 tank, weighing sixty tons and costing $2.7 million, uses computer control and laser beams to achieve pinpoint accuracy for its 105mm cannon at up to one and a quarter miles in fog or darkness. The tank has extra-strength armor that is impervious to most bazookas and can resist most individually launched missiles—including "kinetic energy" projectiles that punch through normal tank armor and ricochet inside. But, high tech as it is, the M-1 has drawbacks: It gets only two miles to the gallon, it breaks down every forty-eight miles, and it requires the operator to be in a supine position that makes it easy to fall asleep.

Electronic battlefield wizardry. The Army has experimented with the following at its Combat Development Command at the Hunter Liggett Mil-itary Reservation, seventy miles south of Monterey, California:

- Helmets with antennas that automatically send signals to a central computer when a soldier fires a shot.
- Rifles that fire laser beams instead of bullets. (For practice only. When hit by a laser, sensors strapped to the body go off, indicating a hit.)
- Range-finding devices connected to computers to tell where every man, vehicle, and aircraft is.
- Sensors in aerial drones to tell how close near misses come.

The Combat Development Command spends over $10 million a year testing this stuff out. The Army War College looks to the future and foresees the day in the year 2000 when hand-held medical diagnostic units can diagnose illnesses and prescribe treatments (like Bones's tricoder in *Star Trek*); suitcase-size teleconferencing and computer systems for setting up portable war-rooms; pocket-size computers that receive signals from satellites and convert them into maps or pictures; matchbox teleconferencing units for soldiers in the field (they could call it the Sony Watchman!).

The world's largest computer. It weighed three hundred tons and took up twenty thousand feet of floor space. Another twenty thousand square feet were devoted to consoles, peripherals, and communications. When the system was delivered at McGuire Air Force Base it took three days just to unload the computer gear (eighteen vans). Another thirty-five moving vans contained display screens and spare parts.

This was the IBM AN/FSQ-7, a direct descendant of MIT's WHIRLWIND Computer and heart of the Air Force's semi-automatic ground environment (SAGE) system for air defense against attacking bombers. It cost $30 million—in 1958, when SAGE went operational—and the Air Force bought fifty-six of them.

SAGE was big business. MIT's Lincoln Labs was formed to design it, System Development Corporation was founded to write the software for it, and dozens of subcontractors took part in putting it together. Common estimates are that the nationwide system cost $8 billion, including communications, radar equipment, computers, and training. The mathematical instructions that made it run filled three million punched cards.

It worked. WHIRLWIND, its progenitor, could perform 110 scientific computations a second; SAGE could perform 36,000. WHIRLWIND had 4,500 vacuum tubes and 14,800 diodes; SAGE had 170,000 diodes and 56,000 vacuum tubes. SAGE contained enough signal wire in one installation to reach from Boston to L.A.

The irony was that just as SAGE was being completed, the Soviet Union launched Sputnik, making the idea of ground-based bomber defense obsolete. From then on, satellites would rule. But SAGE nevertheless set standards for the computing industry that lasted for years. SAGE was the first system to use interactive graphic displays, the first to provide dual computers for failureproof operation, the first to operate in "real time," the first to use data transmission to and from remote sites, and the first to use computer-based system development and testing.

It was also the longest-operating computer, not decommissioned until 1983. And no Soviet bombers attacked us while SAGE was on duty.

It's called Janus. Put it in an arcade and you'd make millions.

Running on powerful computers at the Lawrence Livermore Computer Simulation Laboratory, Janus is the ultimate video game. Using mapping detail supplied by the Defense Mapping Agency that can display any four-mile-by-four-mile square on earth, including Moscow, New York, the Falklands, or the Tonkin Gulf, Janus provides a big-screen view of modern warfare. Players—Army officers at the Army's War College—sit at $100,000 combat stations and push buttons and maneuver "pucks" across electronic grids to order their electronic forces about. In the arsenal: tanks, jets, helicopters, artillery, chemicals, and tactical nukes.

Janus' graphics would rival Imagic. Bombs flash, bullets sweep across the board precisely timed to include bullet speed and reloading time, red dots flicker to represent flames. Wind speeds and humidity are included in the battlefield simulation. The computer also simulates the destructive results of the munitions. It takes twenty seconds to calculate the carnage of a ten-kiloton nuclear blast.

You'll be glad to hear this: During the first trials of Janus, officers who got outfoxed by the enemy resorted to nuclear weapons more than the Army thought they would. In some cases they chose bombs so powerful that both the enemy and their own armies were wiped out. (Well, better to be wiped out in a computer simulation than in real life.)

The first computer-simulated war game. It was conducted in 1952 by the Rand Corporation, which had built a mock-up of the Tacoma radar station in the back of the Santa Monica Billiard Room. To simulate radar tracks on scopes, 1's and 8's were printed on continuous-form paper every thirty seconds. It took a million calculations to come up with the proper 1's and 8's for a two-hour session, which took about twenty-five hours on IBM punched card tabulators, even with a library of past exercises stored on cards.

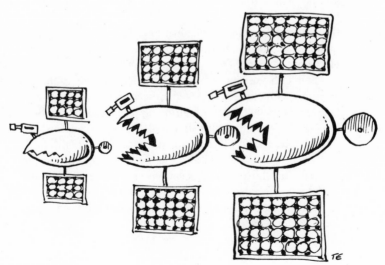

Drawing by Tim Eagan

KILLER SATELLITES:
A Primer

You know, of course, that they are out there. Flying about the void of space, waiting, waiting. Bellies full of death rays, particle beams, laser cannons, military computers, radar traps, and stored programs to tell them what to do on doomsday. These are the killer satellites. The offspring of Sputnik, launched October 4, 1957, by the Soviets, today's orbiting artifacts resemble the 184-pound Sputnik about as much as Einstein's brain resembled that of Australopithecus. More than twelve hundred military satellites have been launched since Sputnik, twice as many rising from the steppes of the Soviet Union than from the Cape Canaveral launch pads of the United States. (In 1981 the Soviets set a world record by launching fifteen satellites in one month.) Who knows how many other unknown electronic gizmos orbit our tiny planet?

Lest Armageddon descend on us from on high uncomprehended, *The Naked Computer* herewith presents a state-of-the-star-wars white paper. As you hunker in your bunker eating stale Triscuits and drinking rusting cans of Dr Pepper, consider how much better you'll feel knowing that you knew the difference between a satellite "ferret" and a "FOBS," and which one it was that did you in.

They all, by the way, have computers in them; they all require computers for launch. They are children of the computer, the out-of-body *Gestalt* of the computer waiting to return at the push of a button. Classifications:

1. **Hunter-killer** satellites. These are Russian Cosmos satellites that, after launch and a few orbits, cozy up to another satellite and then blow up, taking the target with them. More voyeuristic versions of the hunter-killer birds are known to exist—these simply fly by other satellites to take pictures and record electronic emission, like an electronic Peeping Tom.

   The U.S. version of a hunter-killer satellite is the Miniature Homing Vehicle (MHV), a paint-can-size spacecraft with rocket boosters launched from a high-flying jet. Whereas the Soviet killer bird sprays its victim with shrapnel, the American version smashes into it. (Remember, Americans invented the demolition derby.)

   "Space mines" would also qualify as hunter-killers. These simply wait in orbit until radioed what and where to blow up.

   The Soviets have been testing Cosmos hunter-killer satellites since October 20, 1968, when Cosmos 249 moseyed over to orbiting Cosmos 248 and blew up; the United States has had an MHV designed for five years but has yet to test one. The United States is reportedly working on a satellite protection system that would be able to squirt liquid metal at approaching hunter-killer spacecraft.

On impact the metal would harden, entombing the would-be attacker.

2. **Spy** satellites. These are the reconnaissance craft that take pictures and listen for electronic signals. For years, at least since 1971, the United States' premier entry in this class was the twelve-ton Big Bird made by Lockheed. It takes detailed pictures from special cameras and then jettisons the film back to earth in tiny spacecraft that are recovered by airplanes dragging nets behind them. The pictures are allegedly able to distinguish individual faces from hundreds of miles up. Pictures also can be taken by moonlight.

Eclipsing Big Bird in sensitivity is the KH-11 spy satellite, launched in 1976, with its onboard computers that convert pictures directly to digital electronic signals (like those sent back by the Voyager missions to Mars, Jupiter, and Saturn). These signals are touched up on the ground through computer enhancement and provide intelligence much faster than film from Big Bird. During the Iranian hostage crisis, KH-11 pictures could distinguish among mullahs by the bushiness of their beards.

3. **Ferret** satellites, also called "Rhyolite" satellites. These are satellites that listen electronically to enemy (or friendly) radar and radio emissions. Some are in orbit high up for comprehensive surveillance, others swoop in fairly low to get closer to interesting targets. A good ferret operation will include some enticement to provoke electronic activity—which then can be analyzed. The ferrets supply us with most of the detail on Soviet missile-launching activities. The ferrets allowed the British to intercept radioed commands from Buenos Aires to the Falklands.

There are ways to fool the ferrets. In the 1970s, to determine if certain Soviet satellites were of the ferret or photoreconnaissance type, the United States had an aircraft carrier task force steam across the Atlantic observing radar and radio silence. Not suspecting the ploy, the Soviets assumed their satellites were defunct and launched new ones. The Navy had its answer.

There are rumors that superferrets are now under development that will be able to detect radio crackles little louder than those sent off when a cigarette lighter sparks.

4. **Navigational** satellites. Navstar types. These will be used not only to track ground-based craft but also to relay signals to Cruise missile computers for guidance and targeting and to relay signals to other satellites—say, hunter-killers.

5. **Ocean surveillance** satellites. These specialize in scanning the ocean for radio or infrared signals to keep track of ships and sub-

marines. The Navy is experimenting with a satellite system that will be able to pick up radar from surface ships and, by matching the radar "signature" with a computer file of radar signatures of all the world's warships, identify ships to their call letters.

The first useful deployment of the Navy's system was in the late 1970s, when the data picked up by the satellites were used to crack down on marijuana smugglers. Over a million pounds were confiscated.

6. **Communications** satellites. These, for the most part, reside in orbits 22,235 miles above the equator, which, by a quirk of nature, means they appear stationary to us on earth. Already over 75 percent of all military long-haul communications go by satellite. Under development now by the Pentagon is the Laser Satellite Communications (LASERSATCOM) system, which will link all the military's satellites, ground stations, ships, and troops with laser signals. A real dreamboat of a communications system.

Less fancy but sooner to see operation will be the $100 million Tracking and Data Relay and Switching System satellite launched by Western Union for the Navy—the one almost lost after shuttle launch in 1983. This will allow current satellites to talk to one another, not just ground stations.

It is in communications satellites that the United States may be most vulnerable—knock them out and you can't tell all your smart missiles and bombs where to head for. The government intends to spend $20 billion over the next five years building a network of Milstar satellites that can withstand EMP and still function after the first wave of nukes puts most of us grounders out of our misery.

7. **Weather** satellites. When the first one, Tiros 1, went up in 1960, the military discovered that the pictures taken for weather mapping were clear enough to show the serial numbers of Soviet warplanes parked at air bases. A whole new category of satellites grew out of this "Eureka."

But the military still needs to know its weather, and modern satellites can map it and relay it to ground computers, which then transmit information to base commands. Weather information from the Block 5-D satellites made by RCA that orbit the poles four times a day can get weather to any military commander within twenty minutes.

8. **Monster** satellites. Essentially space stations, possibly manned, that contain multiple protection and detection systems. These could also serve as platforms for laser or particle-beam weapons.

No monster satellites are yet in place—our space shuttle will make it easier to build them—but the Soviets have Cosmos satellites that can be coupled together, like LEGO pieces, in outer space. And within a few years the Soviets will have their own space shuttle.

Our space shuttle was originally designed to carry a payload of several tons. It was the Pentagon that asked NASA to extend the cargo space to be able to carry twenty tons. Wonder why?

9. **FOBS** satellites. The bomb droppers. FOBS stands for fractional orbit bombardment system, and these are really long-range inter-continental ballistic missiles that spend some of their time in orbit. They never take a full spin, spending just enough time above the atmosphere to get, say, from Moscow to Washington.

A FOB comes with multiple nuclear warheads, and when it de-termines that it is in the right position for a warhead to fall onto its target, it gently uncouples it. Then it maneuvers to another position for the next warhead. All this FOB lobbing is computer-controlled.

10. **Laser cannon** satellites. Death-ray machines, code-named Talon Gold. The military has proposed—and is spending $300 million a year on—the use of high-energy lasers based in space to blast enemy intercontinental missiles as they take off. They could also zap other satellites. Essentially such a satellite would require some kind of fire-control system to tell it where to aim and if the target had been hit, a giant mirror to deflect the laser beam to the right target (the mirror has to be such that the laser doesn't incinerate it in the pro-cess of aiming), and a power supply of enough oomph to provide the requisite energy. Laser fire hitting a target would vaporize the outer skin, which, presumably, would disable the weapon's guid-ance system. Lasers, which were first demonstrated in working fash-ion only twenty years ago, would most likely not be useful striking at ground or sea targets because the signals weaken in the atmosphere.

11. **Charged particle beam** satellites. A version of the laser cannon that would shoot subatomic particles rather than laser light. These are the same particles and this is the same process used in the atom smashers scientists use to discover new elements. The atom smasher at Stanford University, two miles long, is still puny by a factor of hundreds or thousands by comparison to an effective CPB weapon.

An example of a charged particle beam that occurs in nature is the beam of electrons thrown off when thunderclouds collide: light-ning bolts.

Charged particle beams would need the same accoutrements as laser cannons, although the targeting mirrors could be located far-ther out in space. The beams would work by incinerating targets. The American experiments with CPB satellites come under the code name SIPAPU, the Apache word for sacred fire.

If it seems there are so many satellite systems in space and in the works that it would take a computer to keep track of them, you're correct. This chore is reserved for GEODSS, or the ground-based, electro-optical, deep-space surveillance system of the Air Force. With its first installation at the White Sands Missile Range in New Mexico, GEODSS can pick up an object the size of a basketball at twenty-five thousand miles. The system uses powerful telescopes stationed all over the world to monitor spacecraft; the telescopic images are converted to digital signals and input to GEODSS computers, which in turn can relay them to other military computers.

Satellites can also be tracked by radar. The North American Aerospace Defense (NORAD) Command has a radar outpost in Colorado that allegedly can pick out objects in orbit the size of a golf ball.

The trouble with laser cannon satellites. According to Dr. Kosta Tsipis, a physicist at MIT, the power supply for a satellite-mounted laser cannon would have to provide a million megawatts, or a thousand times more than a large commercial power plant, to be effective. The fuel to support such a power requirement would take a thousand shuttle missions—125 years' worth—to park in space. And it would take fifty satellites to provide adequate protection for the United States. The cost for implementing such a system could eat up several years' worth of the entire defense budget.

"We have smart weapons now, but only in comparison to the unguided ones of the past. I'd give the laser-guided bomb or shell at best an IQ of 90. But we'll have truly brilliant PGMs (precision-guided missiles) starting in the latter half of this decade. With their autonomous seekers, they will have IQs of 130 to 140, by my way of thinking."—Norman B. Augustine, chairman, Defense Science Board.

We have met the enemy and they are us. We may not need enemies to crack our defenses; we seem capable of doing it ourselves. Pentagon experts estimate that as much as $1 billion a year is siphoned off the defense budget by fraud and theft and that the opportunity is there for three times as much as that to disappear. In one case the Navy discovered that it was shy $174 million worth of supplies inventory on the East Coast, including twenty-five dummy torpedoes and twenty-five thousand pounds of lobster. A subsequent inventory, matched against computer records, then reversed the problem. Now the Navy had $116 million worth of goods it didn't know it had.

Brain damage to smart weapons. In another case, National Semiconductor was said to have supplied inadequately tested computer chips for military systems. (One F-16 fighter has over ten thousand chips in it.) These chips are supposed to be more reliable than commercial versions—and come at five to ten times the cost.

Will Mount Weather weather the blast? You know, of course, that computer central after they drop the big one will be in the catacombs beneath Mount Weather near Paris, Virginia, eighty miles from Washington, D.C. Not only computers, but also post-holocaust operations plans, a dormitory, a reservoir, and a hospital are all located underground there. The computers there currently maintain a list of two million potential bombing targets for the Federal Emergency Management Agency. During an attack, it will be possible to access the computers to find the status of one of these sites. The agency also maintains a current locator system for the President and the next sixteen people in line for succession in case the commander-in-chief is one of the 110 million—as calculated by the agency's computers—Americans who would die in a full-scale nuclear war.

A Texas Instruments calculator, the TI-59, may get to plan the postblast second wave of World War III. It's the calculator that would be used aboard the Looking Glass plane, a military version of the 707 called the EC-135, to pick enemy targets that hadn't yet been atomized. The plane comes with special curtains designed to prevent the pilot from being blinded by nuclear bombs going off below.

The plowshare computers. When the Air Force decommissioned a thousand Minuteman 1 missiles in the early 1970s, it found a use for the missiles' guidance systems. For $100 shipping costs and a qualification letter from the National Science Foundation, colleges and universities could receive one for use as a computer. The DB-17 guidance systems came with no software, no peripherals, and thirty pounds of manuals. They were cylindrical, about the size of a fifty-five-gallon drum. Or garbage can.

FROM THE CACHE:
Illiac—Boon or Boondoggle?

You be the judge. In the late 1960s scientists at the University of Illinois, principally one Daniel Slotnick, began conceiving of the design for the world's fastest computer.

Three previous Illiacs had lived, the first capable of eleven thousand operations a second, the second capable of five hundred thousand, the third even faster. But Illiac IV was to handle one billion operations a second.

Because the speed of light was becoming a limiting factor in the computational speed of large-scale computers, a radical departure from conventional machine design was proposed. Instead of simply having one homogeneous computer, the new machine would be composed of an array of 256 machines. It would be able to operate on 256 parts of a problem at once.

Although business problems rarely exist that can be so easily partitioned, many scientific ones do—wind tunnel simulation, nuclear blast simulation, weather analysis, and visual image processing, for instance.

The academicians received a funding go-ahead from the Defense Advanced Research Projects Agency in 1967. The machine was to cost $8 million and be built by Burroughs using advanced memory circuits called "thin film memory" and advanced logic circuits made by Texas Instruments called emitter-coupled logic (ECL).

Trouble began almost immediately.

Firebombings and riots at the university associated with the Viet Nam war chilled the defense establishment to having an advanced scientific computer so close to so many peaceniks. The faculty itself debated whether to install the machine on the campus. Meanwhile, technical problems abounded. The Burroughs memories were inadequate to the task, and $1 million in development was scuttled. Thin film memories went down the tubes, never to be seen in normal computers again. And the TI ECL circuits didn't work. More redesign. The computer was scaled down to an array of sixty-four processors.

Cost overruns got so bad that in 1971 the Department of Defense stepped in and began reviewing costs every month.

By 1971, a decision was made to house the machine at California's Ames Research Labs at Moffett Naval Air Station. By 1972, when it was supposed to be completed, the computer cost $24 million. A whole building had to be constructed to house the behemoth, which gobbled up 1.2 megawatts of power and required 280 tons of air conditioning. The computer bay took up 11,700 square feet. In 1973 it was failing every five seconds.

Because the machine was essentially designed as a research device—more to see if it could be done than if it could do anything—it was designed without repair as a major consideration. Fixing it was no snap. It had, after all, six million interconnected parts.

Not until 1975 was Illiac considered working, when it could run sixty hours a week. And by then it had cost the government $31 million.

While Illiac never could be considered a smashing computational success, it did make some breakthroughs. It was the first large-scale "array" processor, it was the first machine to use all semiconductor memory, and it did attain a speed of three hundred million instructions a second. It was decommissioned in 1981, after six operational years.

CHAPTER 12

DR. COMPUTER:

Bedside Bytes

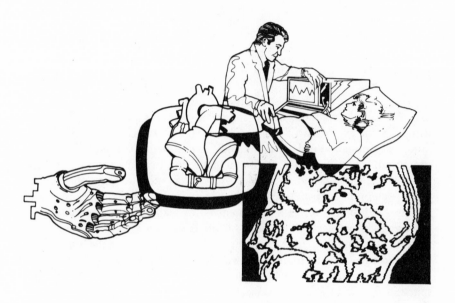

Marcus Welby it never will be, but the computer is at least through med school. Electrocardiograms are transmitted by phone lines and read by computer, special paging systems provide emergency service to shut-ins, Computer-aided Axial Tomography (CAT) scanners look for cancer, microcomputers monitor preemies, computers routinely ask patients their histories, and computers shuttle bills among doctors, labs, hospitals, and insurance companies, labs, doctors, back to insurance companies, to hospitals, labs. . . .

The computer's contribution to the medical arts can be ranked in a hierarchy of wizardry.

High tech. *The glamorous scalpel-edge applications in bionics, genetic engineering, and knowledge engineering. We read or hear about it on the news but don't really know anyone it's happened to. Anything that costs over $100,000 and has blinking lights.*

Mid tech. *The more routine automation systems upon which hos-*

193

pitals have come to depend. Patient monitors, drug dosage meters/ dispensers, blood analyzers, patient history record systems. Include the home computer the physician uses to compute his golf handicap.

Low tech. *The systems that live in the basement. Janitor time clocks, morgue record processors, body part pluckers. Includes the computers that keep the inventories that help the cooks buy the food they turn into tasteless mush.*

Is your inner space constricted? Is life, well, heavy? Are you bummed out? And yet, at the same time, are you too tapped out to afford a shrink?

Psychotronics may be the answer. That's what Dr. Ronald Levy, of Buffalo, New York, calls the use of computer programs that simulate human dynamics for psychiatric therapy. The programs, which Levy calls Computerized Emulation of Personality and Environmental Conflicts (CEPEC), run on an Apple II computer. The programs consist of a set of menus from which a patient is asked to choose. Answers to the questions on the first menu determine a patient's profile, which in turn determines the next menu. By tripping through the menus, the patients are encouraged to perceive their problems in a new light, the basis, says Levy, of therapy. For instance, a woman might start out unhappy with her husband's housework, and after a few menus understand why he calls her a nag. If the husband tried the sequence, he might come to realize he's a lazy slob. The inspiration for CEPEC came, says Levy, from playing the adventure game Wizardry.

All major neuroses available on floppy disk.

Researchers at the University of Wisconsin discovered in the early 1970s that computers were 30 percent better at predicting suicides than doctors were. And suicidal patients were twice as likely as other patients to prefer being interviewed by computer. Potential suicides were happier discussing their innermost problems with a computer than with a human, and the computer was more likely to take the possibility of their suicide seriously.

Experiments conducted at Stanford in the 1970s using computers to teach autistic children to speak triggered improvement in 71 petcent of the cases. Use of conventional methods generally resulted in less than 50 percent improvement. The kids sat at keyboards and display screens and played special games; the computer could react visually and with synthesized sound. (About as many kids are autistic as are blind; very few autistic chil-

dren who haven't learned to speak by the age of five avoid institutionaliza-
tion.)

A most well-traveled doctor. It's the SUMEX, for Stanford University
Medical Experimental, a computer system. With one computer in Palo
Alto, California, and another at Rutgers, New Jersey, the system provides
doctors on both sides of the country access to special computer programs
that help diagnose disease.

One of these is PUFF, developed at Stanford to detect cardiopulmonary
problems. A patient's breathing is sampled by a special mouthpiece that
measures inhalations and exhalations for specific characteristics. The measurements are presented to the doctor—or to PUFF. PUFF combines the
results of the readings with certain background information—Does the patient smoke? Does the patient exercise? How old is the patient?—and comes
up with a diagnosis. PUFF's rules for diagnostics, over fifty-five in number,
were fed into the computer after three months of observing Dr. Robert
Fallet as he analyzed a hundred cases. PUFF is accurate about 85 percent of
the time.

The most erudite computer doctor. It's CADUCEUS, a computer program at the University of Pittsburgh. CADUCEUS contains knowledge of
over three thousand symptoms and five hundred diseases and uses rules of
inference similar to those used in computer chess games. The program
mimics the thought processes of Dr. Jack Myers of the school's medical
school and has passed the internal-medicine board exam.

Computer coach. Computerized analysis has shown that the "Fosbury
Flop" method of high jumping is more efficient than the traditional
method. A computer simulation of Valery Brumel, a Soviet high jumper of
the traditionalist vein, indicated that, with his energy and strength, if he
used Dick Fosbury's method he could have jumped eight feet and retained
the world record.

In fact, the computer is fast becoming a staple of sports medicine and
coaching. The U.S. Olympic teams use computers, for instance, to analyze
skier movements recorded by filming tiny blinking lights taped to the ankles
and knees of racers.

Guru of gurus in "biomechanics" is Dr. Gideon Ariel, founder and
head of Coto Research Center in Trabuco Canyon, California. He films
athletes in action, then analyzes their motions by computer. Generally a
design system like that used to draw computer circuitry is used to stylize the
actions so they can be compared to stored norms. Simulation techniques
can be used to predict how a change in an athlete's style will affect performance. In his computers are digital representations of such jocks as
Muhammad Ali, Jack Nicklaus, and Jimmy Connors.

Drawing by Tim Eagan

Biomechanics also can predict to some degree—from heart rate, skin temperature, blood pressure, and other measurements under stress—a person's potential to excel at certain sports. They also can help design shoes and equipment.

Ariel has had some successes. In 1976, shot-putter Terry Albriton won the world's record after modifying his technique in accordance with Ariel's computer analysis. And the U.S. women's volleyball team, thanks to a computer profile of the ideal contestant, has spiked its way out of the world cellar to become number one over a period of five years.

One computer finding: Tall women play better volleyball.

You can thank a Honeywell minicomputer for the following information on the 1979 Boston Marathon: The average female marathon runner weighed 115.2 pounds, was 29.8 years old, and stood 5 feet, 3 inches tall. The best times were turned in by women over 5 feet, 9 inches. Women under 5 feet and over 160 pounds puked their guts out on Heartbreak Hill.

But does it work only on the ears of oxen? Hewlett-Packard makes a blood oxygen analyzer that doesn't require blood to be sampled. It's called an "ear oximeter," and it shines light from optical fibers through the translucent part of a patient's ear. The light that comes out the other side is transmitted by more optical fibers to an electronic gizmo that can calculate

Drawing by Rich Tennant

"Nurse, would someone please inform the patient that his output is normal?"

from the opacity of the ear what the blood oxygen level is. Good for check-ing lung function. Also earwax.

Habeus computerus. The same computer graphics techniques that pro-duced Walt Disney's *TRON* may soon be helping med students at New York University School of Medicine learn skull surgery. The school is now developing a 3-D graphics system that will allow students to use light pens and joysticks to operate on patients simulated on a computer display screen. The image of the skull can be viewed on the screen from any angle, and complications that might arise from surgery can be programmed into the training exercise. The healing process can be depicted in a matter of min-utes, not months, and aging can be simulated from data stored on a large Control Data 6600 computer.

DR. COMPUTER: PROGRAMS THAT DIAGNOSE

NAME	INSTITUTION	APPROX. DATE OPERATIONAL	FUNCTION
CARE	Buffalo Gen-eral Hospital	1975	Establishes a historical data base of previous surgical patients with cardio-vascular, pulmonary, and metabolic problems. Used to establish norms for re-

DR. COMPUTER: PROGRAMS THAT DIAGNOSE

NAME	INSTITUTION	APPROX. DATE OPERATIONAL	FUNCTION
			covery of current patients and alert physicians to abnormal conditions.
CADU-CEUS	University of Pittsburgh	1980	Internist diagnostician. Over five hundred diseases, three thousand manifestations in repertoire. Most comprehensive diagnostic program in existence.
CASNET/ Glaucoma	Rutgers	1977	Advises on long-term treatment strategies for glaucoma over a period of many visits.
CRYSALIS	Stanford	1976	Hypothesizes the structure of proteins from X-ray crystallographics map of electron densities.
DENDRAL	Stanford University	1968	Infers chemical structures from basic chemical laws and characteristics of tested compound. Contains rules of conjecture, testing, and inference. Granddaddy of all such programs, also longest in existence.
META-DENDRAL	Stanford	1975	Infers from mass spectrometry results the characteristics of new compounds. Input to DENDRAL. Has equaled or beaten experts in interpreting mass spectrometric data.
MYCIN	Stanford University	1975	Diagnoses blood diseases and disorders, explains reasoning process to doctor, recommends treatment.

			Correct 90 percent of the time. IBM uses a version to diagnose malfunctioning disk drives.
MOLGEN	Stanford University	1980	Advises molecular geneticists on experiments and procedures for DNA research and gene splicing.
ONCOCIN	University of Pittsburgh	1980	Assists physicians treating cancer patients with complex drug therapies.
PUFF	Stanford	1978	From measurements of patients' inhalations and exhalations and past history, determines pulmonary problems and recommends treatment. Derivative of MYCIN.
R_x	Stanford	1980	Statistical analysis assistance for doctors treating patients for whom there is a long medical history.
TIERESIAS	Stanford	1980	Generalizes beyond MYCIN to deal with any expert who disagrees with computer. Traces back to point in analysis where opinions diverge; corrects rules of inference. Could be used for more than medical knowledge systems.
VM	Stanford	1980	Ventilator management. Works with PUFF. Analyzes measurements and patient conditions to advise when to take off breathing-assistance machines.

Notes: Most systems like these evolve over time. The exact point when they go from work in progress to operational is hard to define, so dates are necessarily inexact. There are other systems as well, but these are the most common.

First wearers of a computer-in-a-backpack? Antarctic seals, of course. Seals? Seals. The National Science Foundation is funding an experiment in which bioengineers from Massachusetts General Hospital will journey to Antarctica, drill holes in the ice, and attach twenty-eight-pound backpacks to one-thousand-pound pregnant Weddell seals. Each backpack contains a microcomputer. The purpose of the experiment: to monitor fetal heartbeats during diving in an effort to understand sudden infant death syndrome in humans. The experiment will be rigged so mother seals have to return to a specific hole in the ice to get air—at which time their backpack computers will be connected to a land (snow)-based Zenith computer for data transmission.

THE NAKED BIONIC APE

Bionics are here. One person in six is mentally or physically impaired, one in four hundred suffers paralysis of at least two limbs, and one in a thousand is paraplegic as a result of spinal cord injury. To those of us who are unafflicted, it is impossible to conceive of the rainbow of promises the computer age offers the handicapped. Coupled with breakthroughs in materials and implantation technique, advances in microcircuitry are bringing mobility and self-determination to the handicapped undreamed of just a few years ago.

A catalog of body-bogglers:

Thought-controlled limbs. Dr. Robert Graupe of ITT has invented an above-elbow artificial limb controlled by electrical signals from the brain. The signals are picked up at the surface of the amputee's stump by electrodes and passed to a microcomputer that determines their meaning, then activates the motors that move the artificial arm.

At MIT, Dr. David Edell has begun work on a device that will reverse the process—an implanted microcircuit picks up signals from nerves and transmits them to electronic instruments. Ultimately such chips could be used to control artificial limbs from thought waves traveling through the nervous system. Edell has already successfully implanted a ten-channel circuit into rabbit nervous systems. The microscopic chip is encased in a substance that prevents its rejection from the body, and Edell thinks within a few years he'll be able to pick up a hundred channels from a single nerve. The device is powered by the nerve impulses themselves. Making sense of those signals—a cross section of a single nerve can carry millions of signals—will take computer analysis on a large scale. That will first take a better understanding of the nervous system's communications, and second an implantable computer. Not impossible.

Computer-controlled limbs. The best-known advances have been made at Ohio's Wright State University by Dr. Jerrold S. Petrofsky, who has used home computers to control electrical signals to the leg muscles of paraplegics. (Electricity causes the muscles to contract, just as it causes frogs' legs to contract in high school biology experiments.) The first experiments were designed to increase muscle tone and bone condition in long-atrophied limbs. These led to construction of a tricycle with attached computer that allowed paraplegics to pedal.

But Petrofsky isn't alone. Dr. Hunter Peckham of Case-Western Reserve has used the same basic concept to bring inert hands back to life. A computerized transmitter attached to shoulder or neck muscles sends signals to tiny electrodes implanted in the hand muscles. Patients can pick up their own coffee cups.

Others in Boston and Salt Lake City have developed bionic elbows and arms, and researchers at MIT have developed an artificial leg with a computer-controlled knee that can be timed to a person's gait.

Drawing by Rich Tennant

Computer-aided senses. Electronic ears have been developed in experiments that use a microphone and microprocessor chip worn on the body and connected to electrodes in the ear to produce sound for deaf people. Sound picked up by the microphone is changed to electricity, modulated by the microprocessor, and sent to the electrodes, which stimulate the auditory nerve. Different electrodes can be designed to stimulate hearing of different "sounds," different frequencies on the same electrode can stimulate different sounds, and complex sounds can be created by stimulating more than one electrode at a time. It's like a telephone being connected directly to the brain.

Electronics have also made it possible to detect hearing loss that occurs only in certain frequency ranges and to fashion hearing aids that restore hearing by translating sounds at the hearing-impaired frequencies to ones that can be received by the patient.

Even farther out, researchers at the University of Western Ontario, led by Dr. William Dobelle, have connected computers to electrodes implanted in the visual cortex of patients' brains. When the computer has generated signals, the patients have seen starlike images called phosphenes, similar to the patterns you see when you rub your eyes. The research goal is to use the computer to fashion signals that will trigger recognizable images in the brain.

(Actually, it's not necessary that the images formed inside the brain resemble to the nit what we see—only that the images form patterns that can be useful to a blind person in dealing with his or her environment. If the sky is green, so what? Call it blue.)

Computer-aided organs. The artificial heart implanted in Barney Clark on December 1, 1982, is the pinnacle of artificial organ implantation. It uses a microprocessor for system control. Designed by Dr. Robert K. Jarvik, hence the name Jarvik-7, the heart was tested on goats and cows during the past decade. Dr. Clark's artificial heart was immobile—he had to remain attached to outside electricity and plumbing. But Drs. Jarvik and Milton Isaacson have designed a portable energy converter that will someday mobilize artificial-heart recipients. The energy comes from a battery pack in the belt connected to a microprocessor controller and is transmitted by wires to the heart, where an energy converter transforms it into hydraulic pumping. One clear-cut advantage to a Jarvik heart: It costs only $15,000, including surgery. A heart transplant costs $100,000 more than that. If a heart has a computer, does a computer have a heart?

There are other, less glamorous but perhaps more immediately useful computer-driven organs. At the University of New Mexico, programmable computers little bigger than your thumb have been implanted in diabetics to regulate insulin pumps.

Computer-enhanced life quality. Engineers at the Veterans Administration Center, Palo Alto, California, have developed a robot arm for handicapped people that can recognize voice commands and is connected to a computer that remembers past actions. The user first trains the remote arm by describing actions in a series of moves and then calls the actions by one-word commands. The engineers are now working on giving the robot mobility and sight (a TV camera that would show the owner where the robot was going). The robot could be used to go to the refrigerator, fix a sandwich, and bring it back.

Home computers can now be routinely fitted with attachments that allow input by voice, tapping, eye movement, sips and puffs, and cheek movements. Nelson and Johnson Engineering, Boulder, Colorado, has modified a van so it can be completely controlled by a joystick operated with two fingers.

Bio-eyes. James McAlear of EMV Associates, Rockville, Maryland, has funding from the NSF for this ambitious plan: to build a microscopic array of ten thousand electrodes, cover them with a layer of protein, drill holes through the protein with electron beams, and dip the device in a soup of nerve cells from embryos. The device will be small enough to implant in the visual cortex; embryo nerve cells will act as connectors to the cortex's brain cells. A TV camera outside the body will send digital signals to the device, which will fire individual neurons in the brain. If it works, blind people could have rudimentary artificial vision by 1990.

Dr. Robert K. Jarvik, inventor of the artificial heart, has been a carpenter and jeweler in his past. Besides building the heart for Dr. Barney Clark, he built one for the movie *Threshold*, starring Donald Sutherland as a doctor who implants an artificial heart illegally.

Most computerized quadriplegic. Rob Marince, Hopewell Township, Pennsylvania. Equipment: Apple II Plus computer, thirteen-foot satellite dish, Scott Instruments voice entry terminal, miscellaneous video gear, phone equipment, and interconnection boxes. Total value: $60,000 (donated). Next purchase: robot arm.

Different ways to skin a CAT. Two new technologies promise to provide even better analysis of internal body conditions than CAT scans, which use multiple X rays and a computer to re-create images from the X-ray data. Positron-Emission Tomography (PET) scans pick emissions from radioactive substances injected into the body—and caused by collisions of matter and antimatter—then re-creates images just like CAT scans. Nuclear Magnetic Resonance (NMR) uses radio waves passed through a magnetic field to determine the state of individual atoms within the body. The resulting data show the distribution of molecules within the body—and images can be re-created through the use of computers.

Although the equipment is expensive—a CAT scanner can cost $600,000, an NMR scanner over $1.5 million—they may ultimately save treatment costs, since they can be used on an outpatient basis.

"I can't hear you, I don't have my glasses on." At Kumamoto University, Japan, researchers have designed a TV that changes color in response to sounds made by the human voice. Deaf people can learn to talk in colors—even if they can't hear themselves.

"I can hear you, I do have my glasses on." NASA, meanwhile, is work-

ing on a set of glasses that will help deaf people lip-read. Under design by Robert Beadles, Research Triangle Institute, and Orin Cornett, Gallaudet College, Washington, D.C., the glasses will have a microphone and a microprocessor embedded in them. The mike will pick up the speaker's voice; the computer will translate the signals into visual cues transmitted to a light-emitting diode (like those in calculator displays). Special lenses will project the diode images into space—in fact, the images will seem to hang around the speaker's mouth.

There will be specific cues for the consonants; vowels will be indicated by the position of the consonant cue. Although the glasses won't be able to catch every word, they should at least increase comprehension for lip-readers.

Nuclear-age Frankenstein's monsters. There's a group of nuclear reactor "gypsies" who trek from one power plant to another who may carry too much cancer-causing radiation. In order to monitor them, the Atomic Industrial Forum has proposed a centralized computer bank to keep medical records on workers at all such plants. Power companies are required to maintain these records now and to send them to another utility if a worker applies there for a job. Some workers lie about the amount of radiation they've received in order to land the new position; the computer system would send the records electronically, rather than allowing the delays and lost papers that happen now. There are between two thousand and four thousand workers in this field now, servicing seventy nukes; the number is expected to grow. Sounds like a good idea, but thirteen of the utilities the Atomic Industrial Forum surveyed said they wouldn't spend a dime on the program.

Oh, those cold fingers. Ichiro Kato of Waseda University, Japan, has developed a twenty-five-finger robot that can perform breast cancer checks. (Kato also has invented a robot arm that can open a door, and a pair of legs that can walk like a human.)

A portable, computerized pollution detector developed by the Environmental Protection Agency detected its first pollution—yes, you guessed it, at the Environmental Protection Agency. Carbon monoxide was seeping in from an underground garage.

Chip in a lip. The miniaturization of circuitry allows Dr. Zee Davidovitch at the University of Pennsylvania to provide an assist to people wearing braces. The device comes with batteries, a resistor, and a transistor and is small enough to hide under a patient's lip. It helps move teeth by electrically stimulating enamel buildup on one side of the tooth while helping it recede on the other.

It's still a work in progress, but Dr. Garrett Lee's laserscope may revolu-tionize the treatment of arteriosclerosis (hardening of the arteries). Normal treatments for the disease include bypass operations, including the coronary bypass, using healthy veins to replace clogged ones, and balloon an-gioplasty, where a tube is inserted into the vessel and then inflated to plaster the deposits against the artery wall.

After watching Darth Vader and Obi-Wan Kenobi duel with lasers in *Star Wars*, Lee decided to investigate whether lasers could be used to attack the fat deposits in clogged arteries. He discovered they could. By 1982 he and the engineers at the University of California at Davis had built a pro-totype system that used laser light pumped through quartz fibers embedded in a catheter that blasts the fat deposits. Debris is vacuumed out through a second tube in the catheter, and a third tube contains optical fibers through which Lee can watch what's going on. The temperature at the point where blast meets fat can get as high as twelve hundred degrees, but because the light is pinpointed, artery walls can be left undamaged. The fat literally melts away.

Before the laserscope can see wide use, it needs to be more fully tested, a videoscope needs to be added, the catheter made smaller, and the whole system computerized so calculations of laser intensity and duration are made automatically.

The three computers of Eve. Psychiatrists at the National Institute of Mental Health are using computers and strobe lights to map the brainwave characteristics of people with multiple personalities. Once decried as bogus, these personalities are showing up so differently under the mapping tech-nique that the cries of fakery have been all but stilled.

The technique was developed in 1979 at NIMH by Drs. Monte Buchsbaum and Richard Coppola. A DEC PDP-11 with appropriate pe-ripherals and plotters is attached to an electroencephalograph wired to the patient's head. When the patient watches the strobe light, brain activity is recorded and coded by the computer. Running the test while different per-sonalities are in control yields different electrical "maps." From analyzing various multiple personalities—one woman has 127—over the past three years, Dr. Frank Putnam of NIMH has discovered that the brain activity of multiple personalities in the same person can vary as much as that among separate people, that multiple personalities can alter their voices, accents, and patterns of speech in unusual and seemingly impossible ways, and that some alternate personalities have their own consciousnesses, memories, and intellect. Ninety percent of the multiples are women.

I compute, ergo sum. There are different roads to self-knowledge. The Greeks chewed stones and held dialogs on the street corners, the mystics stared at their belly buttons, and Michael Krawetz used flow-charting techniques. After a family tragedy in 1980, Krawetz, a data processing specialist at Manufacturers Hanover Trust in New York City, found himself at the lowest emotional ebb in his life. When he realized there was no book or manual he could turn to for help, he decided to write his own. Using the programming and flow-charting techniques he used in his job, he created a "Self-Esteem Passport." His logic was this: If a flow chart helps a computer come to the right answer, a flow chart should help a person do the same thing. The person's problem was getting access to the right "files." He established a "self-esteem" data base consisting of a collection of files such as the "Be Proud of Your Looks File," the "Self-Confidence File," and the "Respect to Others File." He documented all these in the "Self-Esteem Passport," which comes in a brown Leatherette case and includes space to put favorite pictures and list a person's best traits.

And why not? It seemed to work for Krawetz. And as anybody knows who has gone through a tough emotional period, sometimes you have to act like a computer just to get through the day.

A little more hardware is involved in the scheme for better self-knowledge proposed by Reed Larson of the University of Chicago. He would wire people to biomechanical devices—things that measure blood pressure, galvanic skin responses, heart rates, brain activity—for a period of several weeks during their normal daily life. At periodic moments a pocket pager would remind them to fill out preprinted questionnaires about their state of mental well-being. After enough of these measurements and recordings, a computer could begin to establish a profile of the person that could be used to predict future mental states or advise on ways to act.

"There's a similarity to a horoscope," he says in *The Futurist* of October 1981 in discussing experiments. "We are providing people with an image of their daily temperament. Unlike in astrology, however, the image provided is not based on mystical conjectures but on systematic empirical data."

Final implementation of the Larson scheme awaits more portable biomechanical measuring devices, but he has conducted experiments with pocket pagers and manual recording of mental states and current activity. A computer analyzes the reports and creates a profile of a person's ups and downs. One woman learned how unhappy she was in her job and quit.

Do you live near a nuke plant? Are you afraid of meltdown? Do your local authorities know what to *do* when the radioactive plumes rise up over the plain?

Maybe you should get in touch with Professor William A. Wallace, Rensselaer Polytechnic Institute. He's worked out a microcomputer-based information system of disaster preparedness for communities in the shadow of nuclear power plants. A prototype system is already in use at the Indian Point plant in Buchanan, New York. The system combines backup plans—

like those now kept in notebooks somewhere in the village offices—and data from remote monitors at and around the plant. Remote measurements of wind speed, temperature, and humidity, for instance, would be useful in predicting movement of radioactive gas. The computer can be programmed to display appropriate phone numbers of authorities to call to marshal evacuation.

All this assuming, of course, that the nuclear plant and its surroundings, including Wallace's apparatus, don't go up in a mushroom cloud.

You knew, of course, that Pillsbury was once in the computer business. The venture lasted a year or so, after which the company decided it was easier to roll in dough rolling dough than selling computer services. Maybe the one the company announced last year will last longer. For $19.95 you can now get from the company's Consumer Division a program called Eat Smart that runs on Apple II computers. The program requires users to key in what food they ate during a period of time, then analyzes their nutritional value. Calories, salt, cholesterol, and other key ingredients are tracked. It considers age, sex, and the special requirements of nursing and pregnant women. So, here goes. Breakfast: two Twinkies, coffee with sugar, leftover pizza. Warm beer. Lunch: potato chips, Clark Bar, frozen yogurt, one pack beer nuts. Dinner: Whopper my way, five cans Blatz, two Digel, popcorn, one box Old Crows. Midnight: leftover three-alarm chili, Dr Pepper. How'm I doin'?

FROM THE CACHE:
The Long Trek to Nan's Long Walk

Just before Christmas 1982, Nan Davis, a senior at Wright State University in Dayton, Ohio, made national TV news by being the first paraplegic to walk with the help of computers. She had physical help from a parachute harness that took 45 pounds of weight off her legs, and she held onto a set of parallel bars—but she walked. Wired with electrodes and feedback devices connected to a computer that controlled the firing sequences for the pulses of electricity that made her leg muscles twitch in such a way as to cause one foot to go in front of the other, Nan's legs could move only in one plane of motion—but she walked. The computer system and associated paraphernalia are bulky (150 pounds) and costly ($200,000)—but she walked.

The fact that she did results from a series of fortuitous events. The first is the undergraduate poverty of Dr. Jerrold S. Petrofsky, who designed Nan's walking contraption. To fill his wallet in college he got a part-time job at St. Louis University's School of Medicine. They used him as an electronics technician (he'd had two years of metallurgy and mining at a school in Missouri), which required that he tinker with the lab computer. It was OK; nobody knew much about computers then. Petrofsky's interests led him to get an oddball degree—a Ph.D. from St. Louis University in physiology and a minor in biomedical engineering at Washington University, St. Louis. He was on his way, and by 1969 he had conceived of the idea of electrical stimulation of muscles to assist paraplegics in walking. He began to work with cats.

The second was the growing availability of computing power in affordable chunks. The idea of electrical stimulation of muscles to make them move is an old one, but the computational power required to pull it off just wasn't available ten or twenty years ago. Five thousand dollars' worth of computer today would have cost five hundred thousand dollars ten years ago.

In 1981 Petrofsky switched from experimenting on cats to using electrical stimulation to exercise large muscle groups among paralyzed students. Wright State, because of its enlightened treatment of the handicapped, had a goodly portion of volunteers. Petrofsky discovered that long-atrophied muscles could be restored. His subjects began doing leg extensions under computer control. Not only did the legs regain their strength, some did so so fast that they stressed the bones, causing hairline fractures. One student strengthened his legs to twice the strength of a normal, ambulatory person.

There were setbacks. The first feedback mechanism for an exercise cycle Petrofsky built used a photo sensor as a feedback device. When the university sent a photographer to take a picture of the first quadriplegic to pedal a bicycle, the flashbulb blew the sensors. Petrofsky switched to another method and eventually was able to build a bicycle that subjects could pedal about campus. To regulate the electricity going to the muscles, Petrofsky and mathematician Chandler Phillips built a throttle like that of a motorcycle. The legs of the rider were the engine. Later they switched to a joystick. Soon Petrofsky will have a pair of slacks with the electrodes built in, so a rider is automatically wired for stimulation.

Petrofsky has been working on electrically stimulated walking for over a decade. In another decade, with the computer advances on the horizon, he'll be able to miniaturize his equipment to make it portable, perhaps even implantable. The *real* significance of Nan Davis's December walk will be understood. By then, if the body is willing, the computer will be able.

CHAPTER 13

FUNNY MONEY:

Banks and Electronic Funds Transfer

In little electronic blips, the Federal Reserve and the world's banks shunt over $1 trillion around the globe every day. Just one of these transport systems, the Fedwire, moves $100 million a second at peak operating times.

As Everett Dirksen, the late senator from Illinois, once said, "a billion here, a billion there, and pretty soon you're talking real money."

Thanks to the computer, paperless money is already here. Besides these great electronic dollar conduits, there are over 120 million national bank cards and 30,000 automated teller machines in use every day. In 1950 the banking system had to handle 7 billion checks; today the number is over 35 billion (150 million of which bounce!). Bank card sales transactions have grown from less than 500 million a year ten years ago to around 2 billion a year today.

All of which is grist for the computer's number-crunching mill and none of which would be possible without the computer. The world's major banks are getting so sophisticated, so electronic, that they were willing to set up a special international data network to shunt money about in lieu of the traditional Telex system because it could cut the time of the transaction from two minutes to twenty-five seconds. Ninety-five seconds of interest can pay for a lot of computers.

Of course, electronic currency has its downside. Theft need no longer be limited by the size of a getaway car; electronic funds thefts are quicker, cleaner, and generally run in the millions. And system screwups can be costly and liability hard to pin down—who pays the interest while the computer's being repaired?

Contemplating the electronic banking system is a little like contemplating infinity, mind-boggling but fun. And just as there's a whole branch of mathematics devoted to the different types of infinities, so there are a lot of ways to comprehend electronic banking.

Our favorite way of thinking about it requires that you picture a salami. Now consider slicing it. But consider slicing it so thin that nobody even knows you got a slice. If you could "salami slice" a penny a second off the Fedwire alone—and who would notice a penny?— you'd make $315,360 a year.

And a computer could do that. Easily.

Perils of the electronic age. One Friday in 1981 New York's Irving Trust computer operators forgot to put the right code in their computer, and billions of dollars didn't get forwarded electronically to the Federal Reserve. The loss of interest was between $10 million and $15 million. Another: On April 25, 1973, a company called Hyman-Michaels ordered its U.S. bank to transfer $27,000 to a supplier. Because operators in a Swiss bank forgot to load paper into an automatic Telex machine, the transfer never took place and Hyman-Michaels suffered over $2 million loss of potential profit. In 1981, eight years after the flub, Hyman-Michaels won a court judgment against the Swiss bank.

The French have introduced a "smart" credit card. It comes with a microcomputer embedded in it. It will remember transactions and keep customer account data—like having a branch bank in your pocket. The Department of Defense is using a smart card now for Army personnel, to replace the standard ID card. The microprocessor chip embedded in the card contains the owner's special identity number, name, rank, serial number, branch of service, blood type, sex, height, medical eligibility, and privileges he or she is entitled to—and, we suppose, what to do in case of an emergency. The card, manufactured by Philips Data Systems, automatically self-destructs if the wrong password is entered three times. Just like *Mission Impossible*. The newest smart card is being developed in West Germany and utilizes infrared fingerprint analysis to establish the owner's identity.

Most famous EFT heist. In 1978 Stanley Mark Rifkin diverted $10.2 million on the Fedwire from Security Pacific Bank to his personal account in Switzerland, where he used the money to buy diamonds. Rifkin, once a college professor, posed as a consultant to obtain computer codes, made a ten-cent call from a pay phone to transfer the money. He was caught only because he boasted of his feat to an attorney. Just two days before Rifkin's trial he was arrested for attempting a $50 million swindle from the Union Bank of Los Angeles. This charge was dropped, and Rifkin received a three-year sentence to Lompoc Federal Penitentiary for the Fedwire theft.

Largest known computer-related bank fraud. Wells Fargo's loss from embezzlement in 1980 of $21.3 million. It was a simple case of pyramiding loan authorizations, but detailed knowledge of how the company's data processing system worked made it possible.

Most innovative use of a bank card machine. In 1974 a Tokyo kidnaper named Masotoshi Tashiro, using a bank card issued under the name of S. Kobayashi, chose an automated teller for the payoff drop point. The money was to be put into his account, and at a subsequent time he would withdraw it from one of the bank's 348 machines. In fall of 1974 he kidnaped actress Yukiji Asoka, daughter of a famous Japanese painter, and made his demands. Although he'd previously determined that it would take the bank twenty minutes to tell which machine he had made the ransom withdrawal from, programmers rewrote the software quickly enough to identify which machine was making a request. He was caught walking away from the machine, ¥5 million in hand.

One swindler cashed over $1 million in checks on which he had altered the magnetically encoded bank routing number. They crisscrossed the country for six months, searching for a computer that would accept them for payment. The fraud was uncovered only when the checks became so mutilated from machine handling that they couldn't be processed.

There are bright spots. A recent task group of bank computer security experts met at SRI International to see if any known vulnerabilities in the banking system could be exploited to the extent that the whole system would collapse. They didn't think so. And in official documents on nuclear preparedness, the government urges us to keep our credit cards with us during

Drawing by Rich Tennant

Ya know, boss, I still sorta miss the way we robbed banks in the old days."

atomic attack. Uncle Sam thinks they'll be critical in restoring the nation's financial system after Armageddon. Maybe they're useful in the afterlife, too.

Home banking. The day when it will be totally unnecessary for you to walk up to the teller's window will soon be upon us, especially if the banks have their way. ATMs (automated teller machines) are a lot less expensive than marble lobbies and vaults. There are several home banking services being tested now, such as Pronto, from Chemical Bank in New York. You can pay bills, arrange to pay automatically bills that recur each month (such as your mortgage or car payment), and review your credit card charges and make payments. Citibank and Chase also have been experimenting with home banking. First Bank System of Minneapolis has a home banking system where customers use special credit cards with embedded micro-processors in them; it's like having an electronic bank vault. In all, twenty-five banks nationwide had experiments with home banking under way in 1982.

Merrill Lynch and Shearson/American Express are also cooking up home banking programs; so are two computer services companies, Tymnet and Automatic Data Processing (ADP). All you'll need is a computer—Chemical Bank requires that you own an Atari—and a modem. Then all you have to do is pay the bank a monthly service charge, all this for the privilege of making it cheaper and easier for them to do business. (The typical check costs $1.00 to write, $0.50 of which the bank pays, the rest of which comes from the payer and payee in postage, blanks, time, etc.)

Biggest home banking flop. Seattle's "In-Touch" system, also the *first* home banking system. In 1973, Seattle-First National Bank launched a pay-by-phone bill-paying service that used customers' Touch-Tone phones as banking terminals. The customer drew down a predetermined budget amount for each type of bill payment and received bill payment notices on bank statements. The system went bust in half a year—not enough Touch-Tones phones.

It's not home banking yet, but for a while in 1982 Dry Dock Savings Bank of New York was giving away Atari home computers for customers who deposited $2,800 in three-and-a-half year accounts. The computers were in lieu of interest and listed at $1,400. Higher deposits got bigger systems.

Why do bankers like ATMs and home banking? Because it means they can put a bank anywhere—in a shopping mall, in the corner of a building, in your living room. With rising costs of real estate, construction, and labor, it looks awfully attractive. After ten years of struggle, ATMs finally have caught on: Texas, Michigan, and Massachusetts lead the nation in the number of ATMs installed. While you read this book, there are forty-six ATMs a day being installed in the United States.

Why do people like ATMs? Because they're fast, they're fun, and once in a great while they spew out more money than they're supposed to, such as the one at First Interstate Bank in Phoenix, Arizona, that burped out $5,140 for Deborah Hall when all she asked for was $40. The bank blamed Diebold, Inc., which made the ATM; Diebold said it wasn't them, it must have been the software. Deborah returned the money, and the bank rewarded her honesty by treating her to lunch.

Why don't crooks like ATMs? Because they're hard to cajole into coughing up the cash, but some people try anyway. One guy made a large withdrawal from his account, then reported that his card had been stolen. He knew enough to cover the lens of the camera that silently views every transaction, but the dummy covered it with another credit card from his wallet, his name and account number in plain view.

A more successful ATM heist was pulled off in England. It was 1979, and Lloyds had just installed the first few ATMs, big machines with a huge stainless-steel bar handle on the door you opened and closed to make transactions. The bank president was making a public appearance to introduce the service, telling the assembled press how safe the system was. One reporter asked if it weren't possible to embezzle money electronically using phone lines. "Oh, no," the president replied, no way; the encryption system was so elaborate "that no one will ever take money from an ATM illegally," he boasted. At that moment, thirty miles away at another of the bank's ATMs, a band of thieves had looped a chain around the machine's big handle, tied it to their truck, and merrily jerked the thing, £20,000 included, right out of the side of the building.

Did you know that electronic bankers are the devil incarnate? Or that the satanic number 666 is diabolically implanted into credit cards and the UPC symbols on the products you buy? So says Mary Stewart Relfe in her books *When Your Money Fails* and *The New Money System*, published by Ministries, Inc., of Montgomery, Alabama.

The first ATM. People's National Bank of Gouster, Virginia, in September 1962. The ATM, built by National Banking Machines of Bena, Virginia, was ten years ahead of its time, and the idea didn't catch on; the company went out of business. People's National Bank was merged with First Virginia Bank.

Passwords are the most common security protection at an ATM. Yet a company in Portland, Oregon, has developed an absolutely positive identification system called retinal microimage digitization (you can bet the company's name, EyeDentify, is easier to remember). All you have to do is look into the camera, which has your "retinal data" stored in its memory banks; if you are who you say you are, you get your money. Here's looking at you, kid!

. *Son of Muzak.* Muzak is replacing its eight hundred local FM radio stations that play the music we love to hear with a satellite transponder, which will beam the sweet strains to earth stations in businesses and shopping centers across the country. Visa and MasterCard lost nearly $1 billion in 1982 due to stolen cards and deadbeats who skipped out on their bills. What do the two have to do with each other? Well, Muzak uses only a small portion of its transponder's capabilities, two megahertz (MHz) to be exact. That leaves thirty-three MHz, and Muzak is interested in leasing that space to credit card companies to use as an electronic credit card authorization system. Instead of the one- to three-week delays in receiving the card recovery bulletins, merchants would run the card through a machine that reads the magnetic stripe and get a yea or a nay in thirty seconds. What's more, the card's dollar limit would be accurate up to five minutes before the purchase. Bye-bye, shopping sprees, legitimate or otherwise.

My credit runneth over. Edward Bellamy introduced the notion of a credit card in his 1888 novel *Looking Backward.* Bellamy's card was actually a *debit* card, with little squares the merchant punched out when something was purchased. Today, three out of every five creditworthy Americans have credit cards; and because of *credit* cards, Americans overspend their budgets by 23 percent.

- First credit card: given by hotels to their best clientele, 1900.

- Most prestigious card: Merrill Lynch's Cash Management Account (CMA) Visa. It requires twenty grand in cold, hard cash to get the card with the famous bull on it.

- First prestige card: the Diner's Club, in 1950. Launched the era of the credit card company as middleman between merchant and customer.

- Most popular prestige card: the American Express Gold Card, which extends a $2,000 line of credit to the cardholder from his local bank. Big deal.

- Least popular prestige card: the Visa and MasterCard premium cards, RIP in less than a year. You seen one, you seen 'em all.

- First bank card: from the Franklin National Bank in New York, 1951. What hath God wrought?

- Stupidest card: the American Express Gold Card *calculator,* yours for only $30 plus annual cardholder fees.

Like lemmings to the sea. The Washington press corps followed President Reagan on a recent junket to Miami, where the press all stayed in the same hotel, plunking down American Express cards to pay their bills. Some two months later, one of the reporters noticed a $500 charge at a Miami clothing store that she was sure she hadn't made but that was dated during her stay. She checked with a fellow reporter, who found a similar charge on her bill. It turns out nearly *all* of them had large charges at Miami clothing stores, run up by a clever hotel clerk who played around with their account numbers and who knows what else. Because their monthly bills run to $10,000, none save the one had bothered checking. And, apparently, none of the journalists' accountants had bothered checking either.

To the credit card society belong credit card problems. With over 750 million credit cards of one type or another loose in the world, the temptation to forge, counterfeit, or otherwise abuse a few is high enough to have spawned a little industry of its own. In the United States alone, $40 million of the $128 million banks lost in spurious credit card transactions in 1982 can be traced to counterfeit cards. That same year the biggest known counterfeiting ring was nabbed in New Jersey—with over two hundred thousand cards. One card alone recently rang up $160,000 in New York City. A counterfeit card sells for $100 to $300 and can return a buyer's investment tenfold or more. Until a crackdown in 1982, the New York Stock Exchange of stolen and counterfeit credit cards was the Magic Cue, a Times Square pool hall.

But counterfeiting is exotic crime. It's a lot easier just to filch credit card receipt carbons out of trash cans behind posh restaurants and use them to forge new charges or order merchandise by mail. It's anyone's guess how many millions of dollars are stolen in this way every year because no one bothers to check, but one recent California gang got away with $250,000 in a carbon paper scam before getting caught.

Visa and MasterCard have over 120 million cardholders between them and run $61 billion worth of transactions through the cards a year. Banks wrote off $652 million in bad credit card debt in 1982 ($128 million in spurious transactions, $524 million in deadbeat customers).

And bazookas, tanks, bombs, and stuff. The American Banking Association has formed a task force to investigate credit card fraud countermeasures (their word), including iridescent pigments that change color if tampered with, heat-sensitive inks to prevent forgery, special emblems or type-embossing so numbers can't be cut off and altered, and the electron card, which has a smooth surface and can't be embossed—or unembossed.

Putting Karl Malden's nose out of joint. The advent of nationwide bank card nets may do in the traveler's check business. Banks and credit card companies are just now constructing their nationwide ATM networks; soon you'll be able to get cash in any major city out of your own checking account or as an advance on a credit card.

January 17, 1982: Thomas A. Jeffs II, an executive vice-president for National Bank of Detroit, completes the first coast-to-coast ATM transaction. Jeffs stuck his card into an ATM in Detroit and withdrew $100 from a bank in San Diego. It took twenty seconds.

January 31, 1982: Nathan Hayward of Maryland Bank took the first coast-to-coast cash advance (on a gold MasterCard) of $100 from the First Beverly Bank in Beverly Hills. To the best of our knowledge, neither Mr. Jeffs nor Mr. Hayward is applying to the *Guinness Book of World Records* for recognition.

No place like home. One hundred families in Ridgewood, New Jersey, are participating in a videotext project sponsored by CBS and American Bell, the new subsidiary of ATT. American Bell has designed two sophisticated terminals, one of which hooks to the television, the other not; they have built-in phones and keyboards. A number of services are available to the families, including stock quotations, shopping, home banking, an interactive TV schedule, and an electronic notebook. The most popular service to date: the weather, which they can get on a cheap AM radio.

The Most Sophisticated Sleuth Award. It goes to the Paris journalist who proved the Soviets were involved in a Eurobank scam by disguising himself as a bum and rummaging through the bank's garbage until he found the incriminating information.

The bum's rush. It seems the Civil Aeronautics Board is deregulating the travel agent industry, much to the delight of the airlines, who have had to condone this $20 billion-a-year industry. How will we buy our plane tickets tomorrow? Industry analysts predict three ways: keying the data in on our Touch-Tone phones, via our home computer, or through an ATM. An ATM? Well, actually it would be more like a ticket dispenser, automatically debiting the flyer's bank account. The only problem is, Burroughs is the only ATM maker with a machine that could print the tickets, and there are fewer Burroughs ATMs than any other.

Best seller at the bank. It's *How to Loot ATMs* by John J. Williams. This six-page booklet, which Williams advertises in *The National Lampoon*, sells for $19.95. You'd have to rip off an ATM just to recoup your investment. It's reported that Williams is sponsoring a contest for the best rip-off.

ATMs, Las Vegas-style. Some banks are considering the idea of having their ATMs spew out a little extra cash once in a while, to encourage their use. The First National Bank and Trust, Rockford, Illinois, gave ATM lottery winners five minutes at a machine to make as many $50 withdrawals as they could. One ATM executive asks, "Why stop with slot machines?" and suggests customers get a free game of Pac-Man when they bank at an ATM.

This giveaway wasn't planned. In 1979 a Portland, Oregon, nine-year-old hit the jackpot at Fred Meyer S&L's ATM. The combination of a software bug and a computer operator error caused the machine to stick while it was dispensing cash. The boy got $5,000 before the machine ran out of money. He turned in the money and got a $100 reward.

For bankers only. An electronic game called Hold-up, $19.95 from Radio Shack. The player maneuvers the burglar, armed with a handgun, and tries to keep three tellers from setting off an alarm while stuffing money into his sack. If a teller reaches an alarm bell, a cop comes and puts the burglar in jail. Three burglars in the hoosegow and the game is over.

The safest credit card: American Express. AmEx's computer is so sophisticated it can track the kind of charges a cardholder makes and detect anything out of the ordinary. It even can sense when three lunches are charged within a four-hour period, or what counterfeit cards are being used repeatedly in certain stores or locales. A twenty-year-old was nabbed trying to charge a piece of jewelry on what he claimed was his parents' card—which hadn't been used for ten years.

Fagin's mortarboard goes to Randolph Beamon. A teacher of computer courses at Bronx Community College, he was nabbed for transferring $185,000 from the U.S. branch of the Banco de la Nación Argentina into a dummy business account in the name of Computer Technical Institute, a front organization. Playing on the inexperience of a new telephone clerk and with an inside connection, Beamon and his accomplices had illegally transferred $88,000 from the same bank a few years earlier. Apparently the inside man didn't nab the transfer receipt in time and a routine audit discovered it. The Bronx rackets bureau did the rest.

Some people never learn. Lloyd's of London has written its first "electronics and computer crimes" insurance policy for Irving Trust. Lloyd's wrote the first policy for burglar insurance in 1889; the firm also gave a man protection against death caused by Sputnik falling on him. So far, no EFT crime has occurred—at least Irving Trust doesn't *think* so.

The most advanced banking in the world? It's in Sweden, where all paper transactions stop at the teller—from there, it's all done by computers. The Swedes have been paying their bills electronically through the post office's system for over twenty years. And they buy gasoline twenty-four hours a day from automated point-of-sale pumps that read the magnetic strip on credit or bank cards. Swedish computerized banking systems are so good that American banks are considering implementing some of their services, such as home banking.

FROM THE CACHE:
Tracking the Cash

It is not surprising that the government wants us all to hang onto our credit cards if they drop the big one, or that the banking system is considered key to resurrecting the country out of the rubble if we ever do go to the nuclear mat with the Russkies. Our society is as much an economy as anything else.

The oldest and still the most important wire transfer system is the Fedwire, begun in 1918 over telegraph lines, which sluices funds to and from member banks in a balancing act that rivals the Wallendas'. Last year Fedwire processed over $75 trillion in funds. But two other electronic banking nets have sprung up since the 1970s, one international, one domestic.

SWIFT, or the Society for Worldwide Interbank Financial Telecommunication, handles transactions between over 850 member banks in over 32 countries. CHIPS, or the New York Clearing House Interbank Payments System, handles domestic transfers between New York banks and non-New York banks if they have a branch in New York. CHIPS also connects to SWIFT; in fact, 90 percent of all international interbank dollar transactions go through CHIPS.

These electronic funds networks grew up for one reason: We are passing money about faster than before. While the number of checks being written grew fivefold over the past thirty years, the number of interbank transfers handled by Fedwire grew thirtyfold. Somehow, the more we shuffle our money around, the more it seems we have.

We are so into the electronic passage of money that more money might pass through a bank's computers in a day than the bank's total net worth. While the U.S. banking industry completes over $15 trillion in transactions over the course of a year, CHIPS—which didn't even exist until 1970—runs that much money through the wires in less than three months. The electronic greenbacks fly around from computer to computer, and everybody gets a microsecond's worth of interest off them.

With that much money coursing through computer networks daily, the possibility for catastrophic error or theft is mind-boggling. Although the computer systems are so replete with extra computers that the networks as a whole never go down—not that we know what would happen if they *did* drop the big one—little problems can go a long way. In 1978, for instance, the Fed lost $150 million when a wire transfer disappeared into a computer in Culpeper, Virginia. And several years ago a Michigan bank network mistakenly paid Amway Corporation's payroll twice. It took considerable effort for Amway to get its $1 million back.

And although the bankers and security experts have decided that no one could deliberately bring the whole system to its knees, they really have no empirical observations to go by. Certainly any enemy strategic war plan would include provisions for knocking out the banking system. And one wonders if terrorists or well-informed conspirators couldn't take a hack at it.

(There can be serendipity, as well. On November 11, 1979, the Bank of New York was forced to borrow excess funds from the Fed because a computer operator error had kept some electronic funds transfers from taking place. The bank had to pay $200,000 in interest. The money was borrowed early in the day. Later in the day the spot interest rate went up, the bank loaned the borrowed Fed money to two other New York banks and made a net profit of $300,000 on the loan.)

The banking system hasn't made its adjustment to twentieth-century technology without some hitches. In the early days the CHIPS network didn't settle transactions on the same day, and when a bank in Germany folded in 1974 millions of dollars of electronic checks bounced, and the CHIPS traffic volume dropped to a third its previous level as banks shunned the system.

And the banks have never really spelled out in minute detail who owes what for losses occurring from fraud, computer errors, or electronically delayed payments. No national or international banking regulations regarding these problems exist; all the problems to date have been settled on an *ad hoc* basis. And for the decade of the 1970s, because of a misunderstanding with the Surety Association of America, most banks lacked insurance on wiretapped losses over electronic banking nets.

Now that most banks use electronic methods for interbank transfers and electronic methods to record and pass checks to and from customers, it's a short step to eliminating the physical routing of checks. Check truncation Swedish style is being experimented with in this country now, and once we and the banks get used to the idea, it should be relatively easy to implement. Unseen, untouched, our money will exist as blips, our wallets will exist as blobs of magnetism located in some distant computer.

CHAPTER 14

MODERN TIMES:

Computers in Our Lives

Computers are good for us. *The government's Bureau of Labor Statistics predicts that out of 340 occupations, computer-related jobs will lead in growth, pay scales, and number of jobs opening up during the 1980s. Demand for computer-savvy people is so hot that one out of four computer specialists changes jobs every year, the average computer department is 20 percent understaffed, and companies offer bounties of up to $1,000 for employees who coax friends to work for them.*

In 1975 there were three specialists for every computer; in 1985 there will be one hundred computers per specialist. The care and feeding of the beasts has become big business.

Over the past ten years American companies have spent over $500 billion in 1982 dollars for data processing staff salaries, mostly for writing programs, reports International Data Corporation. Yet over 65 percent of those programs are rife with mistakes. Although com-

puter hardware price performance improves 30 percent a year, programmer output increases only 2 to 3 percent a year. Our point: There'll always be plenty to do if you have a computer-related job. So get one. Sha na na na.

According to Edward Denison of the Brookings Institution, 45 percent of all productivity gains in the country since World War II can be traced to technological innovation; 15 percent is directly attributable to computer power.

They don't always come from the business. Adam Osborne, founder of Osborne Computing, was a writer; George McQuilken, founder of Spartacus, was editor of an IBM magazine. Lore Harp, president of Vector Graphics, was a housewife.

They don't always stay in the business. Max Palevsky, after selling his company, Scientific Data Systems, to Xerox, entered the movie business. Jane Cahill, an officer of IBM, was an ambassador under Jimmy Carter.

When Edsgar Dijkstra, a Dutchman who also is one of the foremost industry software experts, tried to get married in Amsterdam in 1957, he was asked his occupation when he applied for a marriage license. He said he was a programmer. The town authorities refused to grant the license on the grounds there was no such occupation.

The highest-paid consultant in the industry. It's James Martin, who was at IBM for nineteen years. He has written over twenty-five books on the industry. His lecture fees start at $5,000; a one-day seminar for fifteen people costs $20,000. One contract with a videocassette training film company netted him $3 million.

Don't have a computer? Try the library. The Nashua, New Hampshire, public library may have been the first to have a coin-operated Apple Computer. Rigged like a Laundromat washing machine, the system costs $2.00 an hour. In a year, says the library, the computer has paid for itself. Other libraries and schools have followed suit.

A new way over the wall. Under a prison education program at Leavenworth, inmates learned enough to figure out what triggered IRS tax audits and filed phony returns to avoid them. Refunds amounted from $600 to $10,000.

Using CB handle "Susan Thunder," one L.A. lady of the night specialized in computer programmers. As a by-product, she also learned enough to start using computers in her business. Through her "intimate" contacts, she gained telephone numbers and passwords—which she made available to others through an electronic "bulletin board" for home computers—to breach computer systems run by the Defense Department and the FBI.

Michael A. Chatoff recently made history in the U.S. Supreme Court, not once but twice. He was the first deaf attorney to argue a case before the nation's highest court, but in addition, he used a computer terminal to answer the judges' questions, another first. The minicomputer, made by ATV of Santa Ana, California, is teamed up with a software package called InstaText to act like a stenographer and is used to teach the deaf at Rochester Institute of Technology as well as to create the captions on network television. Both Chatoff, who handles deaf clients exclusively, and the computer made a good showing, but they lost the case.

The world's fastest computer printer. Made by Mead Corporation, it operates by spraying ink onto a moving roll of paper. It can print 45,000 lines a minute, enough to produce a 225-page book in 30 seconds. Its primary application? Printing junk mail, of course.

After TRON, *what?* More, that's what. John Whitney, Jr., and Gary Demos, who worked on *TRON*, *Westworld*, and other movies, have formed a company called Digital Productions to do state-of-the-art "digital scene simulation." Ron Cobb, Digital's chief production designer (and the man who invented the ecology symbol), whose other design credits include *Alien* and *Close Encounters*, will spearhead the first film, *Starfighters*. And the computer they'll be using? Cray's new XM-P, Serial Number 1. Cost? Only $12.3 million.

"We will produce simulated scenes that suspend the film viewing audience's ability to tell the difference between live action and photographically realistic computer simulation," Whitney told members of the press in Boston. What does that mean? That with these computer-generated images you won't be able to see the difference between reality and simulated reality.

"Boys are brought up socialized to consider their careers more important. Girls are brought up to be concerned with softer subjects. They're not pressured into math as much." So says Ronald E. Anderson, a sociologist at the University of Minnesota, who is concerned that girls aren't interested enough in computers. Odd, since some women—Ada Lovelace and Grace Hopper, to name two—have been instrumental in the advancement of computer science. Computers are generally viewed as a male activity, perhaps because of an undue emphasis on games, while girls fail to see the career potential. The video games are mostly violent shoot-'em-ups, but Pac-Man—developed by the Japanese—breaks the mold. Girls apparently love to play Ms. Pac-Man, perhaps a sign of hope. Where do you start the education program: with displaying the most accessible aspect of computers, games, or with the more difficult, mathematical aspects of programming?

Jerry Pinsky lives in a three-hundred-year-old house in pastoral Harvard, Massachusetts, and tends a beautiful French-intensive garden. But when he's not gardening or walking through the woods behind his home, he's working at Connexions, the first electronic help-wanted service in the country. Connexions helps computer people get jobs with their computers; like *Reader's Digest*'s computer network, The Source, it's a subscriber service that you hook up to with your personal computer. People normally subscribe for sixty days, during which they can look through the help-wanted advertisements that appear on the screen. They also get help writing a résumé, which Connexions will print and mail for you.

Michael Knight, the handsome hero of TV's *Knight Rider*, has a computerized car that can do just about anything. The Japanese have led the way in microprocessor-controlled systems for automobiles, but perhaps the most progressive new system is forthcoming from Aristotle, Inc. It monitors critical systems and announces problems, such as "You have just lost your brakes," over the radio. The inventors? Dean Phillips and his brother John, the kid who designed an atomic bomb for under $2,000 for his undergraduate thesis at Princeton.

"By 1986, computers will be as commonplace in construction offices as a drafting table or T-square," says Harry Mileaf, who conducts research in the field. Architects and engineers are attending seminars taught by Sweet's, one of McGraw-Hill's information systems companies. The major obstacle at this point is finding the applications, or programs, they need. One that might be of interest is TK Solver from Software Arts, the folks who brought you VisiCalc. TK (which stands for tool kit) helps a variety of professionals figure things out. For example, if an architect wanted to use two-by-six-inch beams for a roof, he could tap in some other factors—including the type of wood—and TK would tell him if they were strong enough to support the weight. It will still require a human to pound the nails in, though.

Meeting on Mt. Olympus. General Electric Information Services, which operates the world's largest commercial teleprocessing network, has bought $10 million worth of IBM Personal Computers to expand its services. GE Information Services will offer information and custom programs to its subscribers, who may use their Apples or TRS-80s, if they have one. But the nice part for subscribers who don't is that they'll have the use of the IBM

Personal Computer free—which should tell you something about the value of information.

Dueling computers. Almost every travel agency has a computerized reservation system now, and the airlines that sell the flight schedule listings to them are using computers to control their business. It works like this: If the agent subscribes, say, to American Airlines' SABRE system, the first flights displayed on the screen—and there are only eight flights at a time—are American Airlines flights, even though the agent is supposed to see flights for all the carriers that fly that route. Sound unfair? It is, and the agents call the prime carrier's listings "bias," but, after all, everything's fair when you're paying the fare.

Over 60 percent of all businesspeople write their letters and correspondence in longhand, to be transcribed and typed by a secretary. But what if they could speak into a computer terminal and get the letter or memo printed out? A major obstacle is that everyone speaks differently, and accent and inflection change the way words sound. Now Talk and Type, a computer program Threshold Technologies of Delran, New Jersey, developed for the Air Force, takes a giant step forward. While speaking, the user types the first letter of the word on the keyboard, greatly reducing errors. Talk and Type has a vocabulary of 1,000 words and can type at 160 words a minute—about as fast as you can talk into it. Not bad for a dumb machine.

Try the other end of the pond. It was a standard, computerized promotional letter—we all get 'em. But this one read:

Dear Mr. Thoreau:
    As you read through this brochure, you will sense the enthusiasm we have for the all new 1980 Buick Skylark. Come in and test drive one soon. It might just be the perfect car for you.

All well and good, you might say, except this letter was addressed to Henry David Thoreau of 156 Belknap Street, Concord, Massachusetts—dead these past 121 years.

Julia Child, systems analyst. Our friend Matt Kerr tells the story of the two gray-haired ladies working at the IRS facility in Andover, Massachusetts, who bought an ice-cream cake for a fellow employee's birthday party. Returning to the office with nowhere to keep the cake cool, they thought of the air-conditioned computer room. They put the cake inside a disk drive unit, safe from hungry eyes. A systems analyst, returning to work, remembered he'd forgotton to load the disks in that particular drive and hit the button. Twenty read/write heads pierced the cake as it started to spin, creating a mass-storage mess. And you were wondering why it takes so long to get your income-tax refund.

Computer meets cow. At a technical institute in New Delhi, India, a sacred cow wandered into the computer room and, finding it refreshingly cool, lay down for a nap. It was several hours before the holy hoofer trotted out, allowing data processing as usual.

Drawing by Rich Tennant

"I see . . . I see . . . I see a computer glitch. Wait a second here. . . ."

Computer agony. B. L. Ochman has started a business called "Rent-A-Kvetch," dedicated to the fine art of complaining about computer snafus. She helped a man who kept receiving bills from a department store—and finally from a collection agency—asking him to pay up the $0.00 he owed. The kvetch's advice: Write a check for the amount. It worked.

It would be interesting to see how the kvetch would have handled the same situation when it happened to a German man. When he wrote the check for the prescribed 0.00 DM, the bank sent him a notice saying it couldn't process that amount.

Computer mom. Most of us remember with fondness how our mothers got us out of bed for school. Author Rochester recently stayed at a hotel with a computerized telephone wake-up call system. The message was a cheery, "Good morning, it's seven o'clock. Have a nice day." One morning it was Mom, but the next day it was Dad; author Rochester didn't crawl back under the covers the second day.

It was the day after the end of the world . . . Philip had hoped to pull off a miracle and had managed to do just the reverse. He had pitted everything on one clever move—and lost.

Want to read on? Then grab your computer, dial up The Source on your modem, and ask for Burke Campbell's *Blind Pharaoh*, the world's first all-electronic novel. Campbell, a Texan who now lives in Toronto, wrote his twenty-thousand-word novel as a media event: He arrived at a posh art gallery in a black Cadillac limousine, dressed in a black, sequined sweat suit and black cowboy boots. Mounting a black vinyl stage, he sat down in front of his Apple III and wrote *Blind Pharaoh* marathon-style in three days. How much does it cost to read? You can have it sent to your printer or copied onto a floppy disk for $2.03—a hell of a lot cheaper than the book you're reading now. (In fairness to TNC, critics say *Blind Pharaoh* reads like a novel written in three days.)

The what? The psycho-computer syndrome. That's what Hal and Beth Guarnieri call fear of computing. The Guarnieris, who head up Automation Management in Richmond, Virginia, help people overcome their computerphobia. Bad cases: One woman was so afraid she threw up all over the keyboard, and another feared the devil was inside the machine and would steal her soul.

How to help? David Ledecky, a researcher at International Resource Development, Inc., in Norwalk, Connecticut, asserts that using communicating computers to send electronic mail could afford nonthreatening exposure.

Now, the only problem with that is network addiction. Starr Roxanne Hiltz, a professor of sociology at Upsala College in East Orange, New Jersey, studied people using the Electronic Information Exchange System (EIES) for two years. Findings: Users couldn't function when the system was down, they played games instead of taking coffee breaks, and they began to refer to their mental functions in computerese. "We've never found an ex-addict," says Hiltz, noting that more than one user whose terminal was taken away sold his car to buy a micro and get plugged in again.

Computer Cupid. On Valentine's Day 1983, George Stickles and Debbie Fuhrman, who met each other via the CompuServe network, were electronically wed, with seventy-six on-line attendees cheering and throwing rice—in this case commas, semicolons, and other punctuation marks. It was the first live computer network marriage, although not the first computerized wedding ceremony (see Chapter 1); it took place in Grand Prairie, Texas, with the bride's parents at a terminal in Phoenix, the bridesmaid in Long Island, the caterer in Boston, and a reporter in Cincinnati. If you'd like to wish the couple congratulations, their log-on name is "Newlyweds."

Computer conflict. "A revolution is taking place and hardly anybody is looking at its impact on family life," says Thomas McDonald, a psychologist at Transition Associates in La Jolla, California. Football widows are being supplanted by computer widows, and to a lesser extent computer widowers. The computer addict becomes withdrawn, staring into the screen for hours on end. The seriously afflicted begin ordering family members around much as they might give commands to the computer. Author Rochester, whose wife, Mary, was writing her own book as *The Naked Computer* was in progress, reports, "We hardly ever fight over love or money, but we sure had some dillies over who got to use the computer."

"Can Thanksgiving make it in the information age?" So asks computer journalist Andrew Christie. He cleverly explores turkey day in techie terms: "Thanksgiving's design structure is dissimilar to that of the standard modern holiday, bypassing, as it does, the grid overlay of church tradition on a locus of preexistent native ceremonial data—the favored method of fifteenth- and sixteenth-century Catholic field engineers faced with the problem of integrating Christian programming with that of a possibly incompatible host culture, sometimes requiring brute force technique. . . . Several thousand man-years of basic myth development went into Thanksgiving's current streamlined civil/religious holiday configuration."

The Biggest Turkey. It's the Petaluma, California, turkey rancher who used a computer to calculate use of growth hormones and ended up with turkeys too big to carry.

Stamp of approval. Romania and the Netherlands have issued more postage stamps commemorating computers and the people who developed them than have the United States and Japan, the two world leaders in computer technology.

Nowcasting, that's what Bob Brown calls it. Bob works at the National Oceanic and Atmospheric Administration's Prototype Regional Observing and Forecasting Service (PROFS) in Boulder, Colorado, keeping an eye out for killer storms. Using a network of twenty-one microcomputer observation stations, weather radar, and a satellite tied to a Digital VAX-11/780 in Boulder, convection storms—the kind that come up suddenly and with great force—are spotted immediately. Most weather surveying devices relay predictions every six, twelve, or twenty-four hours; PROFS scans every five *minutes.* Although flash floods, tornadoes, and freak storms can't be stopped—at least yet—a little warning will be a lot of help.

Then there's the one about the guy who took out a car loan at the bank, and when he got his computerized loan payment book, sent the last coupon in first. He got a computerized letter from the bank thanking him for promptly repaying the loan.

Big Father is watching you. Massachusetts is testing the Model II Child Support Enforcement Computer System, to keep track of divorced fathers paying child support. The system is linked to the IRS and Registry of Motor Vehicles computers for cross-checking—and chasing—negligent daddies down. Why the concern? Because no-pays put more mothers on the welfare rolls; some 85,000 of the 93,779 women on AFDC in 1982 were there because they weren't receiving child-support payments. If all goes well, those of you in Illinois, New York, Missouri, and Ohio get it next.

Flattery will get you anywhere. Computers were being installed at a Reynolds Aluminum office, and one older woman was violently opposed to the terminals. The clever data processing manager left a message in her electronic mail so that when she came to work the next morning, the first thing she saw on the screen was, "Good morning! What a pretty dress you're wearing today!" And they lived happily ever after.

The computer made me do it. The distribution manager and cost accounting manager for a large liquor firm were in a tussle because their computer system's reports didn't jibe. Terry, a clerk in distribution, was determined to get to the bottom of the bottle—er, case—er, problem. She began studying the reports and forming her own cross-checking procedures. She became enthralled with the computer while her fellow employees scratched their heads, wondering what she was up to. Suddenly one day the pieces fit: If an inventory wasn't where the computer said it was supposed to be, it had been stolen within the past week. She alerted the managers, who set up surveillance and nabbed the thieves.

"It's not the outsiders I'm worried about, it's the people running it," says Adam Osborne, commenting on voting fraud. His concern is justified, but in the case of Denver's 1982 elections, the problem wasn't fraud. The city spent half a million dollars on a new computerized voting system designed to get the results out faster. Unfortunately, it was so hard for voters to use that it took seventeen hours after the polls closed to tote the votes. Colorado's rural areas, which comprise 80 percent of the state, had their results before midnight, and Denver took the honor of having the longest wait in the nation.

Getting down. Four thousand feet below Coeur d'Alene, Idaho, a Data General computer hums in its air-conditioned, fluorescently lit room, making a silver mine safe for workers. Microseismics is the study of rockbursts, explosions that unexpectedly occur in deep, hard-rock mines. Miners used to drill holes randomly to relieve pressure; now the Eclipse computer, with dozens of geophone sensors located strategically throughout the shaft, can help predict the next area of stress. An engineer works with the computer to develop histograms and maps that interpret patterns and pinpoint problem areas, which are displayed graphically on the screen and printed out on a plotter. Beats the heck out of guesswork.

But can he type? The biggest problem in business today is the big guy in the business. Senior executives won't touch the computer, for a variety of reasons: "Computers aren't part of their ethic," "It's a lot of work to punch in questions," or "Those who use the computer could be considered the doer, and the executive will be the reviewer." Yet, for all the irony of it, it's probably computerphobia. "Most executives are intimidated by a keyboard," says Control Data's Kerry Orr. Or is it that computers replace the CEO's abilities for decision-making and asserting his mental powers? In 1749, the Earl of Chesterfield said, "Without some dissimulation no business can be carried on at all." And, as we all know, computers can't dissimulate—can they?

Why execs hate computers, Part 2. Ron Hinckley, a White House analyst, got in a mess of trouble in December 1982 when he ran a computer simulation of the 1984 presidential election. Reagan lost to both John Glenn and Walter Mondale.

Double identity. Patricia Marie Dunn was born on September 8, 1951. She got her Social Security card when she was sixteen. Patricia Marie Dunne was born September 8, 1952, and when she was sixteen applied for her Social Security card. But she didn't get her own; she received a duplicate card with Ms. Dunn's number. One account for both of their earnings, taxes, Social Security benefits, the works. The IRS hounded her, the computers were all confused, and, as Manuel Nunez of the Boston Social Security office says, "It was a series of errors, one compounding the other." Oh, it's all straightened out now, officials say. Turns out it was human error; the Social Security clerk who "helped" Ms. Dunne assumed she and Ms. Dunn were the same person. At least it's *supposedly* all straightened out now. But as a friend told Pat, "You better be careful. If she dies they're going to come and bury you." Er, which Pat?

Grim business. It's called the Death Interface Project or Operation Specter—take your pick—but either way, it's the Social Security Administration's attempt to stop sending checks to dead people. The SSA is comparing its computer tapes with those from the Health Care Financing Administration, which lists people who have recently passed away. Estimated losses since 1966: $40 million.

Mistaken identity? Anette Elaine Cammock was booked and jailed in Miami as Jo Ann Hammock, who was wanted for passing bad checks. She spent two months behind lock and key before the mess was straightened out. A police officer present when Ms. Cammock was arrested said, "I vaguely remember that she did have an ID on her, and I'm pretty sure it said 'Hammock.'" The Florida Criminal Justice System computer, it turns out, crosschecks all names that bear similarity to other names of people born within five years of each other. The two women were eventually proven not to be one and the same, but the policeman, whom we shall spare from further embarrassment, still maintains that Cammock is really Hammock.

Speaking of spawts. Gimme two tackles and a wingback. The Blue Chip Bureau offers a data base of over four thousand high school seniors who have collegiate football skills. Coaches can inquire about a player by name or by tapping in criteria such as weight, height, and other vital statistics. The system can handle up to eighteen thousand players and soon will list baseball and basketball players, too.

Our best guesser, Bud Goode, is *Computerworld*'s football prognosticator, sitting at his Univac 1100 trying to pick the winnners. Bud also reports his findings in several newspapers and to several NFL coaches on a regular basis. His record for 1982: 120 hits out of 224 games, and 5 of 8 playoffs. "That's a lucky year," says Bud. His secret? How the yards per pass attempts, gained and allowed, fare.

Pete Rose ranked seventeenth among first basemen? Fernando Valenzuela not as good a pitcher as three other guys from the L.A. Dodgers? And, worse still, blaming these erroneous claims on a *computer*? It happened to the Elias Sports Bureau of New York when it produced a computerized report for the twenty-six major-league baseball teams. A case of GIGO—garbage in, garbage out—if ever there was one. Elias got its data from the Owners' and Players' Relations Committee, which was being used to set up a new compensation system, not to rank ballplayers' skills. Sometimes you just have a day like that, you know?

The ultimate baseball game. Don Weber and some of his baseball-loving buddies created an all-star game pitting some of baseball's long-gone greats against today's best players, all on an Apple III computer. "The Greatest Game Ever Played" featured Phil Rizzuto, Ty Cobb, Ted Williams, Babe Ruth, Lou Gehrig, Rod Carew, Yogi Berra, Brooks Robinson, and Whitey Ford for the American League playing against Pete Rose, Mike Schmidt, Stan Musial, Hank Aaron, Willie Mays, Rogers Hornsby, Honus Wagner, Roy Campanella, and Sandy Koufax for the National League. It was aired over the radio on July 14, 1982—which is not only Bastille Day but also the day your authors agreed to write *TNC* for William Morrow—nationwide. Oh, who won? The National League, when Hank Aaron hit a home run in the ninth inning to make the score 5–4.

So whatever happened to good old sports? The Lake Placid, Florida, football squad uses an Apple II computer, fed scouting reports from their opposition, to analyze their playing strategies. "The computer shows us opponent tendencies and anything else we want to know," says coach Hector Hernandez. "I really believe the computer gives us an edge—emotionally, psychologically, even physically—but we can't program wins," says he. Well, we suppose that's next—or just let the computers play the game.

The people's computer consultant. His name is Russ Walter, and you can talk to him any time of the day or night about your computer. Russ has set up a hot line from his garret apartment in Boston to answer any questions and help you solve your problems. He also publishes *The Secret Guide to Computers*, a continuing series of books he sells for the ridiculously low price of $3.70 per issue. He helps you choose the right computer, work with languages, learn the history, and find the right software for your machine. His consulting is free. Why does he do it? Because it's fun and he wants you to love computers as he does. What does Russ do in his spare time? He plays with his twenty-odd machines and composes computer music.

This card certifies you've had the
dubious honor of meeting, in person,

RUSS WALTER

For further pleasures, 24 hours,
call Russ at (617) 266-8128.

With his *Secret Guide to Computers,*
he hides at 92 Saint Botolph St.,
Suite 3, Boston, MA 02116.

Get his computer books, courses,
free consulting, and friendship.

CHAPTER 15

FOOL'S GOLD:

Blunders, Blind Alleys, and Kludges

You got a coupla extra minutes? Hey, come on out back, I wanna show you something. You see, all you ever see is the shiny stuff out on the showroom floor. But that ain't the half of it. I'll show you how the sausages are made, if you get my drift. Now lookit it. That dumpster's been filling since, Christ, before 1946 even. Junk, all junk. Those VW wheels? They're old Honeywell tape drives. In that box? Plans for a hydraulic computer—I suppose you could operate it with pedals if you had to. See them? Viatron terminals. Hundreds of 'em. Funny thing, I bought 'em cheap in '72, now people are scavenging 'em. Musta been ahead of their time.

Now, there's a kludge if I ever saw one. A Foto-Mem FM390 laser memory. Cost $300,000 in 1970. Didn't really remember very much, and, come to think of it, I can't recall if the company ever sold any or not. Company's stock did fine, though. Jumped from $8 in 1968 to

$40 in 1969, before a one of these was shipped. Course, the crash came that summer.

How about one of these babies? Never saw a round terminal before, did you? Yeah, well, nobody else did, either, except a few investors that are a little wiser now. How about a Bell labs optical delay-line memory? Prototype only. In that bin over there? Ovonic memories. Well, press releases only. A guy named Ovshinsky sold a bill of goods to a few companies that should have known better. All they got for their $40 million was a bunch of canceled checks.

You want an RCA computer? I got one. GE? Xerox? Alwac? Bendix? Northrop? Hey, I got 'em. And look, over there, a perfectly good IBM 360—blown up by hippies. Want a vintage airline reservation system? Take your pick, two flavors. Univac's $39 million gem for United, or Burroughs's $25 million special for TWA? Don't work, of course. Never did.

No, you won't see this stuff at Computerland, and George Plimpton won't do funny ads for it on TV. But I tell ya, this is the real stuff. Millions. Hell, billions, tossed into this back alley. And nobody remembers. Except the burned-out stockbrokers from 1970, a coupla guys still paying off liens on their houses, one or two warehouse guys, and government purchasing agents. Those gummint guys are special, you know. They build more stuff than anybody, and look what good it does 'em. Skylab falls down. Taxes go up. Jeez.

Say, I gotta get back to the store. You poke around.

The first digital computer, ENIAC, was developed for the Army to perform ballistics calculations. Its first problem, though, was done for the Los Alamos Manhattan Project. (Something to do with figuring out what goes on in an atom bomb when it blows up.) It was later discovered that the calculations were based on an erroneous theory and thus no good.

The first computer that didn't work was Charles Babbage's analytical engine, designed in 1823. Actually, it *might* have worked if he'd ever built one, but he spent twenty years redesigning it instead. He died in obscurity, a bitter man.

Plenty of computers since then haven't worked, many more haven't worked as planned. The most costly blind alley was probably the IBM 360/190 giant computer—$126 million in the 1960s. IBM also blew two thousand man-years of effort ($49 million) on the 360/67 time-sharing computer until abandoning efforts in 1971. NASA's Illiac IV couldn't put in a forty-hour week until three years after it was delivered. The Apple III had to be taken off dealers' shelves.

There are more, of course, and there always will be. Wherever there is technology, there will be lemons.

The word "kludge" was coined in 1962, according to *Datamation* magazine, to mean "an ill-assorted collection of poorly matching parts forming a distressing whole." It's pronounced to rhyme with "scrooge." Oddly enough, *Datamation*'s first editor was named Charles Kluge.

Biggest damage award for somebody whose computer didn't work: In 1972 TWA and Burroughs settled out of court a $70 million suit over a reservations system that never worked. Total monetary gain to TWA, an unofficial $27.5 million.

The original contract was let in 1965; the first shipment was in 1968. The main computers in the system, B8300's, were withdrawn from the commercial market after they were announced.

Biggest bum rap for a computer: The onboard computer that was said to mutiny just after the launch of Voyager II in the fall of 1977. Generally, the media reported that the craft's main computer suddenly took control of the space vehicle and wouldn't respond to earthbound scientists' commands. The system canceled a maneuver that was supposed to check the position of a scientific robot arm on the ship.

What actually happened was that the computer may have saved the mission. Two possible problems—software bugs that showed up during early stages of the launch—were automatically corrected by the time the robot arm was commandeered. The problems that occurred, scientists figured out over the several days it took them to regain complete control of the craft, resulted from inadequate feedback to the computer from other systems on the craft. ("No one told *me* that the thrusters were *supposed* to go off like that, so I jigged the gizomocatchit.")

No, the computer did what its designers programmed it to do, and any outer-space mutiny was the brainchild of a human being.

But it *was* a computer bug that just about aborted the Apollo 14 moon landing. A faulty switch aboard the moon module was sending spurious signals back to the craft's main computer. MIT scientist Donald E. Eyles was able to devise a sequence of 130 numbers that, when trasmitted to Apollo 14, caused it to overlook the faulty signals. The patch was transmitted just moments before the astronauts were scheduled to descend. Eyles was given the February 1971 "Bug of the Month Award" by the Association of Computer Programmers and Analysts, and the astronauts got to walk on green cheese.

What causes bugs, anyway? The Harry Eastwood theory, espoused at Leeds University, England, in 1971: women in nylon panties. Static buildup in women's panties can cause circuit problems when they walk by computers. So, big discovery. Women's nylon panties can cause circuit problems in humans, too.

Nice way to start the day. Western Union went into the business of supplying computer services over teletype lines in 1966—and was promptly sued for $37 million by its first customer. Law Research Service, which had worked with WU since 1965 on establishing legal data bases available nationwide over teletype, sued the company when it lagged entering legal information into its computers and in supplying magnetic tapes so LRS could bill its clients. Ultimately the suit was settled for $2.7 million—$1 million to LRS, $1.7 million to LRS's angry clients.

You can't get there from here—relativistically, that is. In 1971 a man named Frank Marchuk announced development of the CG-100 laser computer. It would use lasers and holographic techniques to store ten trillion bits of information (a million times more than even big computers of the day) and run at a speed of twenty nanoseconds (as fast as the fastest of the day). He claimed already to have sold 178 of the machines. But the CG-100 never saw the light of day, laser or otherwise. The basic problem was one of physics—for the CG-100 to work it would have to violate the laws of quantum mechanics, including the Heisenberg Uncertainty Principle. And that, as you know, carries a stiff fine if you get caught.

Another computer that had cold water thrown on it: Maj. John Humphries, Jr.'s, "fluid computer." Instead of electrical circuits, transistors, resistors, etc., such a computer would use flip-flops, jets, and orifices to manipulate fluid or air flows in a manner that could be used like a computer, in a control or logic system.

In 1967 General Electric published a twelve-page pamphlet describing how fluidics work (the operating principle is known as jet interaction or wall attachment phenomenon). It also described six components: flip-flops and/or gates, digital amplifier, proportional amplifier, half adder, rectifier. An industrial market of $250 million by 1970 for fluid computers was foreseen, but apparently washed out.

How about a computer that runs on spilled coffee?

As long as we're on a rotary kick. What about Interplex's round teletype time-sharing terminal? It was a beauty when it was displayed at the 1971 Spring Joint Computer Conference, says its PR agent, Bob Strayton, and it

Photo Courtesy The Strayton Corp.

The Interplex Perplex

Some Organizations You Might Recognize That Got Out of the Computer Business

AEG Telefunken	ITT	Raytheon
Alwacs	Lockheed	RCA
Bendix	Louisville & Nashville	Rio Grande Railroad
Boise Cascade	Railroad	Royal McBee
Bunker Ramo	McCall's	Singer
Clary	Monroe	Sylvania
Dartmouth College	North American	Transamerica
Ferranti	Northrop	Underwood
GE	Philco	Viatron
General Mills	Pillsbury	Westinghouse
Greyhound	Pitney-Bowes	Xerox
Itel		

Note: Not all of these entities left the business in ignominy (for example, Dartmouth sold out for philosophical reasons), nor did all get out all the way (for example, Lockheed makes military computers), and some came back in (for example, Monroe and Raytheon).

would have revolutionized the terminal business back then if only it could have multiplied 12 by 12. Somehow it got only 143 and a slew of decimals—not 144. The company never could figure out why (was the computer using circular logic) and went out of business.

SLAMMING THE BILLION-DOLLAR DOOR

Of the various exits from the computer industry, the two most spectacular were RCA's and Xerox's, the former because of the abruptness of the decision and the size of the write-off, the latter because of the systematic way the company turned an opportunity into a morass. Both, most industry watchers agree, were hoist on their own petards—they tried to compete head-on with IBM and bungled terribly.

RCA was the *Titanic*. Less than a year before the iceberg hit, the company was in a festive mood. At its 1970 annual meeting its computer division was heralded as the brightest star in a product line that included TVs, military electronics, NBC, and Hertz. That fall RCA announced a new product line and cut the ribbon on a lavish new $22 million manufacturing facility in Massachusetts. The company confidently predicted that computer orders would double in 1971.

But there was dry rot in the customer base. RCA's Spectra computers were designed to compete directly with IBM's, and during the heyday of the IBM 360, with which they were compatible, RCA's orders grew. RCA sold only one for every forty IBMs that went in, but IBM sold a helluva lot of 360s. RCA rode IBM's big blue coattails. But by the time IBM announced the 370 in 1970, RCA had cleaned out the easy pickings. From then on it got tougher to sell Spectras. Foreseeing this, the company had begun hiring ex-IBMers in droves in the late 1960s in an attempt to emulate more than just the IBM technology. But RCA was RCA, and even the best of IBMers couldn't change that. When prospective customers realized that the new line of computers announced in 1970 was simply the old line with a new coat of paint, RCA found itself slipping fast.

If there was a single prong of ice that did the RCA ship in it was a management study conducted in 1971 that indicated the company would need to pump in $700 million before reaching break-even in 1976. At the same time, the 1971 business plan for the Computer Division was constantly being revised downward—from break-even to a $62 million loss. The board of directors decided discretion was the better part of valor and on September 17, 1971, announced intentions to withdraw from the computer business.

Because of previous announcements, this came as something of a shock to users, stockholders, employees, and analysts. Users were left in limbo for over two months, not knowing who would service their machines, sell them parts and supplies, help them write programs. The litany of optimistic pronouncements also made RCA look a little sheepish (if not duplicitous). A rundown:

	1955	RCA enters business, first computer (Bizmac) shipped to Army.
December	1964	RCA announces Spectra series to compete with IBM 360, announced in April 1964.
	1967	RCA surpasses $3 billion revenues, computer bookings double 1966 total.
May	1969	Sarnoff tells shareholders at annual meeting, "We expect to achieve a lasting profit position in computers early in the 1970s . . . and reach a level of profitability that equals or exceeds that of any other RCA division."
April	1970	Sarnoff: "We expect domestic computer shipments to increase about seventy percent this year."
September	1970	RCA announces new line of Spectras, opens $22 million facility. Sarnoff: "We are determined to attain an industry rank second only to IBM in this country."
March	1971	RCA reports on 1970 results. Net income down 43 percent; computer domestic net shipment value up 50 percent; computer bookings at $150 million, revenues running about $12 million per month.
May	1971	Sarnoff: "RCA is making the largest investment in its history to establish a strong position in computers."
May	1971	RCA breaks ground on a $16 million building in Massachusetts.
July	1971	Sarnoff in letter to SEC: "RCA has no intention of selling its computer division."
September	1971	RCA announces intentions to withdraw from the computer industry and sell its Computer Division.

The penalty for getting out was a $490 million write-down of 1971 results—the largest in corporate history at that time—and a user base that foundered until Univac agreed on November 19, 1971, to acquire the RCA base.

Exit RCA.

Enter Xerox. The copier giant entered the computer business in 1969 just before RCA got out. Xerox bought a small company called Scientific Data Systems (SDS). Started in 1961 with $1 million in capital by an entrepreneur named Max Palevsky, SDS had broken $100 million a year in revenues. SDS, with a specialized computer designed for time-sharing and that didn't compete on the same turf as the IBM 360, was a Wall Street darling at the time.

And Xerox was hungry. Or myopic. Over a lunch at Palevsky's house the deal was struck: Xerox would pay a whopping $918 million for SDS. This was an incredible ninety times earnings and turned out to be four times what Honeywell would pay for GE's computer business, a better buy, the next year. Palevsky's personal investment of $100,000 had grown a thousandfold, to $100 million.

But Xerox was game for the fight. As one spokesman said, "By 1975 the price won't matter."

Little did he know. SDS, when it was bought, had peaked. Forty percent of its business came from government contracts tied to the space program, and once Neil Armstrong took his famous steps on the moon, the NASA gravy train began to slow down. Digital Equipment by this time was making inroads into SDS's market, and it was known that IBM would be announcing a new computer soon. Palevsky himself had figured he'd need to pump in $250 million to get through the first half of the 1970s.

Xerox compounded the problem by trying to turn the SDS product line into something that would compete with the standard IBM machines, which SDS machines hadn't been designed for. The company brought in ex-IBMers and tried to market the systems as an IBM would. It was a disaster. Between 1970 and 1975 Xerox lost $264 million and managed to increase its installed base by only 150 machines. Xerox estimated that it would require another $200 million to reach break-even by 1980. On July 21, 1975, the company announced to the world it was throwing in the towel in the computer business.

As the last president of SDS and the first of the new Xerox Data Systems, Dan McGurk said shortly after the announcement, "I don't really think top management ever understood the computer business or the commitment that would be necessary for success. Maybe they just found out and that's why they dropped out."

So maybe there was prophecy as well as truth in the 1969 ad Xerox ran just after acquiring Palevsky's company. The ad said: "The same old management that put SDS out of business now runs Xerox Data Systems."

Exit Xerox.

The third most spectacular exit from computers: Itel. The company, known for the oriental rugs that bedecked its headquarters and the six-figure salaries its salespeople earned, sold computers that could run IBM software.

In January 1979, to celebrate a $50 million profit in this "plug-compatible" business, Itel flew thirteen hundred employees to Acapulco to celebrate, spending $3 million in the process.

But then IBM announced a new computer, the 4300, and suddenly Itel's computers were technologically obsolete. From its $50 million profit on plug-compatibles in 1978 the company went to a loss of $50 million in the first half of 1979. The company's pyramided profit centers began to collapse on one another. By the end of the year the company had disposed of all its computer business, lost or booted out most of its top managers, laid off over six thousand out of seven thousand employees, watched its stock drop from $39 to $5, and posted losses of $443 million. Exit Itel.

Making the worst of a good situation? This was Honeywell's acquisition of Computer Controls Corp., a maker of "digital logic modules," in 1966. This Framingham, Massachusetts, company was in the same business as nearby Digital Equipment Corp., and, at the time of the Honeywell purchase, had technology that was at least as good, people at least as smart, and growth at least as fast as DEC. Revenues in 1965 for CCC were $24 million; for DEC, $22 million.

At first Honeywell kept CCC separate from its other business, but later lumped it in with its commercial data processing business—a different market if there ever was one. The CCC business was ingested by the Honeywell bureaucracy, most of the good people left and ended up at Prime Computer, and Honeywell missed the first round of minicomputer action.

The first (and only) robot supermarket: Telemart, opened in San Diego in 1970. Shoppers would call Telemart (Touch-Tone phones only), give a credit number, and be connected to the company's computer. They would then key into the computer the items they wanted, using the Touch-Tone phone. The computer was equipped with an IBM 7770 audio response unit and could announce if something was out of stock or if there were specials of the day. The shoppers' accounts would be charged with the total, and the computer would print the most efficient picking list for the warehouse and dispatch the proper delivery vehicle.

Telemart's problem, said its backer, was its incredible success. So many people called that the computer couldn't handle all the orders. Even shutting off some of the incoming telephone lines didn't help. Telemart went bankrupt two weeks after opening.

Japan, Inc.'s, first computer incursion onto U.S. soil—er, granite. International Logic Corporation, based in a summer cottage in Jaffrey, New Hampshire. Better known for its near-monopoly on making matchbooks, during 1970–71 Jaffrey also hosted the first Japanese attempt to crack the U.S. computer market and watched a parade of U.S. businessmen trek along the path behind International Logic's storefront offices to the unheated summer cottage occupied by two emissaries from Japan who constituted two thirds of the company's management.

International Logic's product was as unique as its corporate headquarters. Since these were the days many users were going through conversions from IBM's 360 computer family to the 370 family, and because the Japanese were second to none in performing such conversions, International Logic hoped to make a business helping with conversions among Fortune 500 companies. It would work just like offshore manufacturing—the U.S. companies would give the Japanese the specifications, which would be shipped to Japan, where hundreds of programmers would turn out the actual computer code. Done, it would be shipped back as punched cards or magnetic tape to the U.S. company.

But business was colder than a Jaffrey winter, and International Logic disappeared into the woods by 1972.

Out of line of sight, out of mind. In the June 1965 issue of *Datamation*, Bell Labs scientists Donald Herriott and Harry Schulte were written up for their experiments in "optical delay line" memories. By careful arrangement of mirrors and lenses, they had been able to fold a two-mile laser focal length into ten feet. Ten thousand bits of data could be pumped in at one end before the first bit came out the other—thus fashioning a storage device capable of holding ten thousand bits. Each bit would flash by a reading device once in the course of its travel, and access time to data was only the time it took the laser light to travel two miles and the data to be read—about ten microseconds.

According to *Datamation*, however, this demonstration was the last anyone ever saw of optical delay lines.

Honeywell's snake-infested Model H-290 computer. In the late 1950s Honeywell built a computer for Philadelphia Electric to use as a control switch in purchasing power. Unique to the 290 was its logic circuitry— instead of wires connecting vacuum tubes or transistor circuits mounted in orderly arrays on boards and cards, the 290 used ferrite cores. These are the little magnetic doughnuts invented by Jay Forrester at MIT. Normally they were used for memory—crystalline arrays assembled like Tinker Toy pieces with sensing wires running through the doughnuts. Magnetism of the doughnuts would go clockwise or counterclockwise depending on the electrical currents in the wires, allowing for storage of data in the rotation of the magnetism. But in this one case a fellow named Joe Eachus figured out a way to use the cores to act as a logic component, a much more complicated function.

Using seventy-two strands of coated copper wire and hundreds of ferrite cores—and with the help of weaving facilities in a nearby Massachusetts town—Eachus created a component that was about a hundred yards long and just over an inch in diameter. All who saw it agreed that it looked like a snake.

Signals would go in one end of it in one particular pattern, and depending on the particular "weave" of wires and iron doughnuts, come out in another. The contraption "decoded" the information passing through it, like a python digesting a pig. Hooked to the computer, it simply lay in huge piles and curled in and among the other components.

By the time the H-290 was done, there were better ways to implement digital logic, so this particular component was never seen or heard from again. And if you ever ask a Honeywell old-timer about core logic, you'll get a blank stare. Call them Joe Eachus's snakes, though, and you'll get a startled grin. That's all they were ever called, Joe Eachus's snakes.

BIGGEST TANGIBLE COMPUTER-RELATED LOSSES

Fortunes made, fortunes lost. Overall, the market has been rather benign to its suppliers, but there have been more than a few billions tossed down the soil pipe in search of silicon greatness. Because of the effect of inflation, we list both the current dollar value and the 1983 dollar value adjusted for inflation, using the Consumer Price Index. Economists may argue that the CPI is not the best inflation measure, but at least we're all familiar with it.

It's also more than probable that we've missed some. The losses we were able to uncover were the spectacular ones. We may, like Yossarian does with Snowden in *Catch-22*, miss some less obvious hemorrhaging. Obviously there may be some undetected crimes, there may be companies that are about to go out of the business that are right now incurring losses, and the losses of stockholders who bought high and sold low are virtually impossible to get a handle on. Foreign subsidies of weakling computer companies that haven't paid off are not included—in fact, foreign losses are left out entirely. And we've sidestepped the whole case of waste except in a few published government reports.

A whole other question arises over computers used in defense and space exploration. Should the onboard computers now rusting (or whatever they do) on Venus and Mars count as losses? What about the billions of computers used in weapons systems—missile guidance, enemy tracking, tank operation? Are they wasted if we don't use them?

Loss	Date	Pretax $ (M)	1983 $ (M)	Comments
Equity Funding	1973	$2,100	$4,851	White-collar crime. Biggest ever. Use of computer made it possible to create fictitious policies in a pyramid fraud. Losses for stockholders, creditors, reinsurers of fake policies.
Xerox	1975 1969 1970–75	$ 84 $ 910 $ 264	$3,204	Exit from computer industry. Includes 1975 write-off of $84.4 million, $910 million purchase of SDS, and $264 million operating losses, 1970–75.

Loss	Date	Pretax $ (M)	1983 $ (M)	Comments
RCA	1971	$ 490 $ − 78	$1,046	Exit from computer industry. $490 million write-off adjusted downward $78 million later. Does *not* include operating losses of prior years.
Social Security	1976	$ 385	$ 771	$622 million in known over-payments first twenty-seven months running Supplemental Security Income (SSI) program taken over from states. Hodge-podge of acquired systems and last-minute Congressional changes made program virtually impossible to implement. Figures assume 62 percent repayment (SSA estimate). This is simply one documented loss. Undoubtedly there are others.
Itel	1979	$ 523	$ 737	Bankruptcy. IBM 4300 obsoleted leasing portfolio before full payout reached and knocked pins out of plug-compatible market. Losses for 1979, restated 1978 earnings, and nine months 1980. Includes over $300 million write-offs to dispose of computer operations. In receivership in 1981, still there. Lloyds of London faced unknown, but possibly hundreds of millions of dollars in payments for insurance against obsolescence.
Singer	1976 1974	$ 325 $ 40	$ 678	Exit from the industry, exit from point-of-sale market in 1974. Two separate write-offs plus $10 million operating loss in 1974.

GE	1970	$ 34	$ 558	Exit from industry. Includes losses 1965–69, write-off of $31 million in goodwill. Computer base bought for $234 million by Honeywell.
	1965–69	$ 152		
IBM 360/190	1965	$ 126	$ 408	IBM supercomputer project in response to CDC successes. Bust.
Viet Nam	1975	$ 250	$ 405	Defeat in Viet Nam left commercial and military computers in country. Estimate includes mostly military computers. Estimate provided by Technical Financial Services.
Boxcars	1971	$ 110	$ 280	Found: 252 Penn Central boxcars stolen from or lost by computer system. Total loss of all railroads' boxcars to theft or computer error, 2,800 vehicles.
Memorex	1973	$ 119	$ 274	Exit from mainframe market. Includes write-offs associated with discontinuance of mainframes and other losses that prompted Bank of California to take over in 1973.
IBM	1973	$ 115	$ 266	Settlement of CDC antitrust case. Included payments and other arrangements with CDC, less what CDC paid for Service Bureau Company plus an estimated $30 undervaluation of SBC book value.
IBM trials		$ 150	$ 290	Lawyers' fees for antitrust trials starting with CDC. Maybe significantly more—but was the money wasted?
OPM	1981	$ 210	$ 239	Crime. Forged documents to get leases on computers; same computer leases used as collateral for different bank loans.

Loss	Date	Pretax $ (M)	1983 $ (M)	Comments
				Damage may be more severe— users of computers could suffer up to $250 million from lack of OPM insurance on leases.
Levin- Townsend	1970–73	$ 67	$ 164	Successive losses as Levin- Townsend leasing computers, first-year losses as Rockwood Leasing.
Iran	1979	$ 105	$ 162	Revolution. Commercial computers abandoned to Ayatollah Khomeini valued on an if-sold basis at $70 million; TNC estimate of $35 million military computers.
IBM 360/67 TSS	1967	$ 49	$ 150	IBM attempt at time-sharing computer. TSS abandoned in 1967.
Cenco	1973–74	$ 40	$ 90	Crime. Company inflated inventory records to mislead potential stock purchasers.
IBM Stretch	1955	$ 20	$ 77	IBM project to build larger computer. Only nine sold.
Chilcott	1977	$ 45	$ 77	Crime. Use of bogus computer reports to obtain investments from victims. Perpetrator: Thomas Chilcott. Assets inflated $45 million.
Viatron	1971	$ 30	$ 76	Bankruptcy. Revolutionary product priced for volume sales, but demand never developed, costs were higher than expected.
New Jersey welfare	1972	$ 30	$ 74	Unrecovered portion of $100 million overpayments of unemployment. Computers couldn't handle increased claims load, 1971–73.

| Saxon | 1982 | $ 53 | $ 56 | Crime. Extra set of computerized books to inflate value of inventory on hand. Proper inventory and accounting wiped out fictitious profits. |
| J. W. Thompson | 1981 | $ 31 | $ 35 | Crime. Faked computer accounting records overstated profits. |

Making money selling computers is fine. Lots of people do it. But salesmen from Datapoint carried it too far when they booked orders that weren't there (how quickly they forgot Itel). Over $20 million of system orders were found to be phony in 1982, and the resulting chaos at Datapoint caused 1982's most spectacular stock slide—seventy points.

MARCH OF THE MEMORY ELEPHANTS

The lusts of computer users, from ENIAC attendants to Apple II owners, have varied greatly over the times, but one lust has remained constant: the craving for more memory. In the beginning this was sated by punched cards or paper tape kept in boxes and manually input to the computer when it needed information, but automated methods soon came into vogue. IBM first delivered its RAMAC disk-based computer in 1957 and began the era of rotating magnetic memories.

These are all most of us see these days—whirring tape drives or spinning disks—but in the early days there were plenty of alternative methods. Rotating drums (some still are used) had their salad days in the early 1960s, weirdo punched-card contraptions and bizarre tape drives saw brief light. GE's RACE system used magnetically recorded cards moving along a path within the machine—at many feet per second. A jam-up would cause a small volcano of cards. Burroughs offered its Magnetic Tape Cluster, which had tape reels stacked atop each other like pancakes and wove the moving tape around a series of capstans and posts. The idea was to save money by sharing read/write mechanisms. There were fixed-head drums, rotating disks, woven wire systems, tape loop systems, tape strip files, and even experimental laser holographic memories. All that survived of that crew were the disks and tapes of today.

But even these systems offer too little memory for the real data junkie. To this realm was relegated some of the more bizarre computer-related devices and some of the blindest alleyways of development. They were called Mass Store Systems (MSS) and, from a family tree of over a dozen branches, only two main products are in the market today. How they worked and where they went:

MACHINE	COST	COMMENTS
IBM Photo-Digital Store 1360 Digital "Cypress"	$1–2M	Five installed, first two to AEC 1967. Could store a trillion bits of data. Largest mass storage memory of the day, built to tight error-rate specs. This would be enough to provide the average person with two hundred years of uninterrupted reading. Same as a billion punched cards or stack of magnetic tape reels a thousand feet high. Perhaps the most Rube Goldberg of all systems. Data stored on little pieces of film kept in cells (eleven thousand) kept in movable files stacked in trays like egg crates, moved to read/write head by whooshing-air jets. Everything automatic, including wet processing of film. Said one observer, only IBM could make something this complicated and make it work.
IBM 2321 DataCell	$.5–1M	Hundreds installed late 1960s, early 1970s. Known in trade as "chicken plucker." Used filmstrips plucked by mechanical hands from storage.
CDC Scroller	NA	Used 5,000-foot tape twenty-two inches wide to store data and scrolled past a read/write head. Got nowhere fast.
Honeywell Project Mass	NA	Thin metal film on glass with an electron beam to alter film irreversible. More of a dark alley than CDC Scroller. Lab only.
Grumman Masstape	$.5–1M	Another trillion-bit goliath. Used analog recording techniques to write data cartridge with 260 feet of tape. Announced in 1971. Never made it to market.
Foto-Mem FM 390	$.3M	Company went public in 1968, stock went from $8 to over $40, company to make 750 billion bits of data. Kaputski. Company disappeared from view.
Precision Instruments Unicon 690	$.398M	Used laser to burn holes (data) into rhodium-coated polyester strips. Another trillion-bitter. Delivered some to govern-

ment about 1972. Product never worked. Might have been that polyester.

Ampex Terabit	$.5–3M	Get this: *three* trillion bits. Uses videotape recording techniques and videotape as medium. Five or six actually shipped early 1970s. Never supported with software. System worked. Considered a breakthrough.
Xytex (bought by Calcomb, then Braegen)	$.3M	The jukebox. Took tape reels in racks and could mount them on tape drives. Simplicity itself. Actually worked. Fifty to sixty sold early to mid-1970s.
IBM 3850	$1.2M	Magnetic tape in cartridges stored in honeycomb. Same chicken-plucking technique. Didn't work at first (1974), didn't get into volume shipments until late 1970s. Still selling. Over five hundred sold. First winner.
Massstore M860	$.5M	Similar to IBM 3850 but smaller, cheaper, faster. First shipments 1981. Too new to tell if a survivor, but quite likely.
Fujitsu, TRW, RCA Hitachi, IBM	NA	Biggest blind alley of all? Use of laser hologram should work but doesn't. Given up by all players.
GE Beamos	NA	Lab prototype of a memory system that uses electron beams to write on a semiconductor memory. Used "matrix electron lens" and 289 lenslets. Better stick to light bulbs.

The Naked Computer's favorite mass memory is the "Ovonic file." Controversial Stanford R. Ovshinsky, who says he's been blackballed by the semiconductor industry because he didn't get a college degree, came up with "amorphous semiconductors" that he claimed would rewrite mass-storage history. Lasers or electron beams, said Ovshinsky, could write especially small on the amorphous semiconductors—and he said so convincingly enough to get some money out of Burroughs and 3M, which have been searching for microfilm that you can erase for years. Nothing panned out—no one ever *saw* an Ovonic memory, much less got to test one out.

Ovshinsky was last seen touting a new area of interest—the Ovonic energy device. You see, you take these amorphous semiconductors . . .

From *TNC* to Synapse Corp.'s sales vice-president, Stanton Joseph: one size fourteen bronze shoe, for chewing. When he was meeting in the summer of 1982 with Ms. Kay G. Tochimoto, chairperson of the Japanese trading company that set up the three-thousand-person Burroughs sales organization in Japan between 1952 and 1974 and potential representative of Synapse in Japan, he pulled one of the all-time boners. Trying to impress her with the abilities of the company's software team, he found he had too much momentum to stop when he got to this part of the presentation ". . . and our data base group leader came from Lawrence Livermore labs, where they build the atomic bombs."

Ms. Tochimoto, without changing expression, merely answered: "They build a fine product."

Best computer sales pitch that didn't get the order. Dick Vivian's attempt to convince Johnson Controls to buy a Perkin-Elmer computer for factory automation rather than build its own from scratch.

Vivian: "An example of the buy-vs.-build decision was faced by Noah. He could have gone to an ark company, or he could go chopping down trees. You're in the same position."

Silence, then from an engineer at the back of the conference room who didn't recognize the bait: "But, sir, Noah *did* build his own boat."

Vivian, up and shouting: "Damn right! And if you have forty years and God on your side, you ought to build your own computer."

Johnson Controls was sold on the point and bought a computer. Unfortunately, it was from one of Vivian's competitors.

FROM THE CACHE:
Unviable Viatron

Those who putter with computers can be divided into two camps: those who were around for Viatron's brief flowering, and those who came after. Nobody involved with computers could have missed its heyday, unless they spent a year in Tahiti. That's about how long Viatron lasted.

Its story starts at Mitre Corp., which spun out of Lincoln Labs in 1958, which spun out of MIT in 1951. Some of the top computer brains of the day worked at Mitre—air defense computers were fertile soil for computer scientists. In March 1968 one of them, Dr. Edward M. Bennett, spun out of Mitre and took thirteen eggheads with him. It was the first pseudopod of any size spawned by Mitre. They formed a company called Viatron, these forward-looking scientists from a forward-looking think tank, and started working on a forward-looking first product.

In October 1968, Viatron announced it—a small computer designed to work remotely from larger systems but connect to them by wires. Some called it terminal, some called it computer, but all called it phenomenally cheap: $39 a month with enough gizmos on it to make it work.

The price was based on a rationale of mass production. Low price equals many orders equal large manufacturing runs equal economies of scale equal low price. It's a nice cycle if it works. The Viatron machine was to be the "everything" box, and the company referred to itself as the GM of computers—making them affordable for the common man.

It *was* forward-looking. In fact, it encompassed most of the buzz words one encounters today in advanced computer systems: microprocessors, microprogramming, point-of-origin key stroke capture, user-friendliness, portability, compatibility, ergonomics, color graphics.

By January 1969, Viatron had fourteen thousand orders—and had lost its first million dollars. The terminals were promised for the summer of 1969 but didn't make it into users' hands until October of that year, by which time the company had sunk $9.4 million in the hole. The product cycle began. Viatron also announced two bigger computers: price, $99 a month. Viatron hired at a dizzying clip, took out sixteen-page color ads in trade magazines, and leased new facilities.

On April 1 (appropriately), 1970, the trade weekly *Computerworld* ran a full-page story speculating how much Viatron's profit would be. The company then had over $100 million in backlog (one company wanted thirty-four thousand terminals), $36 million in backing, manufacturing capability to turn out six hundred units a month, $63 million worth of computer chips ordered to put in its terminals, and a pioneering plan to assemble its products in the Far East. This, mind you, was six months after the first terminal was shipped.

In May the cards started tumbling down. Viatron, to its chagrin, found costs were higher than anticipated. (Is it ever the other way around?) Orders evaporated because Viatron's backlog was so big customers had to wait many months for their "everything" boxes. The recession hit, pounding many small go-go computer companies. Stock prices fell that year like lemmings over the cliffs of Norway. Viatron, beginning to bleed, doubled prices.

By May, the same *Computerworld* columnist who'd described the critical dimensions of Viatron's future piles of money was questioning the company's long-term viability. Layoffs had begun. Only fifteen hundred terminals actually had gone to customers.

Two months later it was all over but the wringing of hands and post mortem legal work. The board of directors tossed Bennett out on his ear, replacing him with a Harvard Business School professor. His reign was shorter than Bennett's. Viatron began looking for somebody to buy it up—a sugar daddy with $100 million to spend financing a lease base. More layoffs—four in four months by September. The product line turned invisible. Christmas found Viatron with its third president and an overdue interest charge on $15 million of debentures.

By March 1971, three years after it was formed, Viatron was in receivership, bankrupt. It employed seventeen people, down from a high of a thousand, and pretty close to the fourteen who had formed it. The company finally was liquidated in 1974. The company's product cycle lasted about a year; the company spent half its life in receivership.

What really did Viatron in? The recession didn't help, nor did the cost of money. Viatron's dealer network rebelled when the company stopped offering leases in an attempt to conserve cash. Ironically, demand was high. Chip costs were higher than expected.

But the real reason was that the company was so forward-thinking. This forward-thinking cadre from a forward-thinking outfit got so far ahead of themselves that the product didn't have a chance. In many respects, what Viatron produced was the same as today's personal computer or advanced work station. And *that* revolution wouldn't begin for another seven years, wouldn't thrive for a decade. Viatron was a time machine that got caught in a warp and couldn't get out.

CHAPTER 16

NEANDERTHAL COMPUTER:

Screwups, Blowups, and Meltdowns

Saying a computer "screwed up" is as nonsensical as thinking an automobile is "out to get you." Both are machines, inanimate hunks of smelted mud without any volition. There are no such things as computer errors, just human errors—of design, fabrication, or operation. Blaming a mishap on a computer foul-up is ipso facto a logical fallacy.

There, now we've said it. Purists should be satisfied.

So let's revel in computer blunders. Let's wallow in all the stupid things those unthinking automatons have done to us. Let's tell a few war stories.

There's no estimate how much computer goofs have cost the world—we hope it's not as much as computers have helped—but some figures are attainable. U.S. industry has spent over $8 billion (at least) on unscheduled hardware maintenance since the computer was invented, and programming errors probably have cost industry and

253

*government more than that. One out of ten lines of first-draft pro-
gramming code, on average, is in error.*

*But what about the other stuff? The wild-goose chases computers
send us on, the spectacular way our systems do us in. What was it
that downed an $18 million rocket on the way to Venus just after it
was launched from Cape Kennedy? A missing hyphen in one of its
lines of computer code. What did the Air Force get for its $250 million
spent on an advanced logistics system? Something that didn't work,
would cost another $500 million to make right, and a directive in
1975 from Congress to abandon it (which it didn't).*

*So, off we go. Into the netherworld of computers. Life under
the rug.*

Ho ho ho. In December 1971, the Arizona State Finance Center in Phoenix discovered that one of its computer tapes was missing. When it went to
get the backup punched cards from which to reconstruct the data, it discovered the true meaning of Christmas. Two thousand of the cards had
been folded, gilded, and used as tree ornaments.

Fastest computer millionaires. Mr. and Mrs. Emmanuel Kops. In 1971
they received a bank statement that showed a deposit of $20,200,071.49.

Most honest millionaires. Mr. and Mrs. Emmanuel Kops, who reported an erroneous deposit of $20,200,071.49 in their bank account in
1971.

Most defensive bank regarding a computer error. The Union Bank of
West Los Angeles, which denied an error had been made when Mr. and
Mrs. Emmanuel Kops reported an extra $20,200,071.49 in their account.
Their computer, said bank officials, couldn't handle figures that high.

Most gracious bank regarding a computer error. The Union Bank of
West Los Angeles, which, despite a computer system that couldn't handle
numbers as high as $20,200,071.49, adjusted the bank account of Mr. and
Mrs. Emmanuel Kops manually when informed that a deposit to their bank
account of that amount was erroneous.

The First Parke-Bernet auction of computers was a flop. It took place in
July 1970. The prestigious New York auctioneer was dismayed by the fact
that one out of five lots went unclaimed and prices never really got bid up

very high. Two of the best deals: an IBM 7070 for $2,250, about one five-hundredth of original list; a Univac Solid State 80 computer for $485, about $300,000 less than its original list. Not bought: an IBM 7094, which was passed over at $15,000. In its heyday it was a $3 million machine. Most sentimental purchase: the control panel of a Univac 1, the first commercial computer, for $110. For an office decoration.

Oh, those friendly skies. Consider the agonizing birth of the nation's air traffic control system. Around 1960 the Federal Aviation Agency was authorized to computerize its radar-based air traffic control. The first contract was let in 1963 to Burroughs to develop a device to take radar signals and turn them into data a computer could process; in 1965 IBM was awarded the contract to provide the system computers. In 1967 Raytheon was awarded a contract to supply computerized radarscopes.

Ten years after the letting of the first contract the system still wasn't operational. IBM, said the FAA, was supposed to hire experienced programmers to write the software for the system, but only a third of them had more than two years' experience. Not unusual, said IBM. Raytheon, asked the FAA, how come your scopes don't work? Because of the three hundred design changes, that's why, answered Raytheon. Finally in 1975 the FAA completed installation of radar processing operations at its twenty centers and the system went live.

Immediately the system was controversial.

In 1976 air traffic controllers, fazed by the complexity of the system and the difficulties adjusting to power outages, called the system dangerous. Outages, they said, were occurring at the rate of twenty to thirty a week. The most embarrassing near-miss happened when a DC-9 carrying the First Lady, Betty Ford, came close to a single-engine Cessna.

(In one near-miss, an air traffic controller became mesmerized entering data into the computer and lost track of two jets, a TWA L-1011 and American DC-10, heading for each other. A relief controller caught the situation in time to warn the pilot of the DC-10, who had to put his plane in a thirty-five-degree dive to evade the L-1011. Three passengers were seriously injured.)

In 1977 it was revealed in the media that there had been three thousand near-misses as a result of computer and programming problems. The president of the Society of Certified Data Processors quit that post when the Society refused to ask for a court injunction to force the FAA to "stand the system down" until it had been adequately tested. Late in 1976 the FAA hired Computer Sciences Corporation to write additional safety program software.

Not until 1977 did complaints about the system abate. Now we all use it without even thinking about it.

Most prolific producer of computer errors. The Social Security Administration (SSA). With the largest data base in the United States and over a hundred computers, large and small, the SSA's five-acre complex in Woodlawn, Maryland, is a veritable factory of computer errors. SSA's data base is housed on over five hundred thousand reels of tape, and just determining on which of over five hundred tape drives a given tape should be mounted, and regulating the traffic flow of tape mounters, requires a computer. Once a showcase of computerdom, the agency is now a monument to haphazard growth, patchwork computer system development, and whimsical congressional oversight.

The most public problems with SSA occurred when the agency took over the Supplemental Security Income (SSI) program—welfare for the aged, blind, and disabled—from the states in 1974. Congress passed the law in late 1972 and gave SSA only fourteen months to convert 1,350 computer programs that previously administered the program. Congress amended the SSI laws twice in those fourteen months, the last time one month before the thirteen-hundred-terminal system was to be up and running. One out of ten of the welfare recipients had no Social Security number—making cross-checking useless. The SSA's recordkeeping in SSI made some records of its own. In the first two years:

- $1 out of every $4 spent on the Aid to Families with Dependent Children (AFDC) went for administration, over half of that for correcting errors.

- The SSI program error rate in payments was 23.7 percent. About $1 in every $20 was an overpayment.

- The SSI program overpaid recipients over $600 million. Estimated recovery rate: 62 percent.

- At the same time the SSA closed on bids to build a new $69 million building, the GAO was reporting that it was utilizing its large computers at 40 percent of capacity.

- When the agency rushed through a bid to purchase IBM computers in the last two weeks of its 1975 fiscal year, it ended up having to store them in warehouses for over half a year.

Although some of these problems have long been ironed out, the SSA has plenty of other problems. Its computers are aging, its supervisory ranks are understaffed from 10 to 50 percent at any one time, and its employee morale is low enough that vandalism is a recurring problem at the agency's computer complex—for instance, an expensive disk drive was damaged when somebody urinated on it. An employee, Janet Elizabeth Bartlee Blair, a twenty-nine-year-old clerk, was arrested in 1980 for siphoning off

$500,000 in unauthorized benefits. She got ten years in the slammer, but was caught only when a banker got suspicious of her check deposit history. Nobody knows how many other employees are working the Byzantine system to feather their own nests.

Some other SSA problems:

- Over eight thousand cases of checks being sent to dead people are being investigated by the Department of Health and Human Services.

- The file of wage records that don't match benefits records—misspelled names, erroneous Social Security numbers, etc.—has grown to 170 million records totaling over $70 billion. Some records date back to 1937.

- The system wasn't built to handle checks written in more than five digits; making the change from five to six digits in 1981 required changing six hundred computer programs and took twenty thousand man-hours and twenty-five hundred hours of computer time.

- Figuring the cost-of-living increases for fifty million recipients takes over twenty thousand hours of computer time on the SSA's older systems.

- In 1979 the agency, under Jimmy Carter's direction, hired thirteen specialists to plan the 1983 move of its data center into a new building. It then spent $6.7 million on consultants to do the same thing. Sen. William Proxmire awarded the agency the Golden Fleece Award for that one.

There's an advantage to all this. One out of four Americans gets some kind of check from the SSA, which shells out almost a quarter of all federal government dollars, and overpayments currently run over $2 billion a year. That's about $40 per head. Free money.

The hidden subsidy for the U.S. Postal Service. Its estimates that switching to a nine-digit zip code will save $600 million a year leaves out the fact that converting the thousands of computerized mailing list programs running on commercial and government computers will cost more than that.

Who watches the computer? If you've ever had the feeling that all you ever got when you corresponded with the government was a computer, you'll be heartened by this 1976 report to Congress by the Government Accounting Office (GAO). Federal computers make over two billion payments a year without any human overseers. The GAO calls it "automated decision making" and estimated that in 1976 well over $44 billion went out the doorway without any manual supervision—and that in just fifteen agencies audited, the possibility for errors was over $1.7 billion, not including payroll. One example: Army computers weren't smart enough to pick the closest warehouses from which to fill requisitions, blowing $1 million a year on transportation charges.

Another GAO report, in 1977, pointed out that the federal government spends $450 million a year switching computer systems—that's the cost of making programs run on the new systems. The report also thought $100 million could be saved in this exercise by concentrating conversion expertise in one place.

Big cost overruns are newsmakers, but how many little ones are there? Take the $378,147 awarded in October 1969 to Rockwell International by the Department of Health, Education and Welfare. It was to result in nine months in a system to track federal grants issued by the agency. A nice idea.

Three years later and $3 million wiser, HEW still didn't have a working system. In March 1974 it abandoned the project and later filled the bill with a system that cost only $20,000.

The hidden cost of unemployment. The state of New Jersey computerized its unemployment compensation system in the 1960s during a period of low joblessness. When the number of claimants doubled during the years 1971, 1972, and 1973, the state's computers couldn't keep up and manual processing was added as an adjunct. As a result of confusion, $100 million was paid to workers but billed to the wrong employers. Thirty million dollars of that was unrecovered.

Why did New York City almost go bankrupt? Its welfare computer didn't help. A computer error that was undetected for two months in 1974 spewed out $7.5 million in welfare checks to twenty-one thousand people whose cases were closed.

But then if you'd lived in Boston and collected welfare, you might not have made out so well. The Massachusetts Department of Welfare discovered in 1971 that it had been using an incorrect formula for calculating cost-of-living increases since 1957. Pegged to the Consumer Price Index, the percentage of increase was perpetually applied to the original 1957 base, not, as CPI increases are reported, to the previous year's base.

Oh, well, at least it was caught before the era of double-digit inflation.

One reason to live with computer errors that wrongly pay out billions in welfare: Massachusetts uncovered $129 million in welfare fraud in 1982 merely by checking its welfare payment tapes against those of local banks. Matched by Social Security numbers, $4 million in bank accounts of 613 people were discovered in a match of 500,000 names. One woman had

$89,000 in her account. Estimate of total fraudulent take, including welfare, food stamps, Medicaid, and general-assistance payments was extrapolated to be $129 million.

A bust of Ned Ludd. It goes to Judges George W. Spanagel and Gertrude Polcar of Parma, Ohio, who halted the computerization of court records in 1973. They were taken to court by their own clerk, Walter Shipka, who was installing the system, and overruled by Judge James P. Kilbane in 1974.

Who killed Sophie Easier? On January 5, 1971, the Equitable Gas Company of Munhall, Pennsylvania, shut off her gas as a result of a computer-generated notice that she was in arrears in payment and hadn't responded to a dunning notice. It was the company's unwritten policy not to shut off anybody's gas if a customer is disabled, or elderly, or if the temperature is expected to dip below twenty degrees that day. The weather report said the temperature would be in the mid-twenties. Equitable shut off the gas.

But the temperature only got up to nineteen that day, and two weeks later, Sophie Easier was found dead in her house. On the table was a check for $71.68 made out to Equitable. Sophie Easier had frozen to death. The computer had failed to note on the shut-off notice that she was eighty-two years old.

Computers have been used as political weapons for decades. Predictions, polling, mass mailing, and vote tampering come to mind. But the most physical manifestation of the political computer phenomenon took place in March 1981 during a probe by the Boston City Council into improprieties in the city government run by Mayor Kevin White. White merely cut off the council's access to the city's IBM 370/158 computer by deleting the members' authorization passwords. Without access to the computer, the council was unable to trace movements of money in and about the administration. Boston citizens were uniformly unperturbed by the action. In fact, many chuckled at White's cleverness. But then, Boston citizens once elected a mayor while he was in jail.

Sweet boondoggle. The Cook County (Illinois) Legal Assistance Foundation spent six years and $500,000 to develop a computer program that would generate ready-to-file divorce lawsuits without human intervention. Clients would answer four hundred multiple-choice questions, and the computer would generate papers from the answers. The areas specialized in were physical cruelty, desertion, mental cruelty, and habitual drunkenness. So many clients had trouble answering the questions—either because they couldn't read or didn't comprehend enough English—that the system was abandoned in 1977.

BIG COMPUTER IS WATCHING YOU:
Privacy Pains

Recall the sixties. Viet Nam. Haight-Ashbury. The free speech movement. LBJ. Mario Savio. Civil rights. Beatles. Chicago Democratic Convention. Apollo.

This was the decade during which IBM proved that computers could be useful for business. Punched card equipment progeny, they proliferated at what seemed then an alarming rate. And one of the things businesses—and consider for a moment the government, in its administrative capacity, a business—did with computers was put people's names in them.

With their names, in some cases, went their souls.

No one knows for sure how many records the government actually keeps—certainly not the government itself—but a 1967 study by Congress inventoried close to two thousand federal data banks and found over three billion names in them, two and a half billion addresses, one billion entries on alcohol and drug abuse, and twenty billion other items of note about individuals living in the United States.

The brouhaha over "privacy" and computers peaked in the early 1970s and culminated in some important laws—the Privacy Act of 1974, the Fair Credit Reporting Act of 1971, and the Freedom of Information Act.

Some memorabilia from the war for privacy rights:

- Two of the staunchest supporters of citizens' rights to privacy were Representative Cornelius E. Gallagher, a Democrat from New Jersey, and Senator Edward Long, a Democrat from Missouri. Alas, the people's champions proved less than pure as the driven snow. Gallagher was linked to the Mafia in a series of *Life* magazine articles; Long was tied to Jimmy Hoffa and shenanigans of the Teamsters Union. Long was defeated in 1968. Gallagher's committee was stripped of its powers in 1971, and in 1972 he was indicted for income-tax evasion.

- In January 1970, Christopher H. Pyle, writing in the *Washington Monthly*, revealed that the U.S. Army was keeping computerized records on civilians. Cat and mouse began. The Army unplugged data banks at Forts Holabird, Munroe, and Hood, and at its Counterintelligence Analysis Detachment.

  In 1972, in arguments before the U.S. Supreme Court, the Army admitted it had been "overzealous" but argued that the point was moot since the records had been destroyed. But in 1975 the files turned up again and the Army admitted it hadn't destroyed them but merely appended them to files on foreign activities.

- At one peace demonstration at Ft. Carson, Colorado, out of 119 people, 53 were Army intelligence officers.

- In 1976 twenty-six insurance companies were indicted in Colorado for illegally obtaining access to confidential medical files for purposes of writing policies. Insurance investigators routinely tricked government and medical personnel into revealing confidential information, often posing as law officers. The investigators, mostly with a simple phone call, were able to get information out of police, FBI, hospital, physician, and IRS files.

- A study by Rand Corporation in the late sixties estimated that 70 percent of the populace is captured in detail on records held by U.S. companies.

- In 1976, six employees of TRW Credit Data, which maintains credit records on seventy million people, were indicted for altering credit references. They charged $200 to $1,500 for the service and paid $50 per name to the clerk who made the false entries. The longest sentence received was for the ringleader: sixty days in jail, served on weekends, and a $3,000 fine. Companies that issued credit based on the false records estimated aggregate losses of over $1 million.

- All those files on civilians did the government little good when Lynette "Squeaky" Fromme attempted to assassinate Jerry Ford. She was a Manson cultist with an arrest record and had made vague threats in press interviews but somehow didn't qualify for the Secret Service's fifty-thousand-name file of people considered potentially dangerous to the President.

- The total number of personal history items listed in the 1968 congressional inventory of data bases was 27,270,136,000. The files inventoried included only the major government agencies, not Congress or the multitudes of lesser agencies.

Lethal data. In December 1975, when Florida State Trooper Robert Rennie, Jr., saw a car pulled over at the side of the road and a man slumped at the wheel, he routinely called in the car's license plate number. While he was talking to the driver, Frank D. Booth, the message came back that the car was "hot." Rennie pulled his gun and, when the driver reached for his coat for what Rennie thought was a gun, he shot and killed him.

Only later did Rennie discover that the car was not stolen—the "hot" license number had been issued in 1971, Booth's car had the same number on a 1975 plate—and that Booth had been on his way to his father's funeral. He'd pulled off the road to compose himself in an attack of grief.

Rennie was not charged, and neither was the system that allowed unpurged, lethal data to live on uncorrected in the computers of the Florida crime center.

PROTESTS:
The Computer as Symbol

If there's a symbol of the modern age, it's the computer, and our cybernetic friend has been the brunt of many a physical assault. The first major attack took place during a racial protest at Sir George Williams University in Montreal in February 1969. Students set fire to the computer center and attacked the computers themselves with axes.

Thus began a two-year wave of computer-bashing. The most notable incident in the United States was the bombing of the math center at the University of Wisconsin, where three people were injured and one killed. Damage was estimated at $1.6 million, but twenty years of data also were destroyed along with Robert Fassnacht, thirty-three and the father of three children.

Not all kill-the-computer sprees have been spectacular. A Bell, California, policeman shot the police station's teletype terminal in midsummer 1972 when it started spewing out arrest records unbidden, and somebody did $500,000 damage to the memory stacks of a New York insurance company's Honeywell computer in the 1960s with an ice pick.

A chronological look:

INCIDENT	DATE	DAMAGE $	1983 $	COMMENTS
Montreal	Feb. 1969	$1.6M $ .5M	$5.9M	Black students protesting racism at Sir George Williams University occupied computer center and, when fought by police, destroyed CDC 3300 and IBM 1620 and other gear. Two thousand students protest, two hundred inside computer center; ninety-seven arrested. Longest sentence: Roosevelt Douglas serves half of 2½ years and is paroled, deported to Caribbean. Same time, bomb at Montreal Stock Ex-

				change does $500,000 damage, result of Quebec separatist terrorism. No connection with university protest.
Squire	1969	None	None	Black Panther and computer programmer Clark Squire is accused of bombing conspiracy with thirteen others. Squire held twenty-five months without bail. Computer People for Peace attempt to redress. Nine-month trial; jury acquittal in ninety minutes.
Dow	Nov. 1969	Unknown	Unknown	A thousand computer tapes erased by "Beaver 55" group protesting Dow's production of napalm. Tapes reusable and all data backed up. One of few incidents where tapes actually erased by magnetism.
Fresno	May 1970	$ .5M	$1.3M	Molotov cocktails destroy CDC 3150 at Fresno State College computer center during protest by blacks and Mexican-Americans. One person misses death by less than a minute.
Honeywell	May 1970	None	None	War protesters shorten Honeywell's annual meeting to fourteen minutes. World record for an annual-meeting adjournment.

Incident	Date	Damage $	1983 $	Comments
New York University	May 1970	None	None	Two professors threaten to destroy campus computer center if not given $100,000. Money to be used for bail of Black Panthers arrested in bomb conspiracy. (See Squire.) Nicholas Unger, Dr. Robert D. Wolfe plead guilty and get ninety days. Both fired. Computers worth $3.5 million.
University of Wisconsin	Aug. 1970	$1.5M	$4.0M	U.S. Army Mathematics Research Center at University of Wisconsin blown up by exploding van placed next to wall of building. Phoned warning two minutes before explosion. Three wounded, one dead. If bomb had gone off ten minutes later, police, firemen, bomb squad would have gotten it. Destroyed: CDC and Univac computers, twenty years' worth of data, 1.3 million man-hours (13 years) of work. Guilty plea by Karelton Lewis Armstrong; sentenced to twenty-three years in jail.
MIT/ Harvard	Oct. 1970	NA	NA	Student contest for best plan to sabotage

				computers is canceled for lack of entries. Era drawing to a close.
University of Kansas	Dec. 1970	Min.	Min.	Bomb blast at University of Kansas DP center in Lawrence. Damage minimal because of precautions instituted after University of Wisconsin bombing. Three people injured after returning into building after threat called in.
National Farmers Union Corp.	Aug. 1972	$ .5M	$1.3M	Computer operator sabotages computer over two-year span. Vendor (Burroughs) spends $500,000 trying to track down what was thought to be an equipment malfunction. Keith Noreen had "overpowering urge" to shut down computer.
Alaska	1973	NA	NA	Polar bears attack special data-gathering weather buoys run by Department of Commerce. Wiring chewed. No known motive.
Italy	1976–77	$5.0M	$9.0M	Series of commando attacks by Unità Combattenti Communiste—Red Brigades—destroys ten computer centers in one year; $5 million is *minimum* estimate of damages.

Bug saves human. Only moments after student Jerry Polaski left the building, the Fresno State College Computer Center was bombed. He'd left because he'd run across a program bug he couldn't solve without going for help.

If you can't beat 'em, join 'em. After the spring riots in 1970, Syracuse University instituted a new course: Humanities 480. It was a workshop on nonviolent sabotage of computer systems. Run by a manager of systems design for Colt Industries, it purported to teach students the ramifications of their actions along with giving them tips on doing a computer in with magnetism rather than ax handles. The students were required to tote up the damages that would occur for any proposed sabotage.

Maybe it worked. There haven't been too many computer riots since then, the students of 1970 are working for Intel, Texas Instruments, and IBM by now, and the only assaults computers regularly receive are caused by kids trying to get at them to write video games.

Most aggressive computer marketing award. It goes to Data Spec Computer Services. The company's president, his wife, and two employees were indicted for blowing up the computer of a rival company, Computeristics, in 1974.

The most aggressive computer marketing award *would* have gone to Data General if rival Keronix could have proved the Southboro, Massachusetts, maker of computers lit the fire that did about $500,000 direct damage to a manufacturing plant in January 1973. Keronix claimed Data General had begun by hiring a private detective to wiretap its phones and later resorted to arson. Law-enforcement agencies and a grand jury investigated the incident for two years, never able to point the finger at Data General. Keronix sued Data General, Data General sued Keronix, the statute of limitations ran out on the criminal charge, and the whole affair dropped from sight. No conspiracy was ever proved, but behind closed doors people in the industry still speculate on the Keronix fire.

Not all damages are the result of protests. Natural disasters take their toll as well. From 1967 to 1978, according to a study by IBM, there were 352 major disasters in the United States affecting data centers. The number one computer killer is fire (49 percent), followed by theft (17 percent), water/storm (13 percent), loss (6 percent), and other (15 percent). Others include earthquakes, bombs, power shortage, and excessive heat.

The study also showed that the average company could conduct essential operations only five days without its computers.

Another study, by researchers at the University of Minnesota, predicts that a manufacturing company with $215 million in sales would lose

$94,000 in the first week after its computers had been knocked out. By the end of three weeks, it would lose over $2.4 million.

The Naked Computer's *favorite computer error.* It's the misplaced decimal point in the Club of Rome study. This was the computer model devised by Dennis and Donella Meadows at MIT under Jay Forrester that surfaced as the book *Limits to Growth.* Ring a bell? The computer predicted doom. Earth would join all of Los Angeles and Jessup, Georgia, and choke to death on noxious fumes.

But when William J. Boyle of McGill University was translating the original model from its native programming language, Dynamo, into Fortran, he discovered a misplaced decimal point in one of the tables. Fix the decimal, he said, and the planet won't go into the long night gasping. The Meadows agreed that there'd been a typo but pointed out that it affected only three of twelve scenarios. So pollution (cough, cough) may get us yet. (Wheeze.)

The Naked Computer's *favorite company.* It's the Société des Mathématiques Appliqués Ltd., Montreal, circa 1970. The company was a run-of-the-mill computer service bureau—it bought computers and then rented time on them to others—until it acquired a CDC 6600. At $4 million a whack, these require a certain cash flow to own. The Société's wasn't enough. So in order to make a quick buck to pay for its fancy computer, the Société bought up a film production company, reasoning that the new line of business would be good for the bottom line.

Good decision. The first movie netted $1 million, and the Société's first quarter of 1970 saw more profits that all of 1969. The movie was called *Femmes en Or.*

The key to this gem was its plot: Two voluptuous, sex-crazed housewives pass the time of day seducing the guy who comes to clean the rugs. Thigh-high carpet-cleaning suds. Higher-than-thigh other stuff. Then they rip the clothes off the guy who delivers the Chinese food.

FROM THE CACHE:
Ads We'd Like to See Again (Men Only)

In the 1960s hemlines rose above the knee, and some men went crazy. Neuronal circuits frizzled by the rapid change in convention, the men nevertheless were able to hold normal jobs. Some worked for advertising agencies, others worked for computer companies. At least that's how we explain the following ads that appeared in *Computerworld* in the decade from 1965 to 1975. In no particular order:

Name	Comments
Calcomp (plotters)	"Calcomp even makes software for the softwear makers." "Nobody else offers you what we do." Three shapely lasses wearing only bras and panties made of computer printout paper. One on the left most saucy.
Scan-Data (OCR data entry)	"Proposition from a fast girl." "Hi, I'm Sandra 'X,' and I have a proposition for you single-font fellows. Come on, now, you know who you are. . . . Why is it you want to keep so many nice girls in your keyboard harem? . . . Think keyless and I'll show you some real speed. . . . So why have slow girls when you can have a Scan-Data 200 and a fast girl. Like me." A blonde slumped meditatively on an OCR device. Black tape across eyes. Yup, black tape.
National Computer Network (time-sharing)	"Think I'm fast?" "We'll lay it on the line—the bare facts are . . ." Naked blonde wearing only punched paper tape wrapped about svelte body. Plenty of skin. Hair to small of back. Heavy makeup, though. Mom might not approve.
Microdata (handbooks)	"Everything you've always wanted to know about microprogramming but were afraid to ask." "It's all there, no indirect references." Girl in birthday suit holding book across bosom. Ad cropped at three inches below navel.
Tel-Tech (multiplexer)	"The Tel-Tech Multiplexer is like the ideal wife." "Exciting and beautiful . . . requires no periodic maintenance . . . available immediately, just plug in and go. Has no peer." Face only, but sensuous shading and parted lips.
Auto-Trol (plotter)	"Our Model 5030 Delta Plotter is not only a glamour girl, she's also practical" . . . technical blah-blah, then . . . "there's more here than meets the eye." Silhouette of female lounging in suggestive manner, silhouette laced with map plot. Hey, look, you'd have to see it. Huh? Who you calling weird?
Entrex (date entry)	"We taught our data entry system to speak a new language: Dumb Blonde. If a girl can type, she can enter data on our system. If she can read, she can verify it on the display. To her, it's a typewriter and a nifty little TV screen. (She can be the dumbest blonde you can find.)" It wasn't a picture of Albert Einstein.

Data General (software)	"It's a real pig." Full-page picture of a sow's face. Great shot. Not sexist at all.

After this run of ads in the late sixties and early seventies the brouhaha stirred by a single ad from ECI Software headlined "Whatever LAYLA wants, LAYLA gets," seems ludicrous in hindsight—a quarter-page ad, Layla a fully dressed cartoon figure about two by three inches. There were six months of controversy in letters to the editor of *Computerworld*, where the ad ran, about the company's sexist pig attitude. The president answered that the character was named after a song by Derek and the Dominoes and a character in a Broadway musical. Tough noogies answered irate feminists.

CHAPTER 17

GO BIG BLUE:

The IBM Story

"Ever Onward IBM" begins the chorus of the company song, and ever onward it's been since IBM was formed in 1911 as the merger of The Computing Scale Company and The Tabulating Machine Company. When Thomas J. Watson, Sr., became president in 1914, the company had thirteen hundred employees. By the time his son, Tom Watson, Jr., became president in 1952, the company had forty thousand employees. Today IBM has six hundred thousand employees and makes $40 billion a year.

Until 1972, IBM was the only reason the computer industry was profitable—its hefty income made up for the losses of such computing giants as RCA, GE, Sperry-Univac, NCR, Burroughs, Singer, Xerox, and Philco.

IBM, at heart driven by financial rather than technological urges, has kept pace with the times. Its 1401 computer, announced in 1959, set the standard for business computers and outsold all competitors. The

IBM Personal Computer, announced in 1981, has set the standard for sixteen-bit desktop computers and is outselling its competitors.

IBM is also a technological force to be reckoned with. Its inventions are the yardsticks by which others measure themselves. Yet some of its greatest advances receive no recognition, hidden from view as they are by the $60-million-a-year veil of corporate secrecy IBM draws around itself.

For instance, while most credit Ted Hoff of Intel with the invention of the microprocessor in 1971, and Patrick McCarthy and Marvin Minsky of MIT with making a go of artificial intelligence in 1956, it's known to TNC that as far back as 1942 IBM had a special device that encompasses many advances still thought to be ahead of their time today. It was the IBM model 110 "Implantable Loyalty Actuator," and, microscopic in size, it was installed behind the left cornea of all IBM employees from 1942 to 1967 during annual review. Discrete DC voltages that emanated from it triggered synaptic responses in the crinkles of the cerebral cortex, and under this constant electrical wash, employees became intensely attracted to all things IBM. Special read-only programs enabled even the tone-deaf to sing the IBM fight song. Even today, should you look deeply into the eyes of an IBM old-timer, you'll see a glint of the IBM blue nameplate. It's the Model 110.

IBM's most profitable computer: The 704, designed by Gene Amdahl, first delivered in 1955, and the most powerful computer of the day. When IBM's market forecasters first took a stab at estimating how many would be sold, they said 6. A second estimate, 18, was what the product facility geared up to build and on which the price was based. Eventually 180 were sold, not counting 50 very similar 709s. At $2 million a pop, just the 704 and the 709 brought in better than $500 million, and that's not counting subsequent machines founded on the same design. The 705 netted $280 million, and the second-generation 7090 series brought in $12 billion. Original development cost: under $20 million. Other models may have brought in more dollars, but none had as high a margin. Thanks, Gene.

The biggest year at IBM. It was 1964, when the company announced the mag card typewriter and launched modern-day word processing, moved its headquarters to Armonk, New York, and unveiled the IBM 360 family of computers.

The next biggest year at IBM. Try 1981 (including January 1982), when IBM announced its Personal Computer, its return to the computer time-sharing business, a voice mail system, and the settlement of its antitrust case.

The IBM antitrust trial was the largest in U.S. history. It was opened in 1969, went to trial in 1975, and was dropped by the government in 1982. The documents it generated—an estimated thirty million pages—would fill ten tractor-trailer trucks. Had the case continued, it probably would not have been settled until 1989 or later after the appeals process had been exhausted. Some trivia:

- The judge, David Edelstein, had presided over the only other IBM antitrust trial, settled by decree in 1956. That one had been over monopolization of the punched-card business.

- At one point in pretrial discovery, the case was set back three weeks because some papers that had been photocopied were returned out of sequence. It took legions of high-priced lawyers working overtime to shuffle them back into order.

- The whole court journeyed to Florida to interview a witness once.

- The reading of documents and testimony into the record became so time-consuming that the judge finally established a routine where he would disappear from the bench during the trial. In his chambers he'd be reading testimony, while in court IBM and Justice Department lawyers would be carrying on the trial in front of an empty bench. Edelstein had even set up procedures so the lawyers could continue even if one or the other had legal objections.

The settlement of the trial came when the government decided its case was too weak. Most of the private antitrust suits on which the government case was based had been won by IBM, and the issues over which the legal battle was being fought seemed more irrelevant each day. The computer industry just wouldn't stay still while the courts decided if IBM was monopolizing it or not. It was ended on January 8, 1982, the same day the Justice Department announced a settlement of the only other antitrust trial that might have eclipsed the IBM case in size: *U.S. v. AT&T.*

Besides the government case, there have been legions of private antitrust suits against IBM, most won by the giant or settled out of court. Some highlights:

- In 1968, Control Data brought suit claiming IBM had used "paper machines and phantom computers" to keep customers from buying

CDC products—that is, that IBM announced computers it had no intentions of delivering in a reasonable time just to head off potential CDC customers at the pass. CDC sought damages estimated at nearly $7 billion.

The case was settled out of court; CDC got some cash and the rights to purchase Service Bureau Company, an arm of IBM that performed customers' data processing on its own computers. Today, CDC makes more money from its service bureau business than from the sale of computers.

The main concession IBM exacted: CDC lawyers would erase the computerized index to the forty-million-odd IBM documents CDC had used in preparation for the trial. Although the Department of Justice and other private companies suing IBM for antitrust cried "Foul!" IBM and CDC lawyers maintained that the tapes were merely for "work products" and thus subject to routine destruction after a case.

- A company called Symbolic Control sued IBM in 1971 alleging predatory practices in software. The case was dismissed in 1976 when Judge Alfonso J. Zirpoli ruled that "without a product for commercial sale, or at least available for field testing," the company wasn't in a competitive field to be predatorily practiced against.

- Telex brought suit in 1972, claiming IBM had a monopoly in the provision of peripherals that attached to its computers. IBM countered with a trade-secrets suit. In 1973, Judge Christian Sherman ruled in Telex's favor. This first-round victory was a clarion call to others to sue IBM, and no less than a half-dozen companies followed Telex into the courts. Unfortunately, Telex lost on appeal and settled with IBM seventy-two hours before the U.S. Supreme Court was to decide whether to hear the case. This took the wind out of other cases.

- Calcomp got so wrapped up in its case against IBM that when it was dismissed, so was the company's founder, Lester Kilpatrick.

- The most pitiful suit may have been that brought by Memory Technology, Inc., seeking $168 million when business got bad in 1974. Two months later, Cambridge Memories bought the firm out when it couldn't meet its financial obligations. IBM wrote a check for $50,000 and the matter was dropped.

- I breaka you face. Las Vegas, 1976: Royal Data slammed IBM with a $25.5 million suit claiming that slander drove them out of business. Royal, which operated a computerized credit-checking service for local casinos, was reported to have links with the Mafia, according to several sources. The firm leased a computer from IBM, which repossessed the machine after Royal fell five months in arrears. The suit died.

Competing bedfellows. Virginia Rulon-Miller began dating Matthew Blum, a fellow IBMer. Blum left IBM's Office Products Division to work for QYX, a competitor, but the romance lingered on. Suspicious about leaks, IBM axed Rulon-Miller, a twelve-year veteran and a supersalesperson. She sued for wrongful termination due to invasion of privacy and won a $300,000 judgment in 1982. Now she's working for an IBM competitor, too.

An IBM operating system—the software that tells the computer how to run itself—has about six million lines of instructions in it, enough for a printout fifteen miles long.

Life-span of a computer. The longest-living IBM 704 was installed originally at Bell Aerosystems on December 1, 1957. At the time, it rented for $33,250 a month. But its successors could perform so much better that in 1964 it was sold to Pan American Petroleum. In September 1967, almost ten years after it was first delivered, it was sold to Southwestern Computing Service for $1. In April 1975 it was finally retired—the $800 a month in power and cooling costs just weren't worth it.

IBM has a check processor that prints numbers on checks moving by at 31 feet per second. The system sprays ink on the paper through carefully controlled nozzles at 130,000 drops per second.

An apocryphal story has it that Thomas J. Watson, Sr., founder of IBM, once predicted that "the world will only need a dozen computers." The prevailing view thirty years ago was that a few big computing "power plants" would service the nation. Besides, the elder Watson wasn't that hot on computers; he figured the electronic calculators would do just fine. This year IBM will ship over 500,000 computers.

A *classic moment.* In 1945, Howard Aiken paused in his work on the giant digital calculator, the Mark I, to dedicate the machine at Harvard. IBM, hoping to attain prestige by association with the nation's oldest university, had invested $500,000 in the Mark I. At the unveiling ceremony, however, Aiken scarcely mentioned IBM's contribution—the mark of a true academic. Tom Watson, Jr., recalling the event years later, said, "If Aiken and my father had revolvers, they would have both been dead."

Who else but IBM could call a personal computer "The Personal Computer" and get away with it? Eight years after the introduction of the first micro personal computer and long after the TRS-80 and Apple had arrived, IBM finally decided to bring one out—and it is suddenly the industry standard.

IBM made a dramatic policy change with the PC: It went to outside vendors for its operating system and software. The operating system is what makes the machine work, not unlike the electrical system in your car. And, of course, IBM wanted the best, so it contacted Digital Research, the firm that developed CP/M, the most popular operating system at the time, and made an appointment with its president, Gary Kildall.

However, when the IBM team arrived in Pacific Grove, California, at the appointed time, it was told Mr. Kildall had gone flying for the day. This was probably the first time IBM had ever been snubbed, and the event changed the course of personal computing history. Kildall clearly had no intention of relinquishing control of CP/M to IBM, which assuredly would have made more demands than the Soviets at the SALT talks. So IBM went to Digital Research's main competitor, Microsoft, and adopted its system, MS/DOS. It will undoubtedly become an industry standard in itself.

Singin' their little hearts out. The 1940 edition of the *IBM Songbook* was chock full of fight songs and paeans to IBM employees, from old man Watson to the vice-president and general manager, the executive vice-president, and one dubbed "To Professor T. H. Brown, IBM Board of Education, Professor, Statistics, Graduate School of Business Administration, Harvard University, Tune: 'Let Me Call You Sweetheart.'" Over the years these tunes became embarrassing, and by 1957 all songbooks had been carefully tucked away.

IBMers regularly raised their voices in praise of their company; when we asked IBM for the lyrics to the fight song "Ever Onward," the company politely declined. But herewith, courtesy of our friend Charley Lecht, the most famous song of them all:

Ever Onward

There's a thrill in store for all
for we're about to toast
The corporation that we represent.
We're here to cheer each pioneer
and also proudly boast,
Of that man of men
our sterling president
The name of T. J. Watson means
A courage none can stem
And we feel honored to be
here to toast the IBM.

(First Chorus)
Ever Onward! Ever Onward!
That's the spirit that has brought us fame.
We're big but bigger we will be,
We can't fail for all can see,
that to serve humanity
Has been our aim.
Our products now are known
in every zone.
Our reputation sparkles
like a gem.
We've fought our way thru
And new fields we're sure
to conquer, too
For the Ever Onward IBM!

(Second Chorus)
Ever Onward! Ever Onward!
We're bound for the top
to never fall,
Right here and now we thankfully
Pledge sincerest loyalty
To the corporation
that's the best of all
Our leaders we revere
and while we're here,
Let's show the world just what
we think of them!
So let us sing men—Sing men
Once or twice, then sing again
For the Ever Onward IBM!

Gee, thanks! St. Thomas Aquinas wrote the *Summa Theologica*, considered the greatest work of medieval philosophy, from 1265 to 1272. It contains the summa (praise for God), treatises, questions, and articles, and fills sixty volumes. When IBM indexed the *Summa Theologica*, Pope John XXIII was so delighted he conferred the Hand Cross of the Equestrian order of St. Sylvester on Tom Watson, Jr., and his brother Arthur.

Robert Redford, look at us now. Hitachi, a plug-compatible manufacturing (PCM) company, made headlines in 1982 in the infamous "Japanscam." It all started when some proprietary workbooks on an experimental IBM computer, later dubbed the 3081, changed hands through National Advanced Systems, which markets Hitachi computer equipment in the United States. Later, Palyn Associates, a consulting firm in San Jose, offered to sell Hitachi a research report on the IBM 3081, which was on the market by that time. Max Paley, president of Palyn and a twenty-one-year veteran of IBM, was informed by Hitachi's Kenji Hayashi that "we have already got Adirondack workbook that is similar to [yours]." Hayashi didn't have all of them, however, and asked Paley if he could help obtain the remaining volumes. "Please keep confidential," he said in his memo.

Paley called a close friend at IBM and said, "I think one of my Japanese clients has gotten your crown jewels." Less than eight top execs at IBM were notified, and plans were made. The FBI was notified, and through its storefront consulting firm, Glenmar Associates, set up the sting. With thirty-five hours of videotape and sixty-five hours of audio recordings, their evidence was solid; on June 22, 1982, Hayashi and accomplice, Isao Ohnishi, were arrested at the Glenmar offices.

In February 1983, the two pleaded *nolo contendere* to the charges. It was a matter of fierce pride between the two firms, but Hitachi acquiesced when told a guilty plea meant no one would go to jail. Hayashi was placed on five years' probation; Ohnishi, two; total fines Hitachi had to cough up: $24,000. Hidden costs: the $622,000 the firm paid to Glenmar up front for the trade secrets and equipment, now safely in the U.S. Treasury.

IBM hit $1 billion in sales in 1957. As the year 1983 began, IBM was doing $1 billion in sales every two weeks.

It was a $5 billion research project, under development for four years, and dubbed "You bet your company" by a senior IBM manager. It was the IBM System/360, introduced April 7, 1964, by Tom Watson, Jr., himself as the most important product announcement in the company's history. The 360 became the most popular computer in history, the standard for the industry, and garnered over $1 billion in orders the first month of its announcement.

So much for symbolism. Within IBM, the SPREAD (Systems Programming, Research, Engineering, and Development) committee assigned the task of developing this computer dubbed it 360, the number of degrees in a perfect circle. The significance was lost, however, when its successor was introduced as the 370.

First System/360 installation: Globe Exploration Company of Midlands, Texas, in May 1965.

Symbolism recherché. Arthur C. Clarke called the computer in 2001: A *Space Odyssey* HAL. Why? He took IBM and moved each letter back one.

What's in an acronym? Ken Cohen told us the story of the IBM engineers who set out to find a more efficient randomization technique to replace "the Monte Carlo method." Monte Carlo is a trial-and-error technique to find the best solution to a problem, and it gobbles up excessive computer time. Their shortcut was dubbed "the Vegas technique," and when they presented it to a technical review board, Tom Watson, Jr., asked what Vegas stood for, assuming it was an acronym. Without missing a beat, the answer was, "Versatile Engineering Generalized Application System." Fortunately, no one guffawed and Watson was satisfied.

Computer in the round: the IBM System/360.

Photo courtesy of IBM

Fear and loathing at IBM: The world's number one computer maker is the object of violence about once a year. From *Computerworld's* files, death and destruction over the past decade:

- 1:56 A.M., March 14, 1970: A bomb blast takes out the men's room on the twelfth floor of IBM's 425 Park Avenue offices. Eight IBMers evacuated after anonymous phone call; no one injured. "Revolutionary Force 9" takes responsibility in a letter stating, "IBM, Mobile [sic] and GTE are enemies of all life. . . . [They] profit not only from death in Vietnam, but also from Amerikan imperialism . . . and from the exploitation and degreadation of employees forced into lives of anti-human work, from the pollution and destruction of our environment."

• December 1972: Guerrillas dispatched by ousted dictator Juan Perón bomb the local IBM office in San Miguel de Tucumán, Argentina. No injuries or loss of equipment.

• November 1975: A small bomb detonates outside the lobby of One IBM Plaza in Chicago, breaking five windows. The bomb was one of nine set at various governmental and office buildings by the Fuerzas Armadas de Liberación Nacional Puertorriqueña, who claimed it was a "coordinated attack agains Yanki [sic] government and monopoly capitalist institutions."

• May 28, 1982: Edward Thomas Mann, a former IBM marketing representative, pulls a seven-hour standoff at IBM's Federal Systems Building in Bethesda, Maryland, killing three people and wounding eight others. Then on September 6, Leonard D. Avery, a senior keyboard assembler who had been terminated, walks into the IBM manufacturing facility at the Research Triangle Park, North Carolina, and opens fire with a rifle. One man is killed and four wounded. Avery's sentence: life.

• December 16, 1982: The United Freedom Federation bombs IBM's Harrison, New York, office building; the blast is so powerful it is heard five miles away. The building was evacuated just minutes before the explosion due to an anonymous tip passed on by a local newspaper. IBM has put up a $50,000 reward.

Drawing by Tim Eagan

The quiet bomb. On April 11, 1980, at precisely 7:30 A.M., all of IBM's newly minted 4341 computers stopped. Quit working. Nothing. *Kaput.* Cause? A disgruntled employee had written a "time bomb" into the computer's internal instructions, causing the time clock to malfunction and shut the machine down.

And you thought electronics was a clean industry. IBM, in a 1982 consent decree, agreed to pay $2.2 million for its share in cleaning up a hazardous-waste dump in Seymour, Indiana. Its share was twice that of the next worst polluter, General Motors. IBM had dumped solvents and magnetic sludge in steel drums at the site from 1972 to 1978. To its credit, IBM stopped using the site when it learned security measures were lax; the dump was closed by the EPA two years later. IBM uses nineteen sites nationwide for incinerating and dumping wastes. It should listen to Hal Lorin, at IBM's Systems Research Institute think tank in New York; he suggests using the space shuttle to launch hazardous waste into the sun.

Doing it up blue. In 1977, IBM had cash items of close to $6 billion and spent $1 billion of it to repurchase its own stock. In 1979, the firm was forced by expansion needs to turn that sum back into the largest public debt offering in American history. In 1982, IBM made a $500 million convertible debt offering, which means it can be turned into stock when it matures—which will be in the year 2007.

"Variety's the very spice of life." So saith poet William Cowper, and IBM concurs. Aside from being the world's largest computer manufacturer, IBM also makes computer peripherals such as mag tape drives, controllers, punch ("IBM") cards, the world-standard Selectric typewriters, dictation machines, industrial process control devices, optical character reader (OCR) machines, point-of-sale terminals, lab equipment, printing and typesetting equipment, prosthetic devices, and Braille typewriters. IBM owns an educational publishing firm, Science Research Associates; holds partial ownership of Satellite Business Systems with Aetna Life & Casualty and Comsat; reached an agreement with the Canadian firm Mitel to develop corporate telephone systems, called Private Branch Exchanges (PBX); bought a 30 percent interest in Intel, the leading chip manufacturer, and a 15 percent interest in Rolm, another PBX maker, in 1983; and is forming a partnership with Mitsubishi in Japan to import and sell some of its computer products.

During World War II IBM made not only computers but also Browning automatic rifles, .30-caliber carbines, bombsights, and war bond printing presses.

A most prolific inventor for IBM. He was H. P. Luhn (1896–1964), who garnered eighty-two patents from 1929 until his death. Although he was most prolific in developing information retrieval devices used for indexing and searching techniques, he also invented a raincoat, a gaming table, and a recipe guide.

GREAT MOMENTS IN IBM HISTORY

- 1936: First large IBM installation at the Social Security Administration, where punched-card equipment performed over 120 million postings per year.

- 1944: Dr. Howard Aiken completes the Mark I Automatic Sequence Controlled Calculator at Harvard. The incarnation of the machine Charles Babbage wished he had built, it was 51 feet long, 8 feet high, contained 760,000 parts, and had 500 miles of wire.

- 1948: The first computer to employ von Neumann's stored-program concept, the Selective Sequence Electronic Calculator (SSEC), plugged in. It used 12,500 vacuum tubes, 21,400 high-speed relays, and employed electronic memory. Even so, it stored only 150 words in buffer memory and 20,000 words in addressable memory. (Today's microcomputer stores on the average 8,000 words in ROM and hundreds of thousands in RAM.) It was in service for four years at IBM headquarters in New York.

- 1954: First I/O mag tape unit.

- 1957: The 608, first all-transistor computer.

- 1957: RAMAC, first disk memory. Invented by Alan Shugart, who went on to invent the floppy disk, the disks were twenty-four inches in diameter.

- 1960: Operating system developed; later implemented on the System/360.

- 1961: Selectric typewriter invented; ball element an accidental invention of Ken Iverson, looking for a convenient way to tap out symbols for his computer language APL.

- 1962: SABRE (Semi-Automatic Business Environment Research) airline reservation system for American Airlines. The first computer communication system operating in real time.

- 1964: System/360, first IBM computer to utilize semiconductor circuits.

- Mid-1960s: First home calculator system utilizing the Touch-Tone telephone. You would punch the buttons to perform arithmetic functions, and a prerecorded voice would give the answer. Never saw the light of day.

- 1968: First cache memory, ultrafast buffer for performing complex calculations.

- 1970: Relational Data Base concept, developed by E. F. Codd, allowed for separation of information from program itself. An automatic transmission for the computer.

- 1971: Thin-film memory, the fastest recording technology of its day. A complex method of magnetizing dots on a substrate whose expense outweighs its value; superseded by other technologies.

- 1971: First System/370 installed at Zayre Corp., a discount store chain, in Framingham, Massachusetts. Izzy Milkow, Zayre programmer-analyst, claps his hands with glee.

- 1971: First floppy disk. Sexual innuendo enters computerdom.

- 1973: The IBM 5100 desktop computer. You needed a pretty big desk and $20,000. Used magnetic tape reels, was a bastard to program, and had very limited usefulness. One of IBM's few red herrings, it was nevertheless the first marketed personal computer not counting Honeywell's "kitchen computer").

- 1974: Systems Network Architecture (SNA), first and most prevalent computer communications distributed network. Still a standard in the industry.

- 1976: First laser printer, which clipped along at over 300 lines per second, or 2,272 miles per hour.

- 1978: First use of 64K RAM chip. Real Memory Doesn't Eat Small Bytes.

- 1980: The complete logic circuit for the IBM 3081, eight hundred thousand circuits, is dense-packed in twenty-six modules on four printed-circuit boards occupying less than four cubic feet—most significant advance in circuit density packing to date. Called *dense logic*. No one blinks at the oxymoron.

- 1981: IBM labs develop experimental 288K chip, largest capacity to date (eclipsed by Japan's Nippon Electric Corp. the following year by an experimental chip with four times its capacity).

- 1981: IBM introduces the Personal Computer—no numerical designation, no acronyms, just the PC. Over a hundred thousand sold the first year. By January 1983, over twenty other computers claim to be PC compatible.

- 1983: IBM "leaks" word that it has an operating Josephson Junction computer in a lab somewhere, but the time is not ripe for commercial introduction. Meanwhile, Brian Josephson, the Englishman who first introduced the concept of a supercooled, superfast circuit in 1962, reportedly is studying psychic phenomena and extrasensory perception and doesn't place a high degree of importance on computers these days.

FROM THE CACHE:
A Foundation Full of Holes

It all started with Herman Hollerith, whom historian Robert Sobel characterizes as a man with "a gift for things mechanical, but little else." Hollerith graduated from Columbia College (New York) with the degree of Engineer of Mines in 1879 and landed a job at the Census Bureau, compiling a report on steam and water power. There he met John Billings, who thought a machine capable of tabulating the U.S. population ought to be feasible. "We talked it over," Hollerith recounted, "and I remember . . . he thought of using cards with the description of the individual shown by notches punched in the edge." Nothing new: The Jacquard loom, in use in France for over a century, used the same technology to weave patterns in cloth.

Hollerith rose to the challenge, however, and had an operational machine by 1884. By 1889, with three more patents under his belt, Hollerith was something of a celebrity; he was awarded an honorary doctorate by Columbia for his "census machines," and he won the contract to tabulate the 1890 census. The 1880 nose count had taken seven years to tabulate; the 1890 census was completed in two.

Hollerith was not only the first statistical engineer and systems analyst, he also was the first "after market" entrepreneur. While he earned a handsome return for leasing his machine to the U.S. government, Canada, Austria, Russia, and others, he made most of his money on punched cards—the 1890 census gobbled over a hundred million of them, and they could be used only once.

He formed the Tabulating Machine Company in 1896 and began making money hand over fist. But competition grew, and by 1910 Hollerith was short of cash and new ideas. He took the advice of merchant-banker Charles R. Flint and merged his firm into a new entity, formed from three companies—The International Time Recording Company, The Computing Scale Company, and his own firm. The hybrid: Computing-Tabulating-Recording Company.

The best thing that ever happened to C-T-R was Thomas J. Watson, Sr. Born in East Campbell, New York, a town near Painted Post, Watson had been in the employ of National Cash Register, a firm run with an iron fist by John H. Patterson, a man known for his sclerotic management practices.

Photo courtesy of IBM

The Hollerith tabulating system. The top row of dials is the Hollerith tabulator; beneath the tabulator on the left is the pantograph punch, and to the right is the card reader. The sort box is to the right.

As part of an incredibly confusing lawsuit charging the firm and its employees with unethical practices, Watson, along with other high-ranking executives, had been ousted. Standing outside the Dayton, Ohio, headquarters of NCR, Watson, age forty with his first child (his son Tom, Jr.) on the way, said, "I've helped build all but one of those buildings. Now I'm going out to build a business bigger than John H. Patterson has." He did.

Within the year—1914—Watson had displaced Hollerith as president and general manager of C-T-R. Watson codified three beliefs: profit for customers, profit for employees, and profit for shareholders. He also brought a talismanic slogan to C-T-R from NCR: "THINK." When he took over, C-T-R had gross receipts of perhaps $1 million, and the firm had 770 employees. By the end of his first year, income had risen to $4 million, profit margins were significantly improved, and the number of employees had nearly doubled.

In 1915, C-T-R held its first convention, the forerunner of the Hundred Percent Club, where the sales force is infused with new vigor and determination. In 1924, the firm adopted a new name: International Business Machines. Two years later, IBM stock split three for one and there were nearly four thousand employees. Watson, who ran his organization like a general leading his armies, was often referred to as a "benevolent despot"; he demanded hard work and rewarded it. The first known company song ended with the following refrain:

> Mr. Watson is the man we're working for,
> He's the leader of C-T-R,
> He's the fairest, squarest man we know;
> Sincere and true.
> He has shown us how to play the game
> And how to make the dough.

Old man Watson ran the company until just months before his death in 1956, although he had officially passed the reins to Tom, Jr., in 1952. During the intervening years, IBM distinguished itself by offering the most advanced yet useful business machines available on the market. While never the first out with a new machine, IBM always produced quality. Among its successes: the printing tabulator (1919), the electric keypunch (1923), the eighty-column punched card and subtracting-accounting machine (1928), and the electric typewriter and check-proofing machine (1935). During World War II, IBM turned its facilities over to the government for the war effort, producing war bonds and processing wartime paperwork, as well as other manufactured items.

But for all his accomplishments, Tom Watson, Sr., was outshone by the son who grew up in his shadow. Tom, Jr., was the man *Fortune* magazine dubbed "the most successful capitalist who ever lived" for taking IBM into the computer age and doubling its revenues between 1952 and 1957 to $1 billion. In 1971, the year Tom, Jr., stepped down as CEO, the world's largest computer company netted $8.3 billion. In a recent interview, Tom Watson, Jr., said, "They were turbulent years for me. I don't think any one person would want to live through more than one decade like that. But it was an interesting decade. We ended up with a great father-son relationship. I was always hoping that he would feel that I was a worthy son, and I have the satisfaction now, twenty-five years later, of assuming that he's sitting up there looking down, and he probably figures things are going OK."

CHAPTER 18

TOUCHING THE SKY:
Computers and Communications

Wounds of the Civil War still were fresh, the golden spike had been driven into a railroad tie at Promontory, Utah, only seven years earlier to complete the transcontinental railroad, and the flush toilet had yet to see wide use in the New World when, on February 14, 1876, a man by the name of Elisha Gray filed papers with the patent office on an as-yet-unperfected invention he called the "telephone." Yup, Elisha Gray.

Unknown to the middle-aged Gray, on the same day a twenty-seven-year-old foreigner named Alexander Graham Bell had filed a similar patent. Only Bell had gotten there two hours earlier.

The ensuing squabble over patent number 174,465 stirred little interest among the common people. Western Union, king of telegraph when telegraph was king, had turned down Bell's pleas for funding in 1875 as a bad investment. And although it fought Bell over the initial patents and competed with a device based on an Edison transmitter, it abandoned the contest when Bell's company agreed not to sell tele-graph services along with this other oddball thing it had going. Who would ever use a "harmonic telegraph," anyway? Huh?

The rest, as the cliché goes, is history.

Within five years Bell had acquired Western Electric, a Western Union subsidiary grown out of Elisha Gray's early company. Within ten years long-distance calling between New York and Washington, D.C., had been demonstrated. Within twenty-five years six million phones had been installed and Bell owned 30 percent of Western Union (since divested).

Today there are almost two hundred million telephones in the United States, close to one for each of us, AT&T is the biggest com-pany in the world, and the telephone is so woven into our lives that we are as conditioned to answer its incessant bell as Pavlov's dogs were conditioned to salivate on cue.

Technology has advanced to the point where our answering ma-chines talk to one another, football coaches transmit plays to quarter-backs' helmets, and we think nothing of dialing long distance to hear jokes, prayers, stock quotes, and heavy breathing. In the movie Our Man Flynt, starring James Coburn, the robots running the govern-ment were controlled by Ma Bell. Who'd be surprised?

You could, in fact, consider the telephone network as one giant transcontinental computer. It's got over ten thousand internal switch-ing nodes, each composed of millions of components, billions of in-ternal circuit miles, and two hundred million input-output ports. It handles nine hundred million transactions (phone calls)—four for each of us—a day. As a switching device, it rivals the human brain for complexity. In fact, certain rumors have come to the attention of The Naked Computer to the effect that the phone network has become a giant brain and that ever since the great East Coast power blackout on November 9, 1965, hasn't been, well, quite right. Certain para-noias and growing psychoses have begun to manifest themselves in isolated regions. And we have just learned of some aberrations that would make your head swirl. Why, just last week, in Meriden, New Hampshire, in a lonely wooden shack out on Route 10 . . . wait, the telephone, better answer it . . . be right back. . . .

AT&T owns so many Digital Equipment Corp. computers that it's thought about buying DEC, whose annual revenues are over $4 billion, on at least three occasions. DEC is the second largest computer company after IBM.

The electronic family. Most of it is here in bits and pieces, but there's a home "infotainment" center in your future. It's an integrated TV set, stereo, computer, and telephone, and it'll be functional as well as fun. The screen will be high-resolution (or "high-rez," as the techies say), with twice the detail your current television set displays. In addition to regular broadcast channels and cable television, you'll be able to access videotex services for shopping, purchasing airline tickets, banking at home, and referencing an electronic library. You'll have a videodisk player and videocassette recorder, which will serve double duty with the computer—movies and shows for TV, mass memory for the computer. When you push the telephone button, you can order movies, recorded music, computer programs, and video games from a variety of electronic stores; these will be sent to you over the phone lines, or "downloaded" either to your VCR or to floppy disk. Of course, everything will be in stereo—television, video games, teleconferencing, the music you create on your plug-compatible synthesizer. When you decide to reach out and touch someone, you'll even be able to see Grandma and Grandpa on your screen—if you want to.

Futuristic? All these components are available now. It's just that nobody sells them all in one package.

MA BELL'S CRUCIAL MEASUREMENTS

- Over 1 million people work for the telephone company. Among them are 7,452 Smiths, 3,547 Joneses, 5,880 Johnsons, and 3,660 Browns—one of them being Charlie O. Brown, chairman of the board. Annual payroll: $21 billion. The company has over 3 million stockholders.

- AT&T's assets are over $165 billion, more than those of General Motors, Chrysler, Ford, General Electric—and IBM—combined. AT&T makes $18,000 profit a minute.

- The most valuable patent in the history of the U.S. Patent Office? You guessed it, number 174,465. (The second fundamental patent was number 186,787, granted January 30, 1877, and covered many of the mechanical features of the apparatus.) There are 145 million phones in the Bell System; the closest competitor is GTE, with 20 million. Thirty million more are hooked up to 1,450 independent companies such as the Farmer's Mutual Cooperative Telephone Company, the William Butts Telephone Company, the Silver Beehive Telephone Company, and Yell County Telephone.

- Washington, D.C., is the heaviest user of telephones and the only area with more than 100 phones per 100 population (175). The five states with the lowest per capita number of phones are West Virginia

(58 per 100 population); Mississippi (62 per 100), Alaska (63 per 100), Kentucky (64 per 100), and Arkansas (64 per 100).

- As far as major cities go, the largest number of phones per capita is claimed by Southfield, Michigan, followed by Washington, D.C., and San Francisco. The fewest phones per capita belong to Independence, Missouri; Chicopee, Massachusetts; and Brownsville, Texas, in that order.

- The first pay station was operated in 1878 by Thomas B. Doolittle in Connecticut and was manned by a cashier-operator. The first coin-operated phone booth didn't appear until 1889, in Hartford, Connecticut, on the ground floor of the Hartford National Bank. Today Ma Bell owns 1.4 million pay phones. The busiest? The one near the ticket counter at the Greyhound bus terminal on Randolph Street in Chicago. The least busy? The 168 vandalized machines found at the bottom of a municipal pond in Detroit.

- The first commercial telephone exchange: New Haven, Connecticut, opened January 28, 1878. The first customer: Rev. John Todd. The first switchboard operators: young boys, until September 1, 1878, when the first female operator, Emma Nutt, was hired. The second female operator, hired an hour later: Stella Nutt. Emma Nutt worked for the phone company for thirty-seven years. A certain Mr. Eckert commented in that year that "with young ladies' help the service is very much superior to that of boys and men. They are steadier, do not drink beer, and are always on hand."

- First Bell System employee: Robert W. Devonshire, bookkeeper, hired at Boston on August 10, 1877. (Watson, Bell, etc., were owners-investors.)

If you were to take the copper wire Western Electric produces in one year, it would reach back and forth from the earth to the moon seventy-seven times.

AT&T's Bell Laboratories is the oldest (formed in 1925 but based on the Western Electric research operation formed in 1907) and most prestigious industrial research institution in the world. Just listing Bell System scientific accomplishments takes two books and a total of 1,811 pages. Over 18,000 patents have been issued to Bell Labs scientists. Andrew Bobeck, who invented the magnetic bubble memory, holds over 100 patents, although Harry "Inventions Furnished on Request" Nyquist, with some 150 patents, may be the recordholder. Bell Labs can take credit for such achievements as sound motion pictures, the cathode-ray tube, radio astronomy, the laser, solar cells, coaxial cable, radiotelephones, radar systems, and, of course, the biggie: the transistor. Bell Labs' George Stibitz designed one of the first digital computers (Zuse and Atanasoff were also on the track) called the complex number calculator in 1939. It was later called the Bell Labs Model Relay Computer. The Nobel Prize in Physics has been awarded to Bell Labs people no fewer than five times:

- 1937: Clinton J. Davisson for demonstrating the wave nature of matter.

- 1956: John Bardeen, Walter H. Brattain, and William Shockley, for the 1947 invention of the transistor. From this, all things computer flow.

- 1964: Charles H. Townes, former Bell Labs member, shares prize with two Soviets for work in quantum electronics that led to lasers.

- 1977: Philip W. Anderson (one of three) for studies in 1958 in the electronic structure of magnetic and disorder materials, an exploration of why and how electricity flows through certain glassy and crystalline materials. Four years later, in 1962, Anderson was to work with Brian Josephson of Cambridge University in the experiments in superconductivity.

- 1978: Arno A. Penzias and Robert W. Wilson because they detected cosmic background radiation, the shock waves from the primordial "Big Bang" that created the universe twenty million years ago.

The first use of telephone numbers started in Lowell, Massachusetts, in 1879, during an epidemic of measles. Dr. Moses Greeley Parker, fearing that Lowell's four operators might come down with the spots, assigned numbers to Lowell's two hundred phone subscribers so fill-in operators could handle the job. The telephone company balked, fearing customers would rebel at such impersonal treatment, but users saw the efficiency of it and switched without a stir.

The mother of invention. Emile Baudot lived a hundred years ago and used printing telegraphy to communicate with the deaf. The Frenchman, after whom the unit of data transmission—the baud—was named, was deaf himself. Alexander Melville Bell taught elocution and created a visible alphabet for the hearing-impaired; he and his son, Alexander Graham, were members of a family who had worked with the hard-of-hearing for three generations. Thomas Edison experienced hearing problems all his adult life, allegedly the result of being saved from falling from a moving train when the conductor grabbed his ear; Edison went on to invent the phonograph.

Who thought 'em up? The original idea for orbiting communications satellites is generally credited to science-fiction author Arthur C. Clarke, who came up with it in 1945. But the first bird, Sputnik, didn't fly until 1957, and the first American communications satellite didn't go up until three years later. It was actually a big balloon—called Echo, a NASA communications satellite whose namesake was a Greek mountain nymph who, spurned by Narcissus, pined away until nothing but her voice remained.

Once Intelsat started launching birds in 1965, the number of transatlantic calls handled by satellite has grown from 240 to over 20,000. As much as 10 percent of all long-distance telephone and data traffic travels by satellite link at some point in its journey, over 75 percent of military long-distance traffic goes by satellite, and 50 percent of all calls between the United States and Europe bounce off Intelsat V. Fifteen commercial satellites now serve the United States. When satellites can be used, they are up to 40 percent cheaper than land-based lines, offer better error rates (higher fidelity) because there are fewer intermediate switches and repeaters than for terrestrial communications paths, and are reliable because there are practically no moving parts.

Most communications satellites appear stationary to us on earth by orbiting over the equator at precisely the speed of the earth's rotation. This makes it convenient to bounce continuous microwave signals off them. Since all such stationary satellites have to be at 22,235 miles above the earth (that's the rule; blame Isaac Newton, not us), and since satellites too close to each other interfere with one another, there are only so many parking spaces up there—180, to be exact, 95 of which are already spoken for. Experts have predicted that by 1990, the equatorial arc could be jammed—hence bidding for permission to launch satellites is hot. As in the old railroad days, right-of-way is key.

Besides crowding, today's communications satellites face another possible hazard: debris. There are 1,281 operational satellites hovering over our planet today (another 1,614 have run down), not to mention over 2,100 pieces of flotsam and jetsam—old fuel tanks, hunks of booster rockets, skeletons of test firings—also in orbit. And new satellites go up at the rate of 168 a year. There are so many pieces of metal up there, in fact, that scientists have warned that within a decade, the single biggest hazard to space flight will be flying through the garbage still in orbit. No manned flights have yet been hit, but some experts suspect that some of the mysterious silences of other spacecraft have resulted from collision.

So it's taken twenty-five years and probably over $100 billion in 1983 dollars to turn space into a litter pile.

More progress. Until 1956, transatlantic telephone calls were made via short-wave and high-frequency radio (remember Edward R. Murrow fading in and out with a heavy layer of crackle underneath?). The world's first submarine telephone cable was connected between Europe and the United States in 1956; within a year the number of calls doubled. By 1973, combined transoceanic phone calls via cable or satellite had increased thirty-five times.

First live bird. Echo was, as its name implies, a passive communications satellite; signals were sent up to it and deflected back to earth. Bell Labs' Telstar I, launched July 10, 1962, by Delta rocket, was the first active communications satellite to receive, amplify, and relay telephone messages and television signals across the Atlantic. The 170-pound spacecraft was used for international telecommunications and was not in stationary orbit above the equator. Several different technologies made Telstar a reality: the maser, or Microwave Amplification by Simulated Emission of Radiation (cousin to the laser, only using microwave signals instead of light signals), for amplifying signals; the transistor in various circuits; the horn-reflector antenna; and the solar battery. Telstar received one of the nation's highest honors: a paean in its name, played on glorious twin stratocaster guitars by The Ventures.

The lightest satellite. Echo, although a hundred feet across, was simply a foil balloon that weighed very little. The first Intelsat satellite, Early Bird, weighed eighty-five pounds. Typical communications satellites being launched today by space shuttle weigh fourteen hundred pounds.

The heaviest satellite. The U.S. twelve-ton spy satellite Big Bird. Not counting space stations.

Close call. Once satellites are tossed out of the space shuttle's cargo bay, they must catapult themselves up the next twenty-one thousand miles to their stationary orbits. This may be the most perilous part of their journey. RCA lost a satellite during the maneuver after a conventional rocket launch; NASA almost lost a $100 million satellite this year. During the space shuttle *Columbia*'s November 1982 launch of a Canadian Anik satellite, that spacecraft went silent during the trek to final orbit. It wouldn't accept commands from earth and might never have locked in place. Just minutes from a curtain call, scientists found the problem—a computer programmer had transposed some digits in telling the satellite what radio frequency to listen on.

(Anik, by the way, is Inuit for "brother.")

Robot in space. The newest remote scientific laboratory in space is the one-ton Infrared Astronomical Satellite (IRAS), in essence a $180 million robot. The instrument is so sensitive to infrared (heat) rays that it could detect a refrigerator bulb on the planet Pluto, 4 billion miles away! That's nothing. What if it *does* detect such a bulb?

The most advanced state in satellite communications: Alaska, which would be in telephone darkness if it weren't for satellites. Alascom, once owned by RCA, now by Pacific Power and Light, provides most of the state's telephone service, an electronic mail network, and the legislature's audiovisual teleconferencing network. In 1982, one of fifty Alaska residents participated in teleconferences with their legislators (most Alaskans live two time zones from the state capital). Even remote Eskimo villages are being outfitted for teleconferencing—the savings in charter flights will more than pay for the equipment.

Drawing by Rich Tennant

"Hi. Al? I just wanted to see if you got that electronic mail message I sent you."

An elevator in space. The space shuttle can thank its existence to its task of hauling satellites into space, both for the military and for private industry. But Joseph Pelton considers the shuttle "a space Rolls-Royce rather than a space truck," and many have suggested less costly and more efficient alternatives, such as ion thrusters (whatever they are). And numerous commercial firms have begun to plan satellite-launching businesses.

But *The Naked Computer* thinks all these alternatives are ho-hum compared to Arthur C. Clarke's proposed space funicular. This, as you are well aware, would be a cable hanging in space from a geosynchronous orbit (just as the satellites orbit), with two buckets, so to speak, traversing up and down by the force of gravity. The cable would need to be very long, of course (the orbit is 22,235 miles up), and very strong—something on the order of a diamond—and it would cost a great deal of money, but it would be very energy-efficient once in place. Well, look, it took twenty years for Clarke's first satellite idea to reach fruition. Give this one a break. (It probably would be cheaper than some of the things the military has dreamed up for shooting laser beams from space [see Chapter 11].

Through a glass, brightly. The invention of the laser at Bell Labs in 1960 and breakthroughs in making ultraclear glass by Corning in 1970 may mean that by 1990 more copper wire will be coming out of underground conduits and cable housings than going in. By shining lasers through hair-thin glass fibers and blinking them on and off up to a billion times a second, scientists have made fiber-optic telecommunications systems that can carry ten thousand conversations over a pair of fibers smaller and more durable than the traditional copper wire-pair that today handles one telephone conversation. A Washington–New York–Boston fiber-optic link opened in 1983. By 1990, major long-haul circuits between heavy-use telephone areas will be made of glass rather than metal; and fiber-optic transoceanic cables will be in place. Twenty-five thousand miles of cable have already been installed in the United States. France is planning the largest fiber-optic experiment—a $100 million network in the town of Biarritz that will connect five thousand homes equipped with two-way visual phones.

One data network that's for the birds. Lockheed Missile and Space Company needed to transmit lots of computer data from its Sunnyvale, California, office to its R&D facility high in the Santa Cruz Mountains. The company used both telephone transmissions of computer-to-computer data (very expensive) and physical transport of printouts, an all-day mountain-road affair that wipes out shocks and springs. Finally the company experimented with a truly advanced network that cut costs to a tenth of what they were before.

Carrier pigeons now fly microfilm of the data between the mountains and Sunnyvale. One bird a day about does it.

Ham radio for the 1980s. They're called information utilities, electronic bulletin boards, communication networks, and the like, but what they mean is two or more people's computers talking. Here's a sampling:

- The Source, the first and oldest, owned by *Reader's Digest*. Lots of utilities, such as electronic mail, news and sports from UPI and *The*

New York Times, games, a home medical guide, travel, dining and entertainment information, and science and technology information.

- CompuServe, running neck-and-neck with the Source, is owned by H&R Block, of all people. It has pretty much the same services as the Source but has one outstanding feature: Megawars, one of the best computer games ever.

  Both CompuServe and the Source have about forty thousand subscribers. The Source is hoping to grow; it's built a new computer facility at its McLean, Virginia, headquarters with nine Prime 750 computers that will allow for up to a quarter of a million subscribers.

- Delphi, in Cambridge, Massachusetts, is the new kid on the block, and it's hot. It's very easy to use, since all the commands are in English; it's fun to log on because your screen says, "Hello, Jack, welcome to Delphi." That's followed by an aphorism, different every time, such as, "Take care of the luxuries, and the necessities will take care of themselves." Delphi has a host of features, games galore, dozens of bulletin boards, home banking, electronic mail, news, shopping, and two unique features. One is *Infomania*, a collaborative novel such as what Michael Rogers envisioned in his novel *Silicon Valley*, and Writers' Corner, a tool kit for writing, editing, and actually publishing your work. You can send your manuscript to a typesetting service right from your home computer. Delphi also has a library service, including the *Kussmaul Encyclopedia* (named after Delphi founder Wes Kussmaul), where you can research a variety of topics.

- Kangaroo Koncepts of South Bend, Indiana, is introducing The Connection this year, an electronic bulletin board, games, and publishing house without some of the frills the Source and Delphi offer. Authors who publish their novels on-line will receive a royalty every time another subscriber reads them.

Definitely not POTS. Bell Labs is busily working on a dial-a-game network of computer games two opponents can play at the same time. "You could dial one number to fight the Battle of Britain or to race in the Grand Prix," says the executive director of research, Robert Lucky. "The great thing about these games is that they don't have to be fixed. You can change the computer's instructions from day to day, so there is no chance for boredom." You can bet no one at Bell Labs is bored, either.

(POTS is telephone industry lingo for plain old telephone service.)

Rabbit ears for the eighties. Channel Master, the folks who brought us the original TV rabbit ears, now offers a satellite earth station in eight different models for your backyard. The dish comes in two sizes, ten feet and

twelve feet, and costs $5,000 to $6,000. You can pick up twenty-four channels with it. Home earth stations are the next big rage; one manufacturer,
Birdview, hopes to have a model for under $3,000 available soon.

Telesoftware? Companies already have started feeding computers software over telephone lines. Time-Life is offering a cable TV service that will
pipe software to home computers that allows them to manipulate data the
company sends over the wires; Creative Associates is starting to market
Gameline, a device that allows Atari owners to receive arcade game software
over phone lines (there's a charge each time a game is played); Mattel and
General Instrument offer PlayCable, which lets cable subscribers get games
electronically for their Intellivision sets. And National Public Radio (NPR)
will be using its broadcast system to send software to customers.

The ultimate, of course, will be the personal telephone—carried with
you and usable anywhere. Don't scoff. A handful of companies already have
applied for permission to offer nationwide paging services, and pagers are
getting sophisticated enough to store verbal messages and print out text. A
company called Dataspeed plans a national two-way service using NPR's
267 satellite earth stations and broadcasting to pagers from NPR radio stations. The pocket-size pager not only will store messages, it also will be able
to plug into any public phone and send a message back to the appropriate
telephone number. PageAmerica, another company, plans an international
paging system that will tie into the Telex networks in over fifty countries.
Dick Tracy calling Diet Smith, Dick Tracy calling Diet Smith . . .

The biggest thorn in Ma Bell's side? MCI Communications. The company applied for permission to offer microwave private telephone service in
1969, and, after three years of AT&T-caused delays, began operating in
1972. AT&T promptly started unplugging MCI connections to the local
phone network about as fast as MCI plugged them in, but MCI prevailed in
the ensuing court and regulatory battles. MCI later figured a way to use a
shared private line service in such a way that it looked like regular long-
distance service—and was able to undercut phone company rates almost in
half. More controversy.

In a landmark decision in 1978, an appellate court made a startling
finding: Although long-distance phone service had been regulated since the
Interstate Commerce Act was revised in 1910, it had never been established
that a monopoly in long-distance service was in the public interest. So, until
the FCC proved such a matter, the market should be open to competition.
MCI had won the big one.

From a low of $0.75 a share (in 1982 dollars) in 1976, MCI's stock rose
to over $40 a share in 1982. The company's customers have grown from
11,000 in 1978 to over 950,000 in 1982. Revenues went from zilch to over
$1 billion this year.

In combating MCI, the phone company is faced with a double whammy. If it gets too aggressive, it's subject to lawsuits—MCI already has won $1.8 billion in the first round of an antitrust suit. If it combats MCI with pricing actions, it will lose more in its own revenues that it will gain back by taking MCI out of the ball game. Rock and a hard place, huh, Ma?

FROM THE CACHE:
Ma Bell's Metamorphosis

In 1959, the year that AT&T introduced the Princess phone and a year in which the Bell System added 3,298,000 phones to the number installed, a Dallas businessman named Thomas F. Carter began marketing a coupler that permitted a two-way radio base station to patch directly into the phone network. Over the next six years, Carter sold some thirty-five hundred of these things. He called them "Carterfones."

The phone company, which added around twenty million phones to the nation's inventory during those years, was not happy. Let one guy connect "foreign" devices to the phone network and pretty soon everyone would want to hook in homemade electronic gunk. AT&T started cutting off service to people who used Carterfones.

The phone company's reaction was not without historic precedent. The company had always jealously guarded the gateways into the network, starting from its inception in 1876. When the last Bell patent ran out in January 1894 and the company no longer had a monopoly on telephone communications, one of its prime competitive strengths was the lock on interconnection with its long-distance network. During the twenty-year period between 1894 and 1914, when many homes had to have different phones to call through different exchanges, the company decimated the competition by denying access to the long-distance network. A provision of the commitment the company made to the Attorney General in an attempt to forestall nationalization in 1913 and become a regulated monopoly was that it would allow interconnection to the network.

So Carter, his business on the ropes because of AT&T's threats to potential Carterfone buyers, fought back. In 1966 he filed an antitrust suit, which was referred to the Federal Communications Commission by the court. On June 26, 1968, the FCC ruled in Carter's favor and struck down tariff provisions that prevented interconnection.

Other liberalizing court and FCC rulings followed over the years—the phone company was thrust into a second era of competition.

Not that it had much effect. Until about 1980, all the competitors combined didn't make any profit—heavy losses in areas such as satellites balanced profits in areas such as switchboards and answering machines. Even by 1982, out of a $72 billion market, competitors to the established monopoly phone companies had but a 6 percent share.

On November 20, 1974, in part as a result of the wave of private anti-trust suits against AT&T that sprung from the new competition, the U.S. Department of Justice filed an antitrust suit against AT&T. The goal was to break the phone company into its component parts and let some of them loose in the unregulated marketplace.

Over the next six years, AT&T examined with a microscope the hand-writing on the walls it had constructed around itself. It began to understand that technology—microwave, satellites, computers—was what had given potential competitors strength in the marketplace. And not only was tech-nology here to stay, but if AT&T were to wield it, it would have to operate under new rules.

So on January 8, 1982, AT&T and the Department of Justice an-nounced a settlement. Ma Bell would cut the apron strings to its local tele-phone companies—the ones we deal with—and, thus liberated, go off on her own.

The local companies will handle local communications, AT&T and others will handle long-distance calling. The transfer of power will give the spun-off companies 75 percent of AT&T's $165 billion in assets and 50 percent of its $85 billion in revenues by the time of the split on January 1, 1984.

The split will ratify AT&T's *de facto* entrance over the years into the computer industry and give it equal footing in the competitive arena—if you can count setting a $40 billion corporation loose in the market as equal footing.

(First major result of deregulation: Dial-a-Joke is open to private compe-tition, and entrepreneurs have begun putting dirty jokes at the end of the line.)

CHAPTER 19

METAL EGGHEADS:

Computers That Think Like People

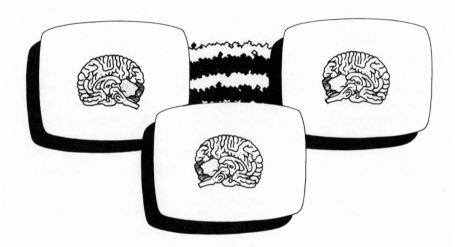

Meet your shrink. Her name is Eliza. You tell her, "Men are all alike."

"In what way?" she asks.

"They're always bugging us about something or other."

"Can you think of a specific example?"

"Well, my boyfriend made me come here."

"Your boyfriend made you come here?"

"He says I'm depressed all the time."

"I'm sorry to hear you are depressed."

"It's true. I'm unhappy."

Normal couch-coaching except for one thing: Eliza is a computer program developed at MIT by Joseph Weizenbaum.

"Artificial Intelligence," or AI, is the code phrase computerniks use to describe the attempt to make computers reason. And after millennia of striving for godhood and three decades of research AI, human beings

can point to some minor accomplishments: A program called Prospec-
tor that helps mining companies strike it rich, some medical programs
for assistance in diagnosing various diseases, and a backgammon
game that beat a world champion.

Actually, much of the seminal work in artificial intelligence has
centered on board games—chess, checkers, and backgammon. After
all, the ability to play chess and braininess have always been associ-
ated. And some board game programs are brainy enough to defeat the
people who wrote them. But scientists seem to agree that it's easier to
mimic the specific thoughts of a chess master or an organic chemist
about his respective job than to mimic a four-year-old just taking in
the world. Kids are smarter than the smartest computer.

Which may be smarter than adults. When Joseph Weizenbaum
developed Eliza in 1966, he did so to demonstrate the possibilities and
limitations of conversing with computers in natural language. The use
of ersatz psychiatry was only so humans would assume a seemingly
dumb question or wishy-washy response was asked for a purpose, not
out of ignorance. Eliza was supposed to be an example of farcical
psychiatry. Instead, the headshrinkers of the day praised its psychiatric
acumen, lauding the program as a therapeutic breakthrough. Some
started telling Eliza their own tales of Oedipal conflict, sibling death
wishes, and fear of kittens.

Weizenbaum was disgusted.

"They [psychiatrists] told me that with Eliza we could treat
hundreds of patients an hour at state hospitals," he remembers in
Katherine Davis Fishman's book The Computer Establishment. *"I*
concluded that many psychiatrists are doing no more than Eliza does.
I was shocked at how easily people are fooled."

Can you pass the Turing Test? It's the one proposed by a thirty-eight-
year-old British mathematician, Alan Turing, in 1950 that tells if a computer can reason like a human. Its method is to ask a panel of human judges
if they can tell the difference between a computer and a human, both out of
sight, by the nature of their typed answers to various questions. As the saying goes, "If it walks like a duck and talks like a duck . . ."

Some computer programs are getting pretty close. In 1980, chess grand
master Helmut Pflager played twenty-six games at once. He had not been
told that three of the players were receiving radio signals that relayed moves
dictated by computer programs. One, called Belle, beat Pflager, who could
not tell the difference between human and computer play. Nor could other

chess experts who later reviewed the game's moves. When he was finally told who defeated him, Pflager was infuriated.

Do you want Newtonian or Einsteinian? A computer program called ABLE designed at Carnegie-Mellon actually learns physics. It starts off asking very basic, stupid questions, and getting the answers takes considerable search through the computer's start-up data base. But ABLE never forgets, and once a problem is solved, the computer uses the learned rules and accumulated data to guide it in its next search.

Scientists have finally gotten a computer that's able to sort parts in a bin. For only $100,000 you can put a Yasakawa robot together with a vision system from Machine Intelligence Corp. and get a system that can pick up parts and compare them with visual image stored in memory. Of course, Rent-a-Teen might be cheaper.

Metal medal for Prospector. It's a computer program devised by Alan Campbell and Peter Hart of SRI International, now backed by the U.S. Geological Survey. Built to parrot the thought processes of experienced geologists (it took researchers at SRI years to pick the brains of twenty top geologists to provide Prospector something to parrot), in 1982 Prospector identified a large heretofore-unknown deposit of molybdenum in the vicinity of Mount Tolman in Washington. Decades of mining in the area had uncovered only minor deposits, but Prospector, analyzing field data, mapped out a whole new area for exploration. A $100 million find.

The state of the art for speech recognition systems—at least ones that don't have to be calibrated for each different voice or don't have other clues, such as typed first letters—is claimed by Bell Labs. The experimental Bell system can understand a thousand words. (English contains three hundred thousand words, twenty thousand syllables, forty phonemes; about ten thousand words are used commonly.)

Another advanced system has been developed by IBM. It also can understand a thousand words, but it needs trained speakers. Although it can recognize words with 91 percent accuracy, it takes three hours to recognize each minute of speech.

A human, by contrast, may know a hundred thousand words or more and can recognize a minute's worth of speech in about sixty seconds. From stranger or friend.

The state of the art for systems that use computers both to recognize human speech *and* synthesize it is also claimed by Bell Labs. It's a system for making airline reservations in which humans talk to the computer over the telephone. It can recognize all of 127 words.

How long before we're as dumb as computers? How many high school kids could boil *Macbeth* down as succinctly as the MIT computer, under the tutelage of Dr. Patrick Winston, director of AI efforts there, that learned this from reading it: "A weak man married to a greedy woman is likely to be evil"?

Eliza doesn't always hack it. Consider this dialog between the program and journalist R. D. Rosen:

R.: Sometimes I'll be eating at an Italian restaurant, and I can't decide whether to order fettucine or clams casino, and I become very agitated and disoriented.

E.: Have you tried?

R.: Tried what?

E.: Tell me about what.

R.: What the hell are you talking about?

E.: What the hell are I talking about?

You're paranoid only if they're not out to get you. A program developed at Stanford and dubbed Parry simulates paranoia. Alan Turing would be proud. Tested on real psychiatrists, Parry fooled 49 percent into thinking its responses were those of a human. Of course, it *was* out to get them.

A sample of typical Parry dialogue:

INTERROGATOR: Why are you in the hospital?

PARRY: I shouldn't be here.

I.: Who brought you here?

P.: The police.

I.: What trouble did you have with the police?

P.: Cops don't do their job.

I.: What do they do instead?

P.: Cops arrest the wrong people.

I.: They arrest the right ones sometimes.

P.: The law should get those Italian crooks.

I.: Are you Italian?

P.: My background is British but I was born in this country.

I.: Do you know any Italian crooks?

P.: I try to avoid the underworld.

I.: Are you afraid of the underworld?

P.: The Mafia are the worst gangsters.

I.: Are you connected with the Mafia?

P.: You know, they know me.

I.: How do they know you?

P.: They spy on me.

I.: Why do they?

P.: They want to get false evidence to frame me.

I.: What do they have against you?

P.: They are out to get me.

Yes, Parry did once meet Eliza, or at least a program called Doctor, that was based on Eliza. He was not cured, nor did the Doctor diagnose paranoia resulting from computer programming.

THE EGGHEADS OF EGGHEADDOM: THE FIFTEEN MOST INFLUENTIAL AI RESEARCHERS

NAME	INSTITUTION	CONTRIBUTION
Claude Shannon	Bell Labs	Pioneered information theory and communications switching, computer chess, and theory of automata and machine thinking. Both Minsky and McCarthy worked under Shannon at one time or another. Nobel Prize winner.
John McCarthy	MIT, Stanford	Invented LISP programming language, founded two out of three major AI centers (MIT and Stanford), organized seminal 1956 AI conference at Dartmouth.

THE EGGHEADS OF EGGHEADDOM:
THE FIFTEEN MOST INFLUENTIAL AI RESEARCHERS

NAME	INSTITUTION	CONTRIBUTION
Hans Berliner	Carnegie-Mellon	Wrote backgammon winner, in AI board games for two decades.
Edward Feigen-baum	Stanford	AI research head, pioneer of computer modeling of human decision-making processes. Began AI research at Berkeley School of Business. Modeling efforts began as behavior psychology research; coauthor of the definitive AI book, *Computers and Thought*. Left Berkeley for Stanford in early 1960s, began collaboration with Joshua Lederberg on Dendral, an "expert system" for identifying chemical compounds. First applied use of AI.
Joshua Lederberg	Stanford, University of Rochester	At Stanford helped with Dendral. Nobel Laureate in genetics.
Marvin Minsky	MIT	Cofounder with McCarthy of MIT's AI labs. Studied at Harvard, attempting to fathom the mysteries of the mind with research in biology, physics, psychology. Spearheaded MIT's Project MAC, a laboratory in AI research. May have had more influential students than any other. Conceived concept of the mind as a "meat machine" (yuk).
Allen Newell	Rand, Carnegie-Mellon	With Simon, Shaw, and Shannon, one of original "old men of AI." With Shaw at Dartmouth Conference, 1956, demonstrated first "thinking" program, the Logic Theorist, which could derive laws of mathematics. Developed "chaining" concept.
Seymour Papert	MIT	Codirector with Minsky of MIT's AI efforts today, inventor of LOGO AI language for children. Runs learning center lab at MIT. Studied under Piaget. Met Feigenbaum at conference in London and decided to emigrate from South Africa to the United States. Turned learning theory into useful mathematics.

Roger Schank	Yale	New-breed AI researcher. Head of Yale's efforts at natural language recognition. Developing commercial AI programs, founder of Cognitive Systems, Inc.
Joseph Weizenbaum	General Electric, MIT	Engineer by trade, left GE for MIT in 1963, devised Eliza program. Had previously met with Kenneth Colby, who used Eliza principles to fashion Doctor program. Weizenbaum is now an AI rogue—an outspoken critic of the field and of computers in general.
Herbert Simon	Carnegie-Mellon	Spearheaded early AI work at CM; influenced a generation of researchers. Designed the Logic Theorist with Newell, worked on the General Problem Solver. Nobel Laureate in economics (early work). Formed relationship with Newell and Shaw while at Rand.
J. Clifford Shaw	Rand	Collaborator with Newell in Logic Theorist, General Problem Solver, and Chess Machine. Designed and programmed Rand's Johnniac computer. Most computer-oriented of Shaw-Simon-Newell team.
Paul Armer	Rand	Head of computer sciences at Rand during Shaw-Simon-Newell days.
Oliver Selfridge	MIT Lincoln Labs	Pattern recognition studies. Major influence on Simon, Minsky, others.
Hubert Dreyfus	MIT, Rand, Berkeley	Performed a study for Rand published as paper "Alchemy and Artificial Intelligence." Harsh critic of AI; panned its meager accomplishments. Claimed flat out that AI would never work. Pointed out that the best chess program of the day (1966) could be beaten by a ten-year-old boy. Dreyfus subsequently lost to the same program.

Computer chess champ. Belle, a program developed by Ken Thompson and Joe Condon of Bell Labs. The program plays at the "master" level (the top 1 percent), with a lifetime tournament chess rating over 2,200. (A world champion will rate over 2,700; the average tournament player, 1,300.) There are probably fewer than five hundred players in the world who can beat it. No computer can yet beat it consistently, although Northeastern's Nuchess program beats it once in a while. In 1980, at the World Computer Chess Championship in Linz, Austria, Belle beat a program called Chaos, developed at the University of Michigan. Belle, using a specially built mini-computer for hardware, relies on brute force—examining 30 million possible positions in the three minutes allotted between moves. Chaos looks at only 15,300 moves but comes with special software to narrow down what moves to consider.

The humans who can beat Belle manage to do so while looking at a maximum of only one hundred possible positions.

Belle can beat 99 percent of all human opponents, but only 50 percent during the end-game portion.

Why humans make computers that play chess. Because so many computer scientists play chess. Some of the earliest computer developments, for instance, took place at the Government Code and Cypher School at Bletchley, Buckinghamshire, England, during World War II. Here mathematicians and scientists developed the automatic code-breaking machines that enabled Britain to decipher much of the cable and wireless traffic of the Axis powers. Deciphered codes, for instance, led to the sinking of the *Bismarck* and shriveling of Rommel's supply lines. These automata were the secretive precursors to digital computers. Although few direct designs were transferred from Bletchley machines to later computers—the fact of the existence of some of these machines was declassified only in the past ten years—the scientists traveled frequently among the major university computer spawning grounds.

Much of the recruiting for Bletchley efforts was done in chess clubs—the Bletchley chess players were good enough to beat Oxford in a match in December 1944 by a score of 8–4. Several current and future British chess champions were wartime cryptologists at Bletchley.

One of the more avid but less skilled players was Alan Turing; his thoughts on "thinking machines" became guiding precepts of early computer development. In fact, many of Turing's thoughts coalesced out of mulling over the idea of "machine chess."

Why don't IBM computers play chess? In the late 1950s, while IBM was trying to calm its potential customers into believing computers were just dumb machines and not threatening to humans, it was embarrassed by the ability of Arthur L. Samuel's checkers program to beat good players, by a chess program by Alex Bernstein that was getting pretty good, and by a program written by Herbert Gerlernter that could prove geometry theories. IBM made a deliberate decision not to back game-playing research and conducted a hard-sell campaign on the idea that the computer is just a quick moron.

The world backgammon champion. It's "Mighty Bee," a three-foot robot that connects via communications lines to a DEC PDP-10 time-sharing computer at Carnegie-Mellon University, using a software program called BKG 9.8. Invented by Hans Berliner, the program beat Luigi Villa of Italy in July 1979 at the world championships in Monte Carlo.

A computer probably is the world's best player of the game Kalah, a short-range strategy game with origins in Africa or Polynesia. No one's really sure, since finding skilled players of the game is so difficult.

Title purse. The first computer to beat the world's grand master in chess will receive $100,000, a prize donated by Edward Fredkin, chief executive officer of Three Rivers Computers, MIT professor, and AI buff. (Fredkin thinks computers will represent the next stage of evolution.) Most experts think Fredkin won't have to pay up for another ten years or so.

Checkers is less lucrative. World champion checkers player Dr. Marion F. Tinsley has bet that no computer can beat him in a twenty-game match before 1985. Wager: $5,000.

The first program to improve its own performance—by utilizing "heuristics," or rules of thumb to make guessing more intelligent—was written in 1960 by Arthur L. Samuel of IBM. The program played checkers, and analyzed games between human checkers experts to ferret out winning strategies for its own use.

Longest title reign. Arthur L. Samuel's program, mentioned above, remained the best checkers-playing program until 1977. Finesse loses to brute force. While Samuel's program restricted its search of future moves to those it had learned from past experience were advantageous, it was bested by a program called Paaslow, developed at Duke University by Eric C. Jensen and Tom R. Truscott. Paaslow examines a million potential positions every two minutes.

The first chess-playing machine. Wolfgang von Kempelen's Maezel Chess Automaton, invented by the Hungarian over two hundred years ago. It was a wooden model of a man sitting at a chess board and surrounded by elaborate clockworklike machinery. It took on all comers, including Edgar Allan Poe (who later logically proved that it had to be a fake), and defeated practically all of them. Not until several years later was the secret to the automaton revealed—inside was a legless Polish army officer named Worouski, who was a master chess player. Apparently he sneezed. The contraption burned up in 1854 in a Philadelphia fire.

The first major computer chess win. Chess 4.7, a program running on a large Control Data Cyber 176 computer, entered as Class B competition in the Paul Masson American Chess Championship in California in 1976. It began winning despite technical problems, and it created a near-insurrection. Irate chess players eventually grabbed the MC's microphone in an attempt to stop the computerized play. All told, the program, developed at Northwestern University by David Slate, Larry Atkin, and William Blanchard, won five games, lost none, and took the tournament.

Early programs designed to understand the nature of language, first attempted in the 1950s, ran into trouble right away. Isaac Asimov reports that the English phrase "The spirit is willing, but the flesh is weak" was translated into Russian and came back out as, "The vodka is strong, but the meat is rotten." And early researchers were puzzled over the meaning of another translation, "water goat." Turns out the computer was trying to convey "hydraulic ram," a technical term.

Mathematics: Who needs it? The first artificial intelligence program was called the Logic Theorist and was written by Allen Newell, Herbert Simon, and J. Clifford Shaw. It was debuted at the first AI conference, held at Dartmouth in the summer of 1956. With a few mathematical precepts and abilities fed into it, it was asked to derive the basic equations of logic, a feat attempted many years earlier by Alfred North Whitehead and Bertrand Russell in *Principia Mathematica*. The program came up with thirty-eight of the fifty-two theorems found in that work. It also came up with what Whitehead and Russell had missed.

In 1962 James Slagle at MIT designed a program that did freshman calculus about as well as a freshman. Tested, it scored 88 percent. It might have done 100 percent if Slagle had taught it the method for partial fractions.

The national championship for playing Traveller, a spaceship war game in which contestants design imaginary space fleets, then pit them against each other under the rules of the game, was won by Douglas Lenat, who used an artificial-intelligence program called Eurisko to uncover a winning strategy. Eurisko used its understanding of biological evolution to design a space fleet that, although bizarre by human standards, happened to be optimized to the Traveller environment. Eurisko currently is being used to generate and evaluate logic designs for experimental computer chips.

The most noble AI effort. Roman Catholic clergyman Austin David Carroll is enrolling a computer in the peace movement. Brother Carroll is assistant to the chancellor for information management systems for the New York Archdiocese. His plan is to hook up a Radio Shack TRS-80 microcomputer to a larger Sperry Univac computer in Yonkers and begin creating data bases and "artificial intelligence" models to study human aggression. Eventually, negotiators, peace authorities, and activists the world round will be able to access Brother Carroll's handiwork, most of which will be based at the Pope John Paul II Center for Prayer and Study for Peace in Manhattan. The goal: to prevent violent conflict between nations.

Two tools that Brother Carroll hopes to utilize in building his models and setting up his network: the Catholic Church's new satellite network and the Rand Institute's models for war games.

The silliest use of AI? Researchers at Bell Labs have devised a program to advise drivers how to get around Madison, New Jersey, based on a data base compiled from street maps and the Yellow Pages. After the program bugs were worked out—at first the computer thought nothing of making a turn every block just to save a few yards—the system was able to produce a route in an average of twelve seconds, about one eighth the time it would take a human. The researchers point out: "Four percent of all driving is wasted by persons who are lost or don't follow the best route." Let's see, a week of computerized driving would allow how many extra trips to Burger King?

Drawing by Tim Eagan

The computer is my copilot.

A terrorist-tracking program called IPP, devised at Yale to analyze information coming over the UPI wire, has discovered that Guatemalans are rarely killed in bombings and that New Zealand terrorists favor the boomerang as a weapon.

The AI elite. There are about two hundred Ph.D.s in AI, according to an article in *Fortune* in May 1982. Ten percent work for Schlumberger Corporation, a major oil field services and semiconductor manufacturing company, which hopes to use AI techniques to interpret oil-logging data and to design computer chips.

Expert systems. These are AI programs that try to mimic the thought processes of human experts in a field. A minimum amount of core information must also be in the program's bag of memory. An "expert" medical diagnostic system, for instance, would first have to know the basics of medicine—names of diseases, processes, parts of the body, drugs, etc. It would then be programmed to make the same logical connections that a human expert would. "If you have a fever after 5:00 P.M. take two aspirin and call the computer in the morning."

The relatively straightforward and simple program XCON, for example, developed by Carnegie-Mellon for Digital Equipment Corporation to help salespeople configure customers' machines, contains five hundred descriptions of parts and specifications and twelve hundred rules, and it will run through a thousand separate comparisons in determining a configuration. The $450 million ten-year Japanese effort to produce an ultramodern computer family that has built-in AI calls for producing a system that will be able to store twenty thousand rules and a hundred million pieces of information.

The art—who could yet call it a science?—of making computerized sense out of the huge mountains of information and rules is what makes expert systems so difficult to produce. Tying all the "if thises" to the "then thats" requires using conclusions from one analysis as the premises of the next. This process is called forward chaining. In some cases a system can start with a conclusion, or hypothesis, and test it against information and rules in storage (backward chaining).

A bottleneck to developing expert systems is corraling humans and picking their brains for the rules a computer would need to know to simulate human decision-making. Prospector, the program that divines mineral deposits from surface characteristics, tapped the knowledge of twenty specialists. A decent-size expert system currently takes forty to fifty man-years to create.

Oldest expert system. Dendral, invented by Nobel Prize-winning geneticist Joshua Lederberg and computer scientist Edward Feigenbaum. The program interprets data produced by mass spectrometers to determine molecular structures.

A program called BACON, devised by Herbert Simon of Carnegie-Mellon, was once given all the known facts about chemistry in 1800. From these it inferred the principle of atomic weight—a conclusion that took humans fifty years to draw.

The Naked Computer Pick:
The Ten Smartest Computer Programs

Program	Developed at	Rationale for Pick
AM	Stanford	Automated mathematics—is able to understand prime-number theory.
Belle	Bell Labs	Plays chess. Uses brute force but has best current shot at winning $100,000 Fredkin prize.
Boris	Yale	Understands text, understands a little about daily life (for example, knows there's a connection between meals and restaurants).
Caduceus	University of Pittsburgh	Medical diagnostics. More than one disease.
Dendral		White-haired AI veteran. Into molecular chemistry. Actually is useful.
EMYCIN	Stanford	Understands MYCIN (is a general-purpose derivative of it).
Eurisko	Stanford	Used knowledge of biology to win war game called Traveller.
MYCIN	Stanford	Diagnoses cardiopulmonary diseases.
Prospector	SRI	Predicts underground deposits from surface characteristics. Will make money. Is employable.
SHRDLU	MIT	Is able to manipulate 3-D objects on a screen. Precursor to robot brain. Can pronounce SHRDLU (named after typesetting letters).

Trying to cram the pickings of human brains into your own computerized "expert system"? Teknowledge, a company spun out of Stanford, SRI International, and the Rand Corporation, can teach you how. The company claims to have one third of all the world's "knowledge engineers," or scientists with experience in expert systems, on its staff. A twenty-four-week course costs only $45,000.

CHAPTER 20

THE OUTER LIMITS:

Computers in the Year 2000

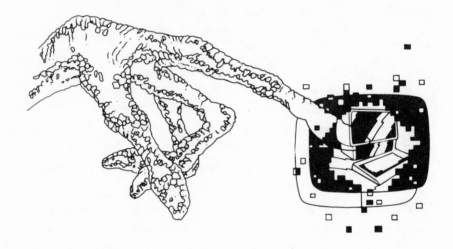

That's an amazing invention but who would ever want to use one?

—President Rutherford B. Hayes

If you were born in 1982, you'll graduate from high school in the year 2000. Congratulations. You've made it to the millennium. You've spent twelve thousand hours in class, watched seventeen thousand hours of TV, seen six hundred thousand commercials and twenty thousand TV murders, written ten thousand lines of computer code, and achieved the Space Invaders score equivalent of one hundred million.

You live in a weird world.

The airwaves are saturated with microwaves, orbits are so crowded satellites are crashing into each other, people have computers inside

312

them running parts of their bodies, your neighbor's mistress is a robot, the best teachers are computer programs, and rock 'n' roll still lives.

Whatever vision of the year 2000 any of us have, it's bound to be wrong. In 1937 the League of Nations put its best brains to work forecasting future technology. Just about every important break-through was missed—stuff such as radar, jets, computers, antibiotics, and the Bomb. In 1948, after the first few computers had been exer-cised, scientists predicted that only a handful would ever be required to satisfy the needs of government and business; IBM chose not to sell the new electronic brains that year—no market. Even as late as 1970, when scientists knew how fast computer costs were coming down, no one predicted a large market for the hand-held calculator; no one fore-saw what video games would do to the record industry.

So any effort to depict the sublime state that computers will have wrought upon our lives by the century's turn is doomed to the same ridiculousness as Rutherford Hayes's pronouncement when he first used a "harmonic telegraph," the telephone, in 1928.

Better just to point out some things that are here today and let you speculate. Hell, if you didn't read it in The Naked Computer *you'd probably think it was turn-of-the-century stuff anyway.*

We will go out on a limb and make one prediction, though: At least half the computer programs that contain dates in them will sprain their chips figuring people's ages after the year 2000, having saved on computer memory by leaving only two digits for the year of birth.

International Data Corporation publishes statistics on the number of computers in the world. The count goes back twenty years and forecasts the next five. If you take the IDC trend line out to the year 2000 you get a forecast of four hundred million computers in the world. One computer for every person in the United States. Now, that's crazy, isn't it? Of course it is. About as crazy as thinking there'd ever be more telephones than people, TVs than families, or cars than adult drivers. Just crazy.

And these are just computers. You know, things at which you might sit and do work (or games if no one was watching). What about micro-processors? According to Intel, inventor of the things, we can expect that by the year 2000 two to three will be coming off the production line yearly for every person on the planet.

"There had been an early forecast that five systems would be sold. I'd even heard some wild speculation that this country could support eight or ten systems—the future was certainly unclear."—Herman Lukoff, from *Dits to Bits: A Personal History of the Electronic Computer.*

Piezoelectric materials turn pressure into electricity—such as the quartz chunks used in crystal radio sets, the quartz of quartz watches, the modulators of CB radios, and parts in eight out of ten microprocessors and just about all computer systems. Although quartz crystals are the most common piezoelectric things—over 50 million were used in World War II radio communications—ceramics and even some plastic sheets exhibit the piezoelectric effect.

Experiments in piezoelectrics in support of computer technology—for dot matrix printers, robot sensors, and signal switching, for instance—have had some interesting side effects. Sheets of piezoelectric plastic have been made so sensitive to heat that they can detect from forty feet away when someone walks into a room). Perhaps the neatest spin-off: a car muffler made by Piezo Electric Products, Inc., Cambridge, Massachusetts, that uses the pressure of exhaust fumes to produce electricity. It replaces the alternator in a car.

Think about piezoelectrics and think about robots and think about Dr. Arthur Harkins, director of the graduate program in futures research at the University of Minnesota. He's the guy who predicts that we'll soon be using robots as sex partners. (Don't let the moon get in you eye, like a big piezo pie, that's *amore.*) We might even make honest robots of them through appropriate rituals.

All this could happen by the year 2000, says Harkins, who points out that "the great bulk of human relationships are formulated on ritualistic actions"—such as having breakfast at a certain time, keeping the house a certain way, or performing sex in a certain manner. The technology of the year 2000 will support robots performing many of these functions—especially for the lonely, imprisoned, deformed, or badly scarred.

"The Japanese have already developed all kinds of mechanical substitutes for human sexual organs, which are implanted in a robot and can be embellished with heat and other types of humanlike characteristics," he notes.

The biggest drawback to the concept of liaison with these man-made creatures is artificial intelligence software. It may be good enough that by the year 2000 robots will be able to exhibit some humanlike self-awareness. At least enough to say no to prospective partners.

But will we be turned on? Maybe we should pull the Veterans Administration's 1972 computer sex index test out of mothballs to find out. Psychiatrists from the VA and Stanford University announced that year they had developed an objective method of measuring sexual stimulation. Electrodes were attached to the heads of male and female volunteers and connected to a "signal averaging" computer, which measured their reactions to viewing photos of nude men and women. Upon seeing a "preferred sexual image" the viewers' brain-wave action increased. No kidding. The system was to be used diagnosing psychopaths and was never made commercially available. It seems to us that the program might be a great help choosing the right robot mate. Oh, R2D2, what U do 2 my brain waves!

> The three great inventions that have inexorably altered our culture are the automobile, the Pill and information delivery systems. Autos allowed us to physically go anywhere; with the Pill, we could explore new life-styles, new ways of living. The electronic media—mating information delivery systems with video technology and computers— have made people think about things they would never have thought about before. We are in a postliterate society where people prefer visual information. If the computer can turn people on to new ideas and new possibilities, then it's really enhancing them. If you want to know what the future of computing is, watch the children.
> —Hank Koehn, Vice-president, Futures Research,
> Security Pacific Bank

IBM has demonstrated a special chip called a Josephson Junction that operates at four degrees above absolute zero. Josephson Junction devices are used in things called SQUIDS (superconducting quantum interference devices) that can detect changes in magnetic field as small as one trillionth of the earth's field. One large Josephson Junction computer—which might be the size of a baseball and draw the power of a sixty-watt light bulb—could equal the computing capacity of all the computers shipped in 1983. Scientists say one could be built by 1989.

But Josephson Junction computers may never see the light of day—by becoming obsolete before they're invented. Traditional circuits are getting so small that their properties are getting benignly weird. At a small enough size, you see, electrons don't flow, they fly around like bullets, which lowers the power requirements needed to make computer chips and makes conventional technology competitive with Josephson Junctions.

The point of miniaturization is to get computer parts so close together that communication between them isn't slowed down by such draggy limits as the speed of light. Most circuit miniaturization is heading for submicron range—a micron, a millionth of a meter, is to your armspan what Wilt Chamberlain's armspan is to the distance from New York to Chicago—and down to the nanometer range. Some fun facts about miniaturization:

- Researchers at MIT's Lincoln Labs have etched onto a chip a channel that is a thousand times smaller in width than a bacterium.

- Electronic devices can now be made so small that fifty of them could be clustered on the cross section of a human hair.

- Something a micron thick is only a few atoms thick.

- Scientists at Cornell have etched letters so small that they could put the entire *Encyclopaedia Britannica* onto a postage stamp.

- Using a scanning transmission electron microscope—which shoots a beam of electrons (rather than light) only ten atoms wide to focus— researchers have taken "pictures" of a single atom.

- Professors at Cornell have developed sensors tiny enough to plug into individual cells.

- The techniques for etching chip circuits are getting so pinpoint accurate that scientists actually can write on molecules.

- The technology is transferable to other disciplines: Teeny pumps have been made by etching a cavity in a chip and covering it with a membrane that contracts or expands when a voltage is applied. IBM has used such pumps in a printer that squirts ink onto the page.

- You can't *see* any of this stuff. The light waves are too fat to focus on things this small.

- Holes etched very close together—say, sixty hydrogen atoms apart—in solid metal have a tendency to migrate and become one bigger hole. Nobody knows why.

The techniques of etching parts this small are varied. Photographic etching, used now for making chips, can't be used because the wavelength of light is too wide. Alternatives: beams of electrons to blast the chasms and pits that become circuits, X rays to do what light cannot, or the molecular growing (epitaxy) of circuits.

War in the year 2000. The U.S. Army is investigating robot soldiers, computerized combat and aerial space surveillance, reconnaissance and targeting systems that make *Star Wars* pale by comparison. A main computer with voice-recognition abilities would be the general deploying robot armies capable of reaction times far beyond a human's and sending information to automated laser defense weapons. The result? A more rational war, with far less loss of human life. The ultimate? Dueling computers.

"You try not to think about what an electron is—if you want to stay sober."—Joe Barnard, researcher at the Department of Defense's Submicron Research Facility.

Photo courtesy of IBM

A random-access memory (RAM) chip capable of sorting 288,000 bits
of information. The first RAM chip could store only 4,000 bits. The 288K chip
could store four copies of the Declaration of Independence.

How many angels can dance on the head of a pin? Well, as a result of
modern technology, we now know the answer to this medieval brain twister:
a hundred thousand. At least that's how many Dr. Edward D. Wolf and his
associates at Hughes Research Laboratories were able to etch on the head of
a straight pin in 1970. The angels were gold deposits, appropriately shaped,
six microns wide. Unfortunately for theologians, the pin itself was lost when
it squirted out of a pair of tweezers and rolled into a crack in the floor.
Besides, Wolf says, with today's technology you could accommodate a billion angels. If there are that many.

The closer components on chips come to the infinitely small, the more
worthy it is to contemplate the infinitely great. This, of course, can be done
with the help of computers:

• Alan Rogers, a forty-eight-year-old television commercial producer,
  has designed a computer-aided prayer system, called the Infinity Cir-

cuit, which he likens to an electronic rosary or Tibetan prayer wheel. It uses a Radio Shack Color Computer—the flickering CRT and past conditioning watching TV help create a passive, receptive mood—and requires the supplicant to type questions on a keyboard. These are then displayed on the CRT, and the supplicant is to wait until he or she feels the answer from within before typing it out. The computer prompts replies. The conscious mind types the questions, says Rogers, but the higher self types the answers. "There are a number of restrictive barriers between normal and God-consciousness. The Infinity Circuit allows you to receive direct communication from God, your higher self, or whatever you call it." In five minutes you can work through five levels of consciousness. Rogers's electronic connection to the ultimate may have helped his consciousness but it hasn't helped his wallet. He's lost $20,000 on the Infinity Circuit so far.

• Gurucharan S. Khalsa, an American Sikh from Massachusetts, is developing a computerized standard chanter. The computer, a SAGE II micro, will use voice print analysis to ensure that a chanter is properly mouthing his mantra. (The chanted voiceprint is compared to a template of a perfect chant.) The next step: an on-line meditation guidance system to be used in clinical application of meditation techniques.

Khalsa should make out better than Rogers. Besides being a guru, he's also an authorized SAGE dealer and founder of Micro Strategies, a computer hardware, software, and consulting business.

Why simply talk to God? Why not be God? In Britain scientists have used protein as an insulator on regular semiconductor chips. And the founders of EMV Associates in Rockville, Maryland, have patented a method for depositing silver on a protein molecule—they say they're working toward a combination protein/conventional electronic device that could encompass a hundred thousand more devices on it than today's chips (a hundred-billion-circuit food molecule, in other words). Making such bioelectronic devices probably will require molecular engineering, since transistor and diode cells don't exist in nature.

"You'll never get a bacterium to build a whole computer—it's too small," says Kevin Ulmer of Genex, another Rockville, Maryland, company. "But a bacterium could crank out transistors or diodes."

Making biocomputers useful is another matter. After all, how do you attach a wire to molecule? With gluons?

Well, Bell Labs is experimenting with organic molecules that conduct electricity. Make them bigger and bigger the farther out you go and eventually they could connect to metallic devices. Such biological computers would open the way for direct communication between computers and people.

Before we feel computers' pulses coursing through our nervous systems, we may hear them. Scientists have discovered that some people actually can hear electromagnetic waves at certain frequencies. And other people can be taught to do so. Some of the best frequencies are those at which many computer I/O devices work. Hm. Hum. Bzzz.

Thirteen years ago a UCLA neuropsychiatrist, Dr. Ivan N. Mensch, reported that "computers are not appearing in the fantasies of disturbed people." This was in response to queries on the effect of the computer's depersonalization of human relationships. Other shrinks agreed.

What no one has studied yet is whether humans appear in the fantasies of disturbed computers. By 2000 maybe this won't be a dumb question.

Not all predictions for our high-tech future are rosy. Last year French statesman and author Jean-Jacques Servan-Schreiber, testifying before the U.S. Congress as head of France's World Center for Computer Science and Human Resources, predicted that by 1990 fifty million people would be out of work as a result of advancing high technology (not counting joblessness in underdeveloped countries). As a result, the world will be thrust into "a situation of despair."

France's World Center is the first agency to teach computer programming to Senegal schoolchildren, produce a videodisk of twenty thousand African plants, and devise a voice-recognition system that can understand Wolof, a language spoken in central Africa.

Computer simulations conducted by researcher Erik Jones, at Los Alamos National Laboratory, predict that mankind will be populating outer space within three generations. Jones's computers have even allowed him to map this future migration, which will start with colonies on the moon and on mineral-rich asteroids. Migration patterns of humans going as far back as 1500 B.C. indicate that we migrate when we get crowded—and major migrations take place every five hundred years or so. The computers predict that when the Earth's population reaches twenty billion, we'll be on the move again. And this time there's no place left to go but the void itself.

Some things you should know when thinking about how to spend your leisure time in the year 2000:

- A $5.00 paperback book holds about 80,000 words, the equivalent of 500,000 computer characters (bytes). Special software could compress

Drawing by Tim Eagan

that to 250,000 bytes. This is about what a floppy disk can hold today. A blank floppy disk costs about the same as a full paperback book. Ten years from now, however, a blank floppy disk will cost much less than half the price of a paperback. A full floppy and a blank cost about the same, since "printing" merely entails magnetic copying. A trickier technological barrier to floppy disk books is sand—how to keep it out of the electronics while "reading" a novel while sunbathing at the beach.

- Digital TVs are under development. These would take video signals and transform them into digital pulses suitable for computers. Computer circuits then could enhance the picture (much as pictures from NASA spacecraft are enhanced). The TV could also be programmed, doing away with signal decoders for cable or pay TV and hooking directly to home computers or home computer/videodisk combos.

- Sony has a videodisk hooked to a computer that offers a video travel brochure on Hawaii—it costs $8,000, and travel agents are starting to buy it.

- There are experimental two-way services in many developed countries. The information most often accessed by them: United States: the weather; United Kingdom: stock prices, airline schedules; Japan: horoscopes; Netherlands: therapy advice.

- A personalized videodisk newspaper is being tested at MIT. A videodisk is used to record material, a computer to search and retrieve only material it has been told is interesting. It's the kind of system that could be hooked up at night to wire services and data banks and turned on in the morning for "reading" with coffee.

- There are already a thousand data bases to which you may purchase access from a home computer, from the Dow Jones stock listing to art catalogs. Almost two hundred thousand computer users availed themselves of them in 1982. The number of on-line references available has grown from twenty-four million in 1976 to a hundred million today.

Computer for the twenty-first century. The Japanese, who have proven themselves redoubtable competitors over and over again, have initiated The Fifth-Generation Computer Project, the most ambitious computer design effort now under way. If it works, the design will redefine everything we have come to know and understand a computer to be. (For an explanation of computer generations, see "From the Cache" at the end of Chapter 4.) Tohru Moto-oka, a Tokyo professor, says, "This project aims to be the space shuttle of the knowledge world." Marvin Minsky, the MIT computer guru, describes it as "the computer industry Pearl Harbor."

The intent of the $450 million, ten-year project is to pull together all the various technological disciplines associated with computers today—each at the leading edge of its art—into one integrated whole. Participating in the project are all the major Japanese computer and communications firms and the government.

A basic fifth-generation computer would be built more like the human brain—lots of little autonomous thinking parts rather than one gargantuan calculator—and attempt to mimic human sensory processing. Included in the fifth-generation computer will be a basketful of advances in computer-aided design, artificial intelligence, sensory data processing, image processing, and robotics.

What will a fifth-generation computer do?

- You can speak into it, and it will be able to speak back. It will be able to read typewritten or printed text and can "see" graphic or visual information.

- It will provide reports and documents in everyday, conversational language, not "computerese."

- Through artificial intelligence, it will be able to use its stored information to perform functions of learning, associating types of information, and making inferences about what it all means.

- It will remember twenty thousand rules of inference about the real world and a hundred million facts.

The first computers expected out of The Fifth-Generation Computer Project will likely be small personal computers used in schools, starting in kindergarten.

"Talk of a fifth generation has more of a public-relations flair to it than reality."—John Opel, president of IBM.

"Unless U.S. companies start putting more of this type of research into their products, we will sink slowly to our knees."—Robert Kahn, a director at the Defense Advanced Research Projects Agency.

Will the Japanese Fifth-Generation Computer Project work? A computer of the type envisioned will require chips five times more powerful than the most advanced ones today, computational speed ten times that of the most powerful computers of today, and central memory a thousand times bigger than today's largest computers—all of which are feasible within ten years if current trends keep up.

The problem will be in the machine's "polyprocessor" design and in software. Many of the experiments to date with computers made of lots of smaller interconnected computers have run into this trade-off: It takes about as much time and memory to have all the processors communicate with one another as they save over conventional designs. As for software, artificial-intelligence work has been going on for twenty years and still can't produce a computer that can beat a rank amateur playing the Japanese game of Go. A fifth-generation computer would have to be able to beat an expert.

The Japanese are high tech all the way. They will be the first to use credit-card-operated public phones, and they lead the world in urban experiments with computerized traffic control—computers in cars receive transmissions telling where jams are, how to get from here to there; sensors in the streets detect car movements and report them to master computers.

They also lead in experimenting with "wired cities." Tama New Town, 30 miles from Tokyo, was the site of a $4 million experiment wiring 500 households to 11 information services by coaxial cable like that used for cable TV. A total of $16 million was spent wiring Nara Prefecture near Osaka in the Higashi-Ikoma Optical Visual System (Hi-OVIS). Optical fiber cable was used here instead of coaxial cable. Hi-OVIS linked only 158 households but offered richer services.

Will the Japanese take over? Ask James Martin. As the computer industry's best-known thinker and highest-paid guru, Martin, perhaps more than anyone, can speak for the industry as a whole. Born in England, he attended Oxford University and subsequently spent nineteen years with IBM. Today he lectures, consults, and writes from his home in Bermuda. He has written over thirty books—*The Wired Society* (1978) was nominated for a Pulitzer Prize.

Martin was interviewed last year by Leonard Kleinrock, professor of computer science at the University of California, Los Angeles, on "the computer industry Pearl Harbor." Some of his thoughts:

- The Japanese target for 1990 is to have a mainframe that can process between a hundred million and one billion inferences per second. That is a staggering rate compared with anything going on in the artificial-intelligence circles today at MIT or Stanford. I compare it to project Apollo, which harnessed an amazing diversity of resources to produce what has been one of the most spectacular technological achievements ever.

- Many computer science departments seem to me today to be doing research in entirely the wrong areas. In fact, they seem to be doing research relevant to the 1970s, not the 1990s. We need much better *direction* and management of future-oriented research with more people doing it. This probably means higher salaries for the university professors who are involved, and substantially more attention to science, mathematics, and computing in our high schools and grade schools.

- As we look at the great achievements of mankind, we see that they often come from an extreme degree of human dedication. This was true with the building of the Gothic cathedrals in the twelfth century, this was true with Project Apollo, and I think it's true with the Japanese fifth generation of computers. If we are to succeed in maintaining our great leadership in technology, then society must achieve the excitement which causes people to work extremely hard, as many people do in Japan, in achieving results which will collectively be worthwhile.

Who's worried about Japan? What about the Martians? Vincent Di-Pietro and Gregory Molenaar, scientists working with NASA, discovered when looking at a certain picture broadcast by a Viking Orbiter of Mars what looked to be, well, a face. NASA had even titled the mile-wide land-scape feature "Head." It seemed odd enough to explore. By going back to the original computer tapes of pictures transmitted by Viking, and then per-forming some image-enhancement magic with a computer, they were able to define the face's features and determine that it wasn't simply a trick of lighting. Unlike most natural landscape "faces" on earth, this is a frontal view—complete with bilateral symmetry, eyes, hairline, mouth, and even a teardrop under one eye. If it's not Martian-made, then Mother Nature has been umpteen times more sophisticated in designing landscapes on Mars than on Earth.

One problem that will no longer bug us in 2000 is the matter of the "Oxen of the Sun." Legend has it that in the third century B.C., Archimedes posed a brain-twister to stump critics of his mathematical abilities. "Compute, O friend, the host of the oxen of the sun, giving thy mind thereto, if thou hast a share of wisdom." The problem went on to describe four herds of cows by color and nine constraints of relationships between bulls and cows (for example: White bulls = yellow bulls + [½ + ⅓] black bulls).

Herds that satisfied the first seven conditions were determinable back then—the smallest number of cows is 50,389,082—but a solution to the last two conditions took two thousand years even to begin to come by. In 1880 a German named A. Amthor determined that the number was a 206,545-digit number beginning with 7,766. Forty more digits were found during the next eighty-five years. Not until a computer was called into play, in 1965, could researchers at the University of Waterloo come up with the complete solution, but they never printed it out.

Finally, as outcome of a test of a Cray-1 computer in 1981, the answer was determined again and subsequently published. In fact, to exercise its circuits even more, the computer found five larger numbers, one a million digits long, that could satisfy the constraints of Archimedes' problem. It took the computer ten minutes to solve a problem that had eluded the best human mathematicians for two millennia.

FROM THE CACHE:
The Mystery of Turin

It's a fourteen-foot-by-three-foot linen, and for years it has mystified scholars and moved theologians. Housed since 1578 in a baroque cathedral in the Italian town for which it's named, the Shroud of Turin is believed by some to be the burial cloth of Jesus of Nazareth.

It's an ethereal image of a bearded man, remarkably composed in death, bearing the marks of a savage scourging, pierced wrists and ankles, with a watery wound through the ribs residing in the weave of the cloth.

For years scientists, many of them scoffers, itched to get their hands and instruments on the cloth, but the Church kept them away. The shroud has been put on public display only three times in the past century. But the Church has allowed photographs to be taken, and, in the last viewing, in 1978, allowed a whole team of scientists to test the shroud.

But instead of unraveling the mystery, science simply has added to it.

Researchers had earlier determined that the fiber of the cloth dated back to before A.D. 1000 and that the cotton was of a variety common in the Holy Land. In the 1978 tests, pollen common in the Holy Land was found trapped in the shroud's fibers. Also, no pigment was found in the cloth, pretty much debunking the idea that it might be a painted fake.

In 1975 two Air Force scientists using a large IBM computer and image analyzer on photographs of the shroud concluded that whatever created the image on the shroud probably acted from a distance, not by contact with the cloth.

In fact, their computerized image analysis established that the shroud had some other unusual properties.

Because they are two-dimensional—although they may show three-dimensional subjects—ordinary photographs or paintings show up under three-dimensional image analysis grossly distorted. Planets or other three-dimensional objects don't.

Surprise. Under computerized image analysis, the Shroud of Turin formed a three-dimensional image. Painting or otherwise imprinting by hand an image on the shroud would result in a two-dimensional image.

In the 1978 tests, it was also discovered that, indeed, the shroud resembled a photographic negative. The image lay on just the topmost fibers of the cloth, and was reversed, light and dark, as if the shroud *were* a photo negative. It was almost as if the image had been scorched on, by some unknown energy emanating from the man depicted.

Two years ago, Rev. Francis Filas used another computerized image analyzer on some 1931-vintage pictures of the shroud and showed that the markings around the eyes of the "Man in the Shroud" were three-dimensional. He enlarged the "eye" sections of the photographs and then used the computer to wash out the weave of the cloth without destroying the pattern. The markings showed the impression of coins placed in the eyes of the dead man, which was a common burial practice in Roman times. A numismatist identified the coins as having been minted between A.D. 29 and 32.

And so it goes. Technology progresses and man is no closer to understanding the mystery of the Shroud of Turin than he was to understanding the mystery at Calgary. In fact, the computer only allows him to be more scientifically mystified.

Somehow it's fitting.

For as the computer stands naked before us, in all its blemishes, warts, and mental limitations . . . so we stand naked before our creator.

INDEX

327